The Ghostly and the Ghosted in Literature and Film

The Ghostly and the Ghosted in Literature and Film

Spectral Identities

Edited by Lisa Kröger and
Melanie R. Anderson

UNIVERSITY OF DELAWARE PRESS
Newark

Published by University of Delaware Press
Co-published with The Rowman & Littlefield Publishing Group, Inc.
4501 Forbes Boulevard, Suite 200, Lanham, Maryland 20706
www.rowman.com

10 Thornbury Road, Plymouth PL6 7PP, United Kingdom

British Library Cataloguing in Publication Information Available

Library of Congress Cataloging-in-Publication Data
The ghostly and the ghosted in literature and film : spectral identities / edited by Lisa Kröger and
Melanie R. Anderson.
pages cm
Includes bibliographical references and index.
ISBN 978-1-61149-452-5 (cloth : alk. paper)—ISBN 978-1-61149-453-2 (electronic)
1. Ghosts in literature. 2. Ghosts in motion pictures. 3. Other (Philosophy) in literature. 4. Other
(Philosophy) in motion pictures. 5. Future life in literature. I. Kröger, Lisa, editor of compilation. II.
Anderson, Melanie, editor of compilation.
PN56.S8G48 2013
809.2'51209375—dc23
2012049550
ISBN 978-1-61149-565-2 (pbk : alk. paper)

∞ The paper used in this publication meets the minimum requirements of American
National Standard for Information Sciences Permanence of Paper for Printed Library
Materials, ANSI/NISO Z39.48-1992.

Printed in the United States of America

Contents

Acknowledgments   vii

Introduction   ix

I: The Gothic and the Ghostly

1   Haunted Narratives: Women Writing the Ghostly in Early
Gothic Fiction   3
Lisa Kröger

2   City of Ghosts: Elizabeth Bowen's Wartime Stories   15
Stefania Porcelli

3   Those "Whose Deaths Were Not Remarked": Ghostly Other
Women in Henry James's *The Turn of the Screw*, Charlotte
Perkins Gilman's *The Yellow Wallpaper*, and Marilynne
Robinson's *Housekeeping*   29
Jana M. Tigchelaar

II: Spectral Figures and Spectral Histories

4   These Ghosts Will Be Lovers: The "Cultural Haunting" of Class
Consciousness in Ian McEwan's *Atonement*   47
Karley K. Adney

5   The Spectral Queerness of White Supremacy: Helen Oyeyemi's
White Is for Witching   59
Amy K. King

6   In the Spirit of Reconciliation: Migrating Spirits and Australian
Postcolonial Multiculturalism in Hoa Pham's *Vixen*   75
Jessica Carniel

7 Haunting Mothers: Alternative Modes of Communication in
    Geographies of Home and *Soledad*   91
    Betsy A. Sandlin

III: Spectral Projections

8 Aesthetics of Haunting as Diasporic Sensibility: Julie Dash's
    Daughters of the Dust   105
    Yu-yen Liu

9 Women as Cultural Wound: Korean Horror Cinema and the
    Imperative of *Han*   119
    Andrew Hock Soon Ng

10 "Help Me": Interrogating Capitalism, the Specter of Hiroshima,
    and the Architectural Uncanny in Kiyoshi Kurosawa's *Pulse*   137
    Paul Petrovic

Bibliography   155

Index   163

About the Editors and Contributors   167

Acknowledgments

Melanie R. Anderson cannot list every person's name in acknowledging the many family members and friends who have been supportive during this project, but there are a few who must be singled out by name. First, many thanks to her coeditor, Lisa Kröger. This project was born one afternoon in Somerville 302 when it was initially decided to do this, and as with all the following decisions, that one was quite easily, and pleasantly, made. Next, she would like to thank two important mentors. Without the guidance of Professors Sherry Cook Stanforth and Sister Colleen Dillon during her undergraduate years at Thomas More College and beyond, she probably would not have pursued this academic path, and as she follows it, she will remember their advice and kindness. Most important, she is deeply grateful for the love, support, and patience of her parents, Paul and Deborah Anderson; her siblings, Justin and Stephanie Anderson; and her grandparents, Earl and Aline Beil. She owes much to their care and constancy.

Lisa Kröger would like to thank her family, particularly her loving and supportive husband, Robbie Kröger, whose words of encouragement keep her going, and her son, Leo, for napping just long enough to let her get the editing and writing finished on time. She would also like to thank her parents, Audrey and Ty Sloan, for supporting her throughout her life and education; her sister, Ginger, for being her friend through it all; her grandparents, Tom and Ruby Erwin; and her family down under. Her mentor, Dr. Colby Kullman, is more than just a professor who led her through her graduate studies; he is a valued friend. Finally, she is grateful for the wonderful friends who have encouraged her to follow this path: to Kelley Hogue, for always making her laugh; to Jenny Hyest, for talking through all the crazy ideas with her; to Emily Jones, for being her partner in crime; and, of course, to Melanie Anderson, without whom this book would not have been dreamed of. She wishes she could name everyone here; a sincere debt of gratitude is paid to all who supported this journey.

Together, Melanie and Lisa would like to thank Benjamin F. Fisher at the University of Mississippi for his mentoring throughout the process, as well as Gray Kane for the inspiration to do this and Annette Trefzer for an illuminating coffee break. An enormous debt is owed to the anonymous readers secured by the publisher for the incisive and illuminating comments that helped strengthen the final product. And most important, a sincere thank-you to the contributors of the essays, without whose creativity, hard work, and patience this book would not exist.

Introduction

A yearning for the possibility of life beyond the moment of death is an integral part of the human condition, and this desire has been an enduring notion throughout the history of civilization and its literatures. From the shades in Homer's epics to Banquo's ghost in Shakespeare's *Macbeth*, to twentieth-century incarnations such as Toni Morrison's enigmatic *Beloved* and the popularity of movies like *The Others* and *Ghostbusters*, the specter has been a constant theme. But why? What is it about the spectral that has held popular attention for so long? What does it symbolize for authors and audiences? What *is* a ghost?

Traditionally, as critic Julia Briggs reminds us, literary ghosts have strict rules for their return. If a person returns from beyond the pale, it can be because he was not buried properly; he has unfinished business; he must atone for some sin or guilt; he must warn the living or provide important information, such as where the second will or buried treasure is located; or finally, he could be seeking vengeance.[1] Because of their tendencies to defy the permanence of death, ghosts have long been considered denizens of the shadows, the areas "betwixt and between." They inhabit a realm between the physical and the spiritual—caught between this reality and the next one. They are not alive, yet ghosts are not entirely dead either. Their very existence is often questioned as they seemingly lie between fact and fiction. As folklorist Gillian Bennett has documented, stories of "real-life" hauntings usually corroborate this liminal trait. Ghost sightings frequently occur in the betwixt spaces of the home: doorways, windows, even stairwells. Briggs notes that ghosts ride the "tension between the known and the unknown, security and exposure, the familiar and the strange, scepticism and credulity."[2] In literature and film, they often signal eruptions that deconstruct binary ways of perceiving the world—methods reified by Western rationality and reason. Perhaps this is why so many horror novels and films involve cases of native hauntings that offer to uncover alternative versions of history. Movies like *The Amityville Horror* (1979) and *Pet Sematary* (1989) feature disturbed Native American burial sites as the genesis of the supernatural activity. In these two films in particular, the mythic otherness of the Native Americans and, perhaps more important, their supposed belief in magic offers explanation for the ghosts that haunt the land. Much more likely, however, is that the ghosts are brought about by a collective cultural guilt. The arrival of Europeans led to the creation of a nation that ultimately attempted to eradicate and overwrite the Native presence, and though past sins may be ignored, these ghosts of cultural conflict and trauma are still haunting our present. There is something there that will not let us forget.

As William Faulkner famously wrote, "The past is never dead. It's not even past,"[3] and the ghost is often an indicator that there are aspects of the past that are not quite finished. Indeed, for theorist Jacques Derrida, a "spectral moment" is a "moment that no longer belongs to time."[4] The ideas of present and past merge into timelessness: "Haunting, by its very structure, implies a deformation of linear temporality."[5] With ghosts, the past is never over, the present is never secure, and the future is certain only of the spectral return. Specters "serve to destabilize any neat compartmentalization of the past as a secure and fixed entity, or the future as uncharted territory."[6] Ghostly entities and moments play with and deconstruct the very concepts of time that Western thought has identified as chronological, and these ghostly encounters account for the actual malleability of lived time and memory. Because ghosts can inhabit both the past and the present, they have the unique ability to act as a conduit, a connection to the past. People often speak of a past that haunts the present; these specters, real or imagined, quite literally make sure that the past will never be forgotten.

Critics, from Briggs and her work on English ghost stories to more recent work by Avery F. Gordon exploring the sociological implications of the metaphorical ghost, have explored the function of the supernatural in literature. For the purposes of introducing the various takes on the spectral that are advanced in the following chapters, a brief survey of selected works in this field of supernatural studies, or "spectrality studies," if you will, is necessary. First, in the introduction to the critical collection *Haunting the House of Fiction: Feminist Perspectives on Ghost Stories by American Women* (1991), Lynette Carpenter and Wendy K. Kolmar focus on the correlation between the liminality of ghosts and an ignored past that begs to be reclaimed in women's fiction. According to Carpenter and Kolmar, women's ghost stories blur the "boundaries between natural and supernatural, life and afterlife."[7] The appearance of ghosts in these stories is often an unsurprising plot event, and the line strictly separating the living from the dead fades considerably to allow for enlightening communication between the two. The communication between past and present, dead and living, is necessary for the completion of the present, living moment. This crossing of the boundaries allows women writers to communicate what cannot be spoken. Somewhat incongruously, truth becomes bolder and clearer when the supernatural element is present. Carpenter and Kolmar list the themes and images from which women's ghost stories draw: "of women victimized by violence in their own homes, of women dispossessed of homes and property, of the necessity of understanding female history, and of the bonds between women, living and dead, which help to ensure women's survival."[8] The communication between living and dead affirms the reality of women and allows for transformation and reclamation. Life as it is actually experienced frequently spills outside of the bounds of artificial methods of ordering reality.

Kathleen Brogan extends these gendered concepts of haunting to a cultural arena. In *Cultural Haunting: Ghosts and Ethnicity in Recent American Literature* (1998), Brogan echoes the concerns with the ever-present past that we have discussed, but she focuses on American ethnic literature. She posits that transitional ghosts become important not only for the reclamation of a group's past but also for the work of communicating that ethnic history to a new generation—a new generation that is often unaware of its past and the effect of the past on the present. According to Brogan, these cultural ghosts appear for specific reasons: "The ghosts in American haunted tales function similarly because they are conjured in response to shared concerns about assimilation and cultural identity."[9] When ethnic identity and unity are threatened, ghosts appear as reminders of a shared cultural past. Ghosts are agents of cultural memory and renewal in a "creative, ongoing process of ethnic redefinition."[10] In addition, dealing with a new environment as a result of displacement calls not only for a redefinition, but also perhaps for an education concerning the origins of one's cultural heritage. Brogan cites, as an example of this relearning and redefining, "geographical and cultural shifting of immigrants who look back to the old country as they negotiate the new."[11] In this situation, the origins may return as ghostly reminders of heritage, but encounters with a completely new environment may seem just as ghostly and unfamiliar. Interaction with ghosts becomes, therefore, not just a negotiation of ethnic identity but of American identity as well in a type of "cultural haunting."[12]

As understood through Brogan's definition, then, a ghost does not have to be the specter of someone already dead: a ghost can be any person, living or dead, who figuratively haunts a culture or society in which they participate marginally. Sociologist Avery F. Gordon's formulation of the concept of a haunting centers on marginal individuals and groups. In *Ghostly Matters: Haunting and the Sociological Imagination* (1997), Gordon describes the concept of a haunting as a social moment:

> If haunting describes how that which appears to be not there is often a seething presence, acting on and often meddling with taken-for-granted realities, the ghost is just the sign, or the empirical evidence if you like, that tells you a haunting is taking place. The ghost is not simply a dead or a missing person, but a social figure, and investigating it can lead to that dense site where history and subjectivity make social life. The ghost or the apparition is one form by which something lost, or barely visible, or seemingly not there to our suppos-edly well-trained eyes, makes itself known or apparent to us, in its own way, of course. The way of the ghost is haunting, and haunting is a very particular way of knowing what has happened or is happening. Being haunted draws us affectively, sometimes against our will and always a bit magically, into the structure of feeling of a reality we come to experience, not as cold knowledge, but as a transformative recognition. [13]

Similar to Derrida's emphasis on spirit work always involving transforma-tion, Gordon's primary emphasis is the transformative power of the haunting experience. She also defines a ghost as not necessarily a returning deceased individual, but rather as a "social figure" and a sign of the haunting that is taking place. When this definition is combined with Brogan's thoughts on cultural hauntings and then framed by Derrida's work on spectrality, the "spectral figure" becomes not a returned lost one, but a liminal figure en-meshed in a specific social situation, effecting change. [14]

Given the theories of Derrida, Carpenter and Kolmar, Brogan, Gordon, and others, the question we asked earlier about the definition of "ghost" has no simple answer. A ghost is not merely the figure shrouded in white that wanders the ancestral home, clanking chains and moaning and wailing; a ghost is not just the phantasm that haunts the living because it cannot cross over to a peaceful afterlife. The ghost is a signal of ambiguity and of the ineffable. It is the sign of something—any person, or group, or cultural moment—that, largely ignored or repressed by the society in which it partici-pates, refuses to be marginalized any longer, but pushes to be recognized. Given this reformulation of "ghostliness," this collection analyzes these limi-nal, elided, and/or repressed individuals and explores the ever-changing role of the ghost. Using the metaphor of the ghost, living characters in these texts find themselves silenced, marginalized, and suppressed by the society in which they take part. Like the traditional ghost, these characters struggle to make their presence known as they learn to manipulate the liminal spaces they inhabit. This social ghosting is not a one-way street, either. As with the conventional haunting, these social ghosts cannot exist without the society that is trying to ignore their presence. Just as these social ghosts are pushing to be seen and heard, their society and culture are pushing back as well. What results is a remarkable cultural tug-of-war that will inevitably end in some sort of confrontation.

In this collection, we offer varying takes on specters in fiction and film from a wide range of time periods and authors, a range that demonstrates the eternal and yet diverse nature of the ghost. In a manner similar to the organization of a monograph, each chapter has been carefully placed to serve as an introduction to the next, and it is recommended that the reader read each in the order presented. In part I of this book, "The Gothic and the Ghostly," the chapters entertain how writers from the Gothic revival of the eighteenth-century to twentieth-century authors, such as Elizabeth Bowen, have utilized the supernatural in their fiction and established a trend in ghostly criticism still at work in contemporary literature. Lisa Kröger identifies ghostly aspects that are present in the relatively understudied texts of women's Gothic fiction, offering an examination of how even traditional hauntings in literature reveal tensions in the culture from which the novel is produced. The remaining chapters in part I expand on this basic principle, exploring how ghosts reveal the pain that emerges when a society attempts to bury traumatic events. In their chapters, Stefania Porcelli and Jana M. Tigchelaar explore the connections among the spectral, trauma, and gender. Porcelli's "City of Ghosts: Elizabeth Bowen's Wartime Stories" focuses on the effects of war, particularly the ripples that a war (in this case the London Blitz) produces for women. Tigchelaar's chapter makes connections among three very different writers—Henry James, Charlotte Perkins Gilman, and Marilynne Robinson—and how they use ghost-like characters, both real specters and imagined ones, to express the repression women often feel in a patriarchal society.

Part II, "Spectral Figures and Spectral Histories," moves into a discussion of the role of ghosts in reconstructing memory and history. In "These Ghosts Will Be Lovers: The 'Cultural Haunting' of Class Consciousness in Ian McEwan's *Atonement*," Karley K. Adney redefines McEwan's novel as a ghost story, a simulacrum of the events that inspired its creation by one of the characters. McEwan's book, then, through its "ghostwriter" Briony, becomes her way of working through what haunts her—her part in the destruction of her sister's relationship. Adney's chapter marks a shift in the collection, as the chapters begin to look away from actual ghosts and hauntings and more toward the theory of ghosted characters, those who may be very much alive but, because of their repressed status in society, identify more with spectral characters rather than the breathing, living ones with whom they share their environment. Amy K. King, in her chapter on Helen Oyeyemi's *White Is for Witching*, examines the idea of the living ghost in her analysis of the protagonist's struggle with pica, an eating disorder. King connects this disorder to the racial tensions and questions of national identity that Oyeyemi explores in her novel. Jessica Carniel and Betsy A. Sandlin both analyze the ghosting effect brought about by cultural expectations. In her chapter "In the Spirit of Reconciliation: Migrating Spirits and Australian Postcolonial Multiculturalism in Hoa Pham's *Vixen*," Carniel reads the fantasy element of Pham's text as an example of social ghosting brought about by the cultural melting pot of postcolonial Australia. Sandlin, in her chapter "Haunting Mothers: Alternative Modes of Communication in *Geographies of Home* and *Soledad*," sees the phenomenon of social ghosting at work in the mother-child relationship that Sandlin believes, despite their best attempt to escape it, haunts the women characters of Loida Maritza Pérez and Angie Cruz, two contemporary Dominican-American authors.

The last part of this collection, titled "Spectral Projections," moves the theory of spectrality one notch past Adney's work on ghost writers as it explores the idea that texts themselves can be ghosts, particularly as they can haunt our imaginations. For this exploration, we transition the focus from book to film. Film, as a medium, lends itself well to spectrality, perhaps better than the written word. Just as a ghost is a reminder of a person who previously lived, images caught on film remind us of life—though, in reality, they are projections of people, places, and histories. In the twenty-first century, life is becoming increasingly virtual. Through the mediums of film, computers, cell phones, and social networks, we are increasingly physically isolated, even while communicating with others. Similar to the images of ghosts appearing to a nineteenth-century witness, now we regularly see and hear people only through images on a screen and sound reproductions in theaters and through Internet and phone communications. Like specters, traces of individuals remain in audio recordings and photographs left behind with the living. Despite Edith Wharton's warning that radio and cinema would gradually defeat the ghost story, film has allowed the ghost story to evolve through its own ghostlike qualities of image. In "Aesthetics of Haunting as Diasporic Sensibility in Julie Dash's *Daughters of the Dust*," Yu-yen Liu posits that the haunting presence of the "Unborn Child" together with the spectrality of the film medium itself recovers and shares important narratives of African American survival and migration. In his chapter, Andrew Hock Soon Ng analyzes the links among female sexuality, the Korean philosophy of *han*, and popular Korean horror films. In the final chapter of the collection, "Interrogating Capitalism, the Specter of Hiroshima, and the Architectural Uncanny in Kiyoshi Kurosawa's *Pulse*," Paul Petrovic delves into the haunted cultural and historical connections between Kurosawa's representation of a technological/supernatural apocalypse and the destruction of Hiroshima at the end of World War II.

Taken as a whole, this collection offers a broad, comparative look at the place of the ghost in literature and film. It shows progress from the ghost as supernatural figure and site of return for traumatic history through more contemporary concerns with the ghostliness of identity. While critics have analyzed compartments of haunted literature, for example, the Gothic, English ghost stories, and women writers of supernatural fiction, there is no comprehensive collection of work that explores the ghost as a connecting figure in all of these historical periods and modes and places these periods and locales into possible conversation with each other. This collection, with its diverse spectrum of work, highlights the continuing importance of the ghost as a pivotal figure in world literature and film. The turn of a century has always been a time full of both hope and worry, and the attendant fear of the unknown always creates an increased interest in the supernatural. Even with the twenty-first century's spike in interest in all manner of horror from vampires to zombies and our rapid technological development, ghosts still fascinate us. They have not been abandoned to the dusty tomes of the past. The ghost is a useful metaphor for the uncertainties of life and death settled deep within the psyche of human beings. Ghosts help pack movie theaters, sell books, and fill television schedules with fantastic and documentary programs. As these chapters attest, ghosts are still returning to give us chills, just in ways that may be more attuned to our cultural and historical moments, and spectrality still offers scholars fertile fields for exploration.

NOTES

1. Julia Briggs, *Night Visitors: The Rise and Fall of the English Ghost Story* (London: Faber, 1977), 15–16.
2. Gillian Bennett, *Alas, Poor Ghost! Traditions of Belief in Story and Discourse* (Logan: Utah State University Press, 1999), 19.
3. William Faulkner, *Requiem for a Nun* (New York: Vintage, 1975), 80.
4. Jacques Derrida, *Specters of Marx: The State of the Debt, the Work of Mourning, and the New International*, trans. Peggy Kamuf (New York: Routledge, 1994), xx.
5. Peter Buse and Andrew Stott, eds., *Ghost: Deconstruction, Psychoanalysis, History* (New York: St. Martin's Press, 1999), 1.
6. Ibid., 14.
7. Lynette Carpenter and Wendy K. Kolmar, eds., *Haunting the House of Fiction: Feminist Perspectives on Ghost Stories by American Women* (Knoxville: University of Tennessee Press, 1991), 8.
8. Ibid., 10.
9. Kathleen Brogan, *Cultural Haunting: Ghosts and Ethnicity in Recent American Literature* (Charlottesville: University Press of Virginia, 1998), 16.
10. Ibid., 12.
11. Ibid., 15.
12. An instance of the use of ghosted characters, and probably a seminal one within studies of ethnic American women writers, is Maxine Hong Kingston's *The Woman Warrior*. In this memoir, Kingston's narrator must deal with her American life and the Chinese background of her parents, and she describes her childhood as one lived among ghosts. For the immigrants, America is full of unfamiliar ghosts, and the consequences of not learning to live in this new environment cause the individual to be silenced and ghosted. A perfect example of this is the character Moon Orchid and her inability to assimilate into American society. When she speaks to her estranged husband, she thinks that she and her sister have "entered the land of ghosts, and they had become ghosts." Kingston, *The Woman Warrior: Memoirs of a Girlhood among Ghosts* (New York: Random House, 1989), 153.
13. Avery F. Gordon, *Ghostly Matters: Haunting and the Sociological Imagination* (Minneapolis: University of Minnesota Press, 1997), 8.

14. Melanie R. Anderson has explored the theme of spectrality and developed the discussion of social ghosts elsewhere in work on Toni Morrison's novels. See, in particular, her dissertation *The Beloved Paradise: Spectrality in the Novels of Toni Morrison from* Song of Solomon *through* Love (2009) and "'What Would Be on the Other Side?': Spectrality and Spirit Work in Toni Morrison's *Paradise*," *African American Review* 42, no. 2 (2008): 307–21.

I

The Gothic and the Ghostly

Chapter One

Haunted Narratives

Women Writing the Ghostly in Early Gothic Fiction

Lisa Kröger

Most readers of the Gothic novel are familiar with the works of Ann Radcliffe. *The Mysteries of Udolpho*, *The Italian*, *The Romance of the Forest* are all texts that are widely read in classrooms and discussed by literary critics today. Less familiar are those women writers who penned Gothic novels during that same time period, namely the 1790s and the decade that followed. One of those texts, Regina Maria Roche's Gothic novel *Clermont,* was published in 1798, only four years following the publication of Ann Radcliffe's *The Mysteries of Udolpho* in 1794. *Clermont* is arguably the definitive text of the Gothic novel craze during the eighteenth and nineteenth centuries, yet readers are often unfamiliar with Roche's novel. If Gothic readers do recognize the title, it is because of the shadow of Radcliffe. *Clermont* is listed as one of the "horrid novels"[1] favored by Isabella Thorpe in Jane Austen's *Northanger Abbey*, the novel that famously parodied the Gothic style of Ann Radcliffe. The fodder for Austen's parody was Radcliffe's particular brand of Gothic, one that has come to be called "Female Gothic" due to its tendency to focus on bumps in the night and other terrors that rarely portended any real danger. *The Mysteries of Udolpho* itself became famous in part because of the "explained supernatural" trademark style of its author; Radcliffe favored hiding the blood and gore from her audience, preferring to keep any violence "offstage"—safely away from her sensitive, and largely female, readership. As a result, Radcliffe and other writers of the same style limit the female characters' struggles to a passive form of confrontation—one expressed through what Diane Long Hoeveler calls a "female-marked communication system—the gossip of servants, the tales and legends that have their own oral histories, the painted miniatures and portraits, as well as visual theatrics,"[2] rather than graphic expressions of rape and violence.

While many authors of the Female Gothic remained true to Ann Radcliffe's model, others, such as Charlotte Dacre and Mary-Anne Radcliffe, to name a few, chose to express the struggle with the patriarchy in more aggressive, bodily terms. Regina Maria Roche fits this trend, as she does not shy away from the blood and gore, though she does maintain an overall Radcliffean Gothic sentimentality otherwise. In a sense, these authors are trying to "un-ghost" the marginalized status of the woman in eighteenth-century society by including violent scenes of bodily harm and mutilation in their novels. I say "un-ghost" because, in every sense of the word, the eighteenth-century woman was nothing more than a ghost. Avery Gordon, in her book *Ghostly Matters*, defines a ghost as a person who "is not simply a dead or a missing person, but a social figure, and investigating it can lead to that dense site where history and subjectivity make social life. The ghost or apparition is one form by which something lost, or barely visible, or seemingly not there to our supposedly well-trained eyes, makes itself known or apparent to us."[3] According to Gordon's definition, a ghost can be any liminal person or social group figuratively haunting the culture that participates in its marginalization. The case could then be made that the heroines are the true ghosts of the Gothic novel, more so than any long-dead specter lingering in the haunted castles that too often set the stage for these tales.

In England in the 1790s, women had virtually no legal rights. As many critics have pointed out before, they were mere chattel for the men in their lives, as marriage often meant procurement of land and estate wealth. Any land a woman could possess was usually inherited from her father, and her husband took complete legal control of any and all properties upon marriage. The family laws were perhaps even harsher. A man could sue for divorce, while "no woman attempted to do so between 1700 and 1801."[4] In addition, "women had virtually no legal right to exercise control over their children's welfare."[5] Any and all decisions were made by the father, and no consent from the mother was necessary. It was not until the Infants' Custody Act of 1839 that a mother had "the right to keep her children under the age of seven with her, in the event of a marital separation."[6] Given the political and social climate of late-eighteenth- and early nineteenth-century England, it is no wonder that women turned to the one medium for expression available to them, and that they would cast themselves as both heroine and ghost of their own "horrid" novels.

To describe the Gothic heroine as ghostly is no true stretch of the imagination. Fulfilling a romantic ideal of womanhood and femininity, these heroines are often described as having pale, almost ivory, complexions. In addition, they are described as fainting away when their emotions get the better of them. Austen seemed to recognize this common trait of the Gothic heroine, as she returns to this idea in *Northanger Abbey*. Catherine Morland is first described as having "a sallow skin without colour."[7] Echoing the same sentiment, Isabella declares that she prefers her men to have "light eyes, and as to complexion . . . I like sallow better than any other."[8] More so than just appearance, the Gothic heroine's actions solidify her status as the true ghost of these novels. Austen again parodies the excessive sentimentality of the Gothic woman when she writes, "And now I may dismiss my heroine to the sleepless couch, which is the true heroine's portion; to a pillow strewed with thorns and wet with tears,"[9] suggesting these heroines do nothing more than lie around, languishing.

If Austen's Catherine is meant to be a likeness of Radcliffe's Emily St. Aubert, then it would not be an exaggeration to suggest that Emily is the pale, wailing ghost of a woman who haunts Udolpho. After all, she has no agency within the novel, as she is taken from La Vallée to Venice and finally the Apennines by the villain Montoni. She never attempts to escape, either on her own or through a clandestine marriage with Valancourt, for fear of upsetting her father's faith in her or soiling her virtuous nature. Instead, once she arrives at Udolpho, described as a castle whose "dismal galleries and halls are fit for nothing but ghosts to live in,"[10] she is the one who busies herself by wandering the secret passages and dark corridors alone—much like the specters rumored to walk the castle halls.

At first glance, Regina Maria Roche's heroine Madeline is just a reworking of Emily in *Udolpho*. She grows up close to her father in an idyllic pastoral home; this setting is Dauphiny, which is essentially "another La Vallée, a peaceful and lovely retreat from the dangerous outside world."[11] She is thoughtful and creative, given to long walks in nature. She has a secret admirer, whose presence is marked by mysterious strains of music and a poem left in her favorite place of solitude (for Madeline, it is the castle ruins; for Emily, the fishing house). Even Madeline's blossoming love affair with de Sevignie closely mimics that of Emily and Valancourt:

> Both de Sevignie and Valancourt are handsome, feminized, highly genteel men of sensibility. Both are wounded early in the story, and their recuperation allows the couple time to fall in love. Distressing separations follow. Both heroes suffer fits of melancholy caused by obstacles to the unions they so much desire. For different reasons both are banished from the heroine's company, but they are frequently seen in the distance in postures of romantic loneliness and suffering.[12]

The similarities are plentiful, and they continue as the novel progresses. To read *Clermont* as only another version of *The Mysteries of Udolpho*, however, would be slighting to Roche's work. A dismissal of Roche as a Radcliffean Gothicist ignores that part of her work that makes her stand out from the rest of the Female Gothic canon. Roche "has more frequent recourse to what

Mrs. Radcliffe called 'horror' than to terror. In that respect, Rochean Gothic becomes more akin to that of the German *Schauerromane* than to the more filmy efforts of Radcliffean romance. Horror, not terror, is a certain un-Radcliffean leaning toward melodrama and physical suffering."[13] While Roche does much to distance herself from her predecessor, her writing shows a complex relationship to the Radcliffean model of the Gothic. Radcliffe's Gothic settings seem almost clichéd to today's reader. Her Gothic heroines find comfort and peace in the unsullied natural world. They write poems in quaint fishing houses deep in the woods and sing songs next to pristine crystal waters. Roche, in choosing the setting for her novels, complicates this Gothic idea of the heroine's relationship to her surroundings, choosing instead to send her heroine boldly outside of the safe confines of the natural world and into the city limits.

Radcliffe firmly presents the thesis that nature is a place of solace while the city is inherently corrupting; someone living too long in the city is going to suffer a fall from grace. Roche breaks away from Radcliffe completely when she moves the action of her novel outside of the forest and into the metropolitan setting of Paris. This setting is not entirely new to the Female Gothic novel, for Radcliffe makes many references to the French city in her novels, though she never stages any of her action within the city limits. Radcliffe frequently refers to the corrupting power of the city, implying that innocence and naiveté would not last long once there (e.g., Valancourt in *The Mysteries of Udolpho*). Roche challenges this idea of the corrupting city— that the city is inherently evil because of its removal from the land, and, therefore, God. Roche seems to highlight her debt to Radcliffe in her description of Paris:

> When dressed, she [Madeline] drew up the window curtain; but how different the prospect she beheld from the prospects she had been accustomed to; instead of sublime mountains towering to the clouds, or rich meadows, scattered over with flocks and herds, she now beheld high and dirty walls, which completely enclosed a small spot of ground planted with a few stunted trees. She sighed, and a tear stole from her to think she might never more enjoy the sweets of Nature.[14]

Roche's reference to the "stunted trees" of Paris at first seems to be a reminder that the city has a dysfunctional relationship with the natural world. Roche seems, however, to be directly challenging Radcliffe's own ideas of the Gothic with this setting change. For Radcliffe, part of the terror at work in the forest is its complete isolation from civilization. For example, Emily is well aware that she is completely under Montoni's control when he takes her to Udolpho. No true harm comes to Emily while she is there, as critics have pointed out. She is the victim only of harsh words and empty threats from Montoni, who is more interested in her land and inheritance than her physical body. Still, the threat of bodily harm is the basis for Radcliffe's terror, and she uses her remote landscapes to intensify this terror. Roche, on the other hand, stages her terror in one of the most populated places in Europe: Paris. Roche is, in a sense, calling Radcliffe's bluff. She shows her readers true scenes of terror (complete with blood and corporal injury), all staged with people around to quite literally hear the screams.

At Madame Fleury's Parisian home, Madeline discovers the images that inspire the most horror. Dupont leads Madeline to a chamber where she discovers "a stain of blood upon the floor."[15] In her horror, Madeline mutters, "Blood sinks deep."[16] The blood reminds Madeline that real bloodshed and real danger are at stake in her struggle against the villain D'Alembert. It becomes fitting that her attacker leads her to this room, the room where a former Gothic heroine lost that same battle. The narrator describes Madame Fleury's home as anything but the quiet refuge Madeline hoped it would be; instead, it is a place more for sin than for solace, where women are in true danger:

> She [Madame Fleury] was a woman of the most infamous description, and avowedly kept a house for the encouragement of vice. Beneath her roof the innocent and lovely Adelaide lost her life; bribed to the horrid deed by D'Alembert, the owner of the inn at which she slept put her into his power, and, on finding no other way of escaping his violence, she stabbed herself to the heart with a knife which she concealed about her; her body was thrown into a vault beneath the house; and it was the traces of her blood which had so much alarmed Madeline.[17]

Adelaide, and her ghostly presence through her blood, which is staining the floor, is a warning to Madeline. She exemplifies the dangers of naïveté. "Innocent" and easily "bribed," she met the inevitable consequence: death. And yet, there is something even darker at work in Adelaide's cautionary tale. Adelaide's blood seems to tell Madeline the same story that the narrator tells the reader, and what alarms her (and us) so much is the idea that the only true sanctuary for women is suicide.

This scene seems to be Roche's ultimate attack on Radcliffe's Edenic landscapes. No garden here for refuge, the Gothic heroine must confront the reality of the realm of sin she finds herself in.[18] The sinful world metaphor is continued as Madeline frantically searches the house for a hiding place. Fleeing from Dupont (or young D'Alembert, as he is later revealed) who has just "propositioned" her, Madeline finds a door that reveals yet another ghost portending her possible fate. This time, the ghostly woman is described as "an old woman wretchedly clad, and worn to a skeleton, kneeling in the corner of an ill-furnished room, before a wooden crucifix."[19] The old woman, later revealed to be Blanche, a woman who is implicated in the corruption and subsequent death of Adelaide, is part of perhaps the most terrifying moment to be found in Roche:

> So saying, she [Blanche] seized a knotted cord that lay beside her, and struck herself with it: Madeline instantly sprung forward—"Have mercy upon yourself (she exclaimed, as she caught her emaciated hand); God only requires real contrition as an atonement for error." The miserable wretch looked wildly at her for a moment; then uttering a piercing shriek, she convulsively wrested her hand from her and fell fainting on the floor.[20]

Blanche's self-flagellation is a direct result of her sinfulness; she feels that her blood can offer atonement for her past deeds. A scene as bloody and horrific as this one could have only occurred within the city. According to the Radcliffean model with which Roche is engaged, the forest in some way is always connected to God, as part of His creation; it is, therefore, always going to be in some small way an extension of the Garden of Eden, a place where innocence can dwell without fear of the corrupting influences of the world. Even in sinister settings like the castle at Udolpho, there is some hope remaining for the heroine in the natural world. Roche, recognizing this duality, is then forced to move outside of that realm in order to bring the implied threats in Radcliffe to fulfillment. Blanche has been reduced to nothing more than a ghost haunting the Gothic estate in Paris. Whereas Adelaide exemplifies the horrific fate of the naive heroine, Blanche shows Madeline the other side of that coin. A woman cannot embrace sin and violence as an answer to her naïveté; she must walk a fine line between chastity and deadly knowledge. The successful Gothic heroine must have a complete knowledge of the sinful world around her while never participating in it herself. It is this precarious balance of knowledge, innocence, and sin that Madeline must successfully navigate in order to survive the nightmare at Madame Fleury's Parisian estate. I posit that she does succeed in her task. By confronting the harsh reality of corporeal violence that does occur in the realm of the eighteenth-century woman, Madeline is able to "un-ghost" herself and take control of both her body and her future. She has vanquished the ghosts of those women who came before her—Adelaide and Blanche—and is able to prove herself a real flesh-and-blood woman, one who can survive the cruel realities of the real world. In the same way, through writing such bloody and bodily scenes, Regina Maria Roche is able to "un-ghost" herself as writer, thus moving out of the shadows of Ann Radcliffe and claiming her own space in literary history.

Roche does not entirely leave her Radcliffean beginnings behind while Madeline is in Paris. It is true that Madeline is in her greatest danger when she leaves the forest for Madame Fleury's in Paris, but a major part of that danger is that she no longer has the realm of the forest to offer her refuge (as it so often does for Gothic heroines). Madeline quite literally has nowhere to hide in Paris. Madeline, like Emily and Adelaide, is triumphant only when she can return to her "earthly bliss"[21] —in this case, the remote and pastoral Chateau de Valdore. Despite Roche's best efforts to distinguish herself from her predecessor, she still relies on the familiar Radcliffean plot devices. As befitting a Romantic novel, *Clermont* must end with a marriage (in this case, multiple marriages) in order for the ending to be deemed "happy." Regina Maria Roche does not deny her readers that expected "happy" ending; she writes that de Sevignie and Madeline were joined in holy matrimony "as soon as tranquility was restored to the inhabitants of the castle,"[22] signaling that Madeline has laid her ghosts to rest and may now begin her true life as de Sevignie's wife.

And, while for some modern-day critics, a marriage may not appear to be the satisfying ending we want (after all, isn't she just trading one form of ghosting for another?), we must remember that this is a marriage on her own terms—not one enforced by societal or economic pressures. One should remember the state of women during this time period—a woman alone is a woman vulnerable to the world around her. She could not hold wealth or land easily, and, as Blanche reminds us, she is susceptible to those who would take advantage of her status. Roche recognizes this, even echoing the sentiment through Madeline's father, Clermont. Clermont worries what will happen to Madeline in the event of his death:

> Unnumbered have been the sleepless nights, the wretched days I have passed on your account; looking forward to the hour which should deprive you of my protection . . . which should leave you forlorn in a world too prone to take advantage of innocence and poverty: the asylum of a cloister was the only one I had means of procuring you; but to that you ever manifested a repugnance.[23]

Madeline's "repugnance" to the idea of a convent has just cause, as convents are presented as unnatural places: "I do not thoroughly approve such institutions; I think they are somewhat contrary to nature; and I can never believe that beings immured for life, can feel gratitude so ardent, piety so exalted to the Almighty, as those who, in the wide range of the world, have daily opportunities of exploring his wonders, experiencing his goodness, and contemplating the profusion of his gifts."[24] Here, Madeline makes her choice. She will not enter a convent, nor will she become the doomed Gothic ghost represented by Adelaide and Blanche. By marrying de Sevignie, she has procured the best possible future for herself. I would caution that de Sevignie is not her traditional hero, though. Jane Austen, in *Northanger Abbey*, may believe that "when a young lady is to be a heroine . . . something must and will happen to throw a hero in her way,"[25] but Roche suggests something else entirely. To be a true Gothic heroine, like Madeline, one must confront her own mortality and embrace her corporeal self, thus establishing her place in the world. The hero is just her reward at the end of the day.

Like those of Maria Regina Roche, the writings of Mary-Anne Radcliffe[26] have been eclipsed by that "other" Radcliffe. Though her name bears striking similarities to the *Udolpho* author's, Mary-Anne Radcliffe does much to distinguish her Gothic prose from that of Ann Radcliffe. Mary-Anne Radcliffe introduces Rosalina, the heroine of her novel *Manfroné; Or, the One-Handed Monk* (1809), to her readers as ghost-like, describing her in languishing terminology and employing adjectives that emphasize her "whiteness": "Rosalina, for some time lost in thought, rested her head on her white arm, till the increasing gloom of her chamber made her look to her expiring lamp."[27] She is later described as having "a bosom fairer than the Alpine snow."[28] While some might read Rosalina's "white" arm and "Alpine snow" bosom as indicative of her privileged status as a British woman in a world rapidly becoming colonized or even as a symbol of her chasteness and everlasting purity (which as we all know is ever so important in a Gothic heroine), I would suggest that the description takes on a new meaning when the novel is placed in the context of Gordon's theories of social ghosting.

Rosalina has no agency within her world. Readers of *Manfroné* are sympathetic to Rosalina early in the novel, as she is presented as economic chattel in a money-marriage exchange between her father (the duca di Rodolpho) and the Prince di Manfroné: "'I congratulate you,' said Manfroné, 'on possessing such an inestimable treasure as you have in so fair a daughter.'"[29] By using words such as "possessing" and "treasure" in reference to Rosalina, Mary-Anne Radcliffe sets the reader up to understand her heroine in relationship to the power struggle between the male characters in the novel. But the exchange between Rodolpho and Manfroné provides readers with another way to understand Rosalina: as a ghost. Much like a true specter, Rosalina haunts her home more than she actually inhabits it. Rosalina often inhabits the role of the spectator, overhearing conversations while hidden from view, as she does when she learns of her impending marriage to the villain Manfroné:

> Pale and ill, she arose in the morning, and was sitting deeply absorbed in pensive ruminations at her casement, which overlooked part of the courtyard, when she saw the duca crossing it, in earnest conversation with the prince di Manfroné. By their gestures, they appeared to be arranging some important affair, and once or twice the eyes of the prince were directed towards the wing of the castello which contained her apartments. She hastily withdrew from the casement.[30]

Rosalina here appears to be almost haunting the scene. She has no active agency as she lurks from the sidelines—a stance mimicking her passive role in the marriage contract she is witnessing. Adding to her ghostliness, Rosalina is again described as "pale and ill."

In a similar scene, Rosalina withdraws from a party thrown by her father, preferring to witness the festivities without actually participating in them.

> When the hour appointed for the banquet arrived, Rosalina descended to the hall: the confusion she felt at being exposed to the gaze of so many strangers, with whom it was crowded, increased the tint of the rose, which since her late illness but faintly blossomed on her lovely cheek and added to her charms. . . . Rosalina hardly dared to raise her eyes during the repast, for whenever she did, she was sure to find herself the universal object of contemplation, from which her native modesty revolted. . . . She hastened from the hall as soon as possible, and gladly sought the welcome retirement of her chamber. [31]

Rosalina moves through the duca di Rodolpho's party as a ghost. She interacts with no one; only the physical sight of her makes her presence known. While Rosalina chooses not to participate in her surroundings, the men around her all take notice of her presence, which seems to captivate everyone in the room, especially "the leaders of her father's forces, who had been before restrained only by their fears of attracting the duca's observation in their conduct towards Rosalina. [They were] now emboldened by the intoxicating juice of the grape, [and] eyed her with such an appearance of insolent familiarity."[32] This scene is important as a metaphor for the female experience in the eighteenth century, as Rosalina is just as responsible for her status as ghost as are the men objectifying her with "insolent familiarity."[33] Rosalina is once again objectified, as she is understood by these men as property to be possessed, but she is also responsible, in a way, for her own ghosting. In this scene, as in others in the novel, she is the one who chooses to withdraw into the liminal spaces of society.

In order to begin to confront (and overcome) her spectrality, Rosalina must confront the corporeal reality found in the violence that surrounds her. Unlike other Gothic heroines, who often faint away when confronted with blood, Rosalina willingly faces the reality of her father's murder. Despite the servants urging her not to go, Rosalina, though "rendered . . . speechless,"[34] proceeds into her father's chamber and views the dead body.

> The breathless body of the duca lay stretched on his couch; the bosom was bare; a dagger was deeply planted in the breast, the hilt of which was encircled by the ghastly fingers of a skeleton hand, and the clothes of the bed were dyed with the blood of the unfortunate Rodolpho. Such was the horrible view which presented itself to the distended gaze of Rosalina. [35]

Unlike many similar Gothic tales, *Manfroné* openly and vividly displays the effects of the violence that occurs within its pages. In comparison to Radcliffe's *Udolpho,* which hides its dead bodies offstage and often describes the scene in vague, clean terminology (e.g., the death of Emily's aunt, Madame Montoni, whose corpse is reduced to an "exhausted frame"[36]), *Manfroné*'s are displayed in gruesome detail in a "distended gaze."[37] Why then is it necessary to change a tried-and-true method of Gothic fiction? Why incorporate such grisly details in what is otherwise a traditionally "Female" Gothic text? I would suggest that Mary-Anne Radcliffe is playing with the body/ghost binary. In short, Rosalina needs to confront the bloody (and bodily) reality here to figuratively "un-ghost" herself. Read in the greater sense, Mary-Anne Radcliffe is "un-ghosting" her audience as well, by writing true horror fiction for an audience that she believes does not need to be sheltered from such details.

Following Rosalina's conversion from specter/spectator to a character with agency and action, she begins to be described in terms more fitting a real person, not a ghost, as is seen in her kidnapping scene.

> Her tender frame was weakened so much by her sufferings, which always were increased when she saw Grimaldi, that he began to fear that he should be deprived of his prey, and therefore kept from the chamber where she was. This had the desired effect; and no longer tormented by his presence, her youth and constitution prevailed, and she slowly began to recover.[38]

Rosalina may not sound like she is better off as a prisoner in Grimaldi's chamber than she was as a ghost in her father's castello, but she is being described in corporeal terms. The choice of the word "frame" suggests skin and bones, although they are "tender" and "weakened." The importance of this scene, as with the one of violence discussed earlier, is that Rosalina *prevails*; her status as "ghost" is not a permanent one. She is not yet a true ghost, and while society may push her to the margins, she is still capable of establishing herself as a person by reclaiming her rights to her body.

As characters, Roche's Madeline and Mary-Anne Radcliffe's Rosalina appear to be the perfect Gothic heroines—pale, quiet, fainting away. Both of these women, though, in the course of their journeys, break free of their stereotypes, boldly confronting the violence that is put in front of them. Just as they resist the title of "ghost," their authors, Regina Maria Roche and Mary-Anne Radcliffe, write themselves out of the shadow of their predecessors. Ann Radcliffe may remain more famous, but these two writers refuse to play the ghosts in her shadow.

NOTES

1. Jane Austen, *Northanger Abbey, Lady Susan, The Watsons, and Sanditon,* ed. John Davie (Oxford: Oxford University Press, 1998), 24.

2. Diane Long Hoeveler, *Gothic Feminism: The Professionalism of Gender from Charlotte Smith to the Brontës* (University Park: Pennsylvania State University Press, 1998), 86.

3. Avery Gordon, *Ghostly Matters: Haunting and the Sociological Imagination* (Minneapolis: University of Minnesota Press, 1997), 8.

4. Valdine Clemens, *The Return of the Repressed: Gothic Horror from* The Castle of Otranto *to* Alien (Albany: State University of New York Press, 1999), 33.

5. Ibid.

6. Ibid., 41.

7. Austen, *Northanger Abbey*, 1.

8. Ibid., 26.

9. Ibid., 68.

10. Ann Radcliffe, *The Mysteries of Udolpho*, ed. Bonamy Dobrée (Oxford: Oxford University Press, 1996), 232.

11. Natalie Schroeder, "Introduction," in *Clermont*, by Regina Maria Roche (Chicago: Valancourt Books, 2006), xiv.

12. Ibid., xv.

13. Natalie Schroeder, "*The Mysteries of Udolpho* and *Clermont*: The Radcliffean Encroachment on the Art of Regina Maria Roche," *Studies in the Novel* 12, no. 2 (1980): 138.

14. Regina Maria Roche, *Clermont*, ed. Natalie Schroeder (Chicago: Valancourt Books, 2006), 334.

15. Roche, *Clermont*, 337.

16. Ibid.

17. Ibid., 364.

18. Roche is confronting an issue that many critics of Radcliffe notice. Radcliffe merely hints at violence in her novels; any scenes of violence happen "offstage," as is common of Female Gothic writers. Ellen Moers has an excellent discussion of the lack of violence in these novels, which she says makes the heroine's struggle a symbolic one, expressed through property plots and will disputes rather than blood and gore.

19. Roche, *Clermont*, 341.

20. Ibid.

21. Ibid., 378.

22. Ibid., 377.

23. Ibid., 32–33.

24. Ibid., 33.

25. Austen, *Northanger Abbey*, 5.

26. To avoid confusion, I will refer to Ann Radcliffe as "Radcliffe" and to Mary-Anne Radcliffe by using her full name. The term "Radcliffean" refers to the Gothic style of Ann Radcliffe and her imitators.

27. Mary-Anne Radcliffe, *Manfroné: Or, the One-Handed Monk* (New York: Arno, 1972), 3.

28. Ibid., 8.

29. Ibid., vol. 1, part 2, 22.

30. Ibid., 25.

31. Ibid., 156–157.

32. Ibid., 157.

33. Ibid.

34. Ibid., 215.

35. Ibid.

36. Ann Radcliffe, *Udolpho*, 375.

37. Mary-Anne Radcliffe, *Manfroné*, 215.

38. Ibid., 233.

Chapter Two

City of Ghosts

Elizabeth Bowen's Wartime Stories

Stefania Porcelli

The presence of ghost-related semantics pervades all of Elizabeth Bowen's works. It especially recurs in her representation of wartime London in the collection *The Demon Lover and Other Stories* (1945). Although some of them barely mention the conflict, these stories of apparitions and dissolutions are all haunted by World War II. As Bowen herself clarifies, "these are all wartime, none of them *war*, stories." Indeed, they are "studies of climate, war-climate, and of the strange growths it raised." Since *The Demon Lover*'s postscript defines London's atmosphere in the early 1940s as a "state of lucid abnormality,"[1] in which people's awareness is simultaneously heightened and anesthetized, it is this ambiguous climate during the war that calls for versatile ghost imagery.

Read as an expression of social or psychological realism by her early critics,[2] Bowen's work has more recently been the object of feminist criticism, Irish studies, and criticism on war literature by women. It has also been compared to postmodern literature and to Samuel Beckett's work.[3] Bowen's ghosts have especially attracted great critical attention, both in relationship to the Gothic and Anglo-Irish literary traditions and as "a symbol of war that will not go away."[4] While trying to consider the collection as "an organic whole,"[5] this study will examine Bowen's multilayered ghost imagery by focusing on some of her short stories that most significantly convey feelings of loss and displacement as experienced by civilians during the Blitz on London.

Most of Bowen's ghostly appearances have been understood as hallucinations caused by the trauma experienced by civilians during the war.[6] Yet, many of Bowen's ghosts can be read as supernatural entities, rather than as

projections of her characters' distressed minds. Accordingly, I contend that
the semantics of the ghost is a structural as well as a thematic element in
Bowen's narrative. It features in her more "realistic" stories as well as in
those writings that overtly reveal her fascination for Gothicism, and it ranges
from the metaphorical implications of the words *ghost/ghostly* to the construction of ghost-characters intruding into people's houses or upon people's
lives. The ghost imagery, I argue, arises from the incursion of the historical
into the private dimension, namely from wartime disruptions of the paralysis
and stagnation that characterizes the family context in these stories.

As Neil Corcoran puts it, however, in Bowen's writings there is more
than "fracture and disintegration."[7] Along with what he calls "a peculiar or
disconcerting ethics,"[8] I would like to call attention to her great insight into
history and politics. Both ethics and politics entail a confrontation with the
ghost: "It is necessary to speak *of the* ghost, indeed *to the* ghost and *with* it,
from the moment that no ethics, no politics . . . seems possible and thinkable
and *just* that does not recognize in its principle the respect for those others
who are no longer or for those others who are not yet *there*, presently living,
whether they are already dead or not yet born."[9]

In Bowen's narrative, the ghost always demands something from the
living that have a great *responsibility*—another category we can borrow from
Derrida[10]—toward both the past and the future.

A SPECTRAL ATMOSPHERE

Fragments and disconnections are prominent in the main part of *The Demon
Lover*. Night is Bowen's usual setting. At night, in the dark of the blackout or
during the German attacks, the city looks like an unnatural place. Feelings of
displacement dominate the streets and combine with the sense of a dissolving
world. "In the Square," *The Demon Lover*'s opening story, features an "ex-
tinct scene," with the "appearance of belonging to some ages ago."[11] Its first
paragraph sets the atmosphere for the whole collection:

> At about nine o'clock on this hot bright July evening the square looked *myster-
> ious*: it was completely empty, and a whitish reflection, *ghost* of the glare of
> midday, came from the *pale-coloured* façades on its four sides and seemed to
> brim it up to the top. The grass was parched in the middle; its shaved surface
> was paid for by *people who had gone*. The sun, now too low to enter normally,
> was able to enter brilliantly at a point where three of the houses had been
> bombed away; two or three of the many trees, dark with summer, caught on
> their tops the *illicit* gold. . . . Most of the glassless windows were shuttered or
> boarded up, but some framed hollow inside dark.[12] (emphasis added)

The ghost here is clearly a metaphor for "touch" or "trace," a suggestion of some quality or element that is fading away; the pale light that still lingers in the square becomes the "ghost of the glare of the midday." Semantically, the word *ghost* connects with other expressions in the passage and creates an eerie atmosphere, where what is no longer there still affects the present. The choice of words such as *mysterious*, *ghost*, and *illicit* countervails the detailed description of the place. Moreover, the phrase "people who had gone" recalls both the people dislodged because of the bombings and those who are dead. The adjective *illicit* imposes a moral judgment on the scene, as if the light had no right to shine on this scene of ruins and on these empty houses.

"In the Square" is built around the opposition "familiar/unfamiliar,"[13] a dichotomy that becomes stronger throughout the collection, according to its "rising tide of hallucination."[14] The characters' sense of displacement links up with women's new attitudes and with the sense of independence they gained during the war.[15] The man called Rupert, back in London to meet his former mistress Magdela, is surprised at seeing "the coldly intimate look he had found new in women since his return."[16] Magdela's reply that "so much has happened. . . . So much more than you know"[17] means more than she actually says, opening up to the experience of other characters in the collection.

Thus, the "ghostly" sounds that one hears in this house are the signs of the "functional anarchy," of social changes, of experience shared with other people, rather than the trace of the past.[18] Both the square and the house of the story are no longer private, but public spaces. Along with the blurring of the boundaries between the private and the public dimensions, the war diminishes the social and cultural distance among people. As the narrator of *The Heat of the Day* (1949), Bowen's wartime novel, affirms, "War at present worked as a thinning of the membrane between the this and the that, it was a becoming apparent."[19] Also the sense of an isolated and final identity is put into question: "Magdela smiled and said to Rupert: 'Yes, look. Now the place seems to belong to everyone. One has nothing except one's feelings. Sometimes I think I hardly know myself.'"[20] The characters' impression that they are strangers to themselves is the ultimate effect of the war on their perception and is one of the reasons for the appearance of ghosts.

The dichotomy of familiar/unfamiliar is even more emphasized in *The Demon Lover*'s last story "Mysterious Kôr," which most poignantly conveys the image of London as an unreal city, "like the moon's capital,"[21] similar to the fictitious city of Kôr, the city of the dead in H. Rider Haggard's novel *She*.[22] The story's central image is London as "a ghostly unbroken reflection,"[23] so unreal as to resemble Haggard's Kôr. Both cities are immaterial. Yet, unlike Kôr, London might be totally annihilated: "This war shows we've by no means come to the end. If you can blow whole places out of existence, you can blow whole places into it. I don't see why not. They say we can't say what's come out since the bombing started. By the time we've come to the end, Kôr may be the one city left: the abiding city."[24] Not only does this passage show an awareness of the destructive potential of new war technologies, but it also asserts the role of imagination as a saving resource for the city's "homeless wanderers."[25] "Kôr's not really anywhere," has "no history," no habitants, and no time.[26] It has been created by imagination and as such it cannot be destroyed by bombs. Literature's creative power contrasts with the destruction brought about by war. Not only first invented by the artist, Kôr can be evoked again by the readers' and by the characters' imagination. It can therefore last forever.

Neither "In the Square" nor "Mysterious Kôr" allows for an obviously supernatural interpretation. Yet, in both stories the ghost-related semantics (and especially the adjective *ghostly*) creates an atmosphere of unreality and dream in the city (and the book). They frame the collection and provide the book with its order based on the "rising tide of hallucination" mentioned above. Hallucinations, dreams, and "fantasies"[27] —in one word, *imagination*—can conjure up figures of ghosts in order to help people cope with the distress of war. "Mysterious Kôr" is the book's ultimate example of how the dreams and fantasies of ordinary people worked as consoling compensation for what Bowen called the "desiccation" caused by war.[28] Indeed, in *The Demon Lover*, ghosts, dreams, and hallucinations are never symptoms of mental disorder.[29] They are in fact the only certainties that "fill the vacuum for the uncertain 'I.'"[30] Being outside of time and space, the ghost is the most profitable representation of the disruption of time and space in the city under siege.

THE LOAD OF THE PAST

A figurative or a real ghost appropriately appears in Bowen's fiction when a traumatic event makes the sequence of time collapse; as Victoria Glendinning states, "Nearly all the short stories [Bowen] wrote during the war (collected in *The Demon Lover*) have this element of time breaking down, a concept of London as a city of ghosts."[31] The metaphor of time breaking down is significantly literalized in "The Inherited Clock," a sort of detective story that hinges upon a mysterious episode that occurred in the protagonist's childhood. Clara has entirely removed it (and the clock at the center of this story) from her memory. Yet, the abnormal perception caused by the war leads her to recover that moment when she was injured because of her cousin's sadism.

> *"I'll tell you something, Clara. Have you ever seen a minute? Have you actually had one wriggling inside your hand? Did you know if you keep your finger inside a clock for a minute, you can pick out that very minute and take it home*

for your own?" So it is Paul who stealthily lifts the dome off. It is Paul who selects the finger of Clara's that is to be guided, shrinking, then forced wincing into the works, to be wedged in them, bruised in them, bitten into and eaten up by the cogs. "*No, you have got to keep it there, or you will lose the minute. I am doing the counting—the counting up to sixty.*". . . But there is to be no sixty. The ticking stops.[32]

The incident is even more upsetting, because the clock had not stopped ticking for more than a century, whereas now "the hundred years are all angry."[33] The time of trauma (i.e., wartime) is discontinuous, full of leaks and anachronistic returns. The story shares, therefore, the modernist obsession with the unnatural return of the past. Time cannot be understood as a linear progression any longer: "Each moment is everywhere, it holds the war in its crystal."[34]

Like "In the Square," "The Inherited Clock" features no human ghosts, but its central character—the clock—is a haunting presence in Clara's life. In Bowen's work furniture frequently haunts its owners, assuming, as Maud Ellmann suggests, "the role of phantom, inducing characters to re-experience a past that they have never lived."[35] Thus, the clock stands in for a revenant from the past,[36] a "*skeleton* clock . . . threatening to a degree its oddness could not explain" (emphasis added).[37] Being "without a face,"[38] the clock is also ineffable, all the more frightening for that reason. Its minute hand makes "spectral advance[s]" and its tick would be heard even if Clara dropped it out of the window.[39] Its power is so strong that Clara herself begins to resemble a phantom: in the blackout "she seemed to pass like a ghost through an endless wall."[40] The simile arises from her being at a loss in the city: "Nothing told her anything, except one thing—unless she had lost her memory, she had lost her way."[41]

"The Inherited Clock" is one of the best examples of the frustration derived from not being able to come to terms with the ghost of the past. Time is here void and useless.

> The newly-arrived clock, chopping off each second to fall and perish, recalled how many seconds had gone to make up her years, how many of these had been either null or bitter, how many had been void before the void claimed them. She had been subject to waiting as to an illness; the tissues of her being had been consumed by it. Was it possible that the past should be able to injure the future irreparably?[42]

The specter, according to Derrida, makes past and future coexist and affect each other: "This being-with specters could also be, not only, but also, a *politics* of memory, of inheritance, and of generations."[43] Having recalled her past, Clara is finally able to project her thought into a less barren future.

Yet, as Bowen herself states, in this and other cases, the past "discharges its load of feeling into the anaesthetized and bewildered present."[44]

Linking past and present through a phantom object or character, Bowen questions the idea of this war as an unpredictable result of the political circumstances, and complicates the discourse about responsibility. Although the central questions of "In the Square"—"Who would think that this was the same world? . . . Who would have thought this could really happen?"[45] — remain unanswered in this first story (and ostensibly allude to "No one" as the only possible reply), one has to read Bowen's writings as a whole to understand that war, in her view, is a consequence of very old processes that involve the oppression of the weakest: "War is not an accident: it is an outcome. One cannot look back too far to ask, of what?"[46] World War II often links back to more ancient conflicts, such as World War I and the Anglo-Irish Troubles of the 1920s; the melting of the present and the past appears as a historical and political reassessment. As Harrison tells Stella in the second chapter of *The Heat of the Day*, "War, if you come to think of it, hasn't started anything that wasn't there already."[47] This explains why in wartime the past often comes back as a ghostly presence. An idealized moment only on the surface, it more often appears as a pattern that the present risks repeating.

The link between the two world wars clearly emerges in the central story of the collection, "The Demon Lover," in which the unfamiliar again impinges upon the familiar. Mrs. Drover's fiancé, who disappeared during World War I, returns after twenty-five years to meet (and maybe to kill) her. Deeply dislocated by the effects of that war and driven out of her London house by "the bombs of the next war,"[48] Mrs. Drover is struck by a strong feeling of displacement when she goes back to collect some of her belongings from her shut-up house: "In her once familiar street . . . an unfamiliar queerness had silted up."[49] Somebody has entered her house and left a letter reminding her of an "unnatural promise."[50] She had promised to meet her former lover again on this precise day. Following the pattern already detected in "The Inherited Clock," Mrs. Drover recovers the past event she had forgotten, this time with a difference: "She remembered—with one white burning blank as where acid has dropped on a photograph: *under no conditions* could she remember his face."[51] In the end she does recognize his eyes, but it is too late: no salvation is now possible, and the story ends with Mrs. Drover's scream of terror, while the demon's car (i.e., the taxi she has called to escape from the house) takes her away, "accelerating without mercy."[52] This story is the only one in which the specter is vengeful.

Despite its disquieting atmosphere and the horror conveyed by its final paragraph, which could lead one to see the story's revenant as "an evil power,"[53] "The Demon Lover" is one of those writings in which, according to Bowen, the ghost is at least "questionable."[54] Although many of her stories might be understood as ghost stories, Bowen's works must be admitted to waver between the realistic and the supernatural. Indeed, this ambiguity is one of her major literary achievements. The best example of such ambiguity is the story "The Happy Autumn Fields," which, suspended as it is between reality and dream, truth and illusion, properly fits Todorov's definition of the fantastic as a literary genre. [55] While evacuating her bombed house, a London woman called Mary encounters—to use one of Bowen's recurrent words and also the title of the first collection of short stories [56] —a mysterious figure from the past. The latter is either a figment of her mind or an "authentic" revenant. Since Mary is said to have been sleeping, the "other" might be a dream. But the narrator seems to suggest that two entities inhabit Mary's body, [57] for example when he or she asserts, "'No idea,' she yawned into Mary's hand. [58] . . . She instinctively tried and failed, to unbutton the bosom of Mary's dress," [59] instead of saying, "'No idea,' Mary yawned into her hands. . . . Mary instinctively tried and failed, to unbutton the bosom of her dress." The unnatural use of personal pronouns in these sentences suggests that *she* and *Mary* refer to two different persons. Yet, Mary is the only woman in the room. I do not think the dream-story interpretation a viable one, but I concede that here the supernatural is only hinted at and never made explicit. The two readings at least intermingle, and rightly so. Bowen's stories never yield final interpretations, and they force the reader to hesitate between rational and supernatural explanations. However, what is at stake here is not the nature of this *she*, but the fragmentation and unreality of both the present and the past: Everything is ghostly, and therefore inconsistent.

GHOSTLY WOMEN

Focusing on civilians, Bowen stresses the effect of the war on people who do not fight but still are involved in wartime activities and distress. Her stories do not feature many soldiers. Most of her characters are children and men who do not fit military life. But her central figures are always women. The war asks for women's self-denial at the same time as war propaganda reveals a patronizing or a suspicious attitude toward them. [60] As women, they undergo a double displacement in wartime, and dislocations always produce a blurred or ghostly identity. As John Hildebilde puts it, "Human contact is often dominated by an emotional and psychic 'presence'—a ghost, whether real or imagined; an absent lover; a missing parent. Somewhere near the centre stands—quite literally—a young woman, who watches and waits." [61] The representation of wartime London in terms of a spectral city acquires new levels of interpretation from the gender issue's prominence in wartime.

Through this lens, "The Demon Lover" also can be understood as the resurgence of preexisting sexual conflicts, in which World War II diabolical-

ly revivifies male aggression.[62] Indeed, Mrs. Drover's lover had never been
kind to her, and he even left a weal on her hand before leaving for the front.
After twenty-five years, he is back as a merciless demon. Conversely, Mrs.
Drover has lived a quite conventional life of marriage and childbearing.
Throughout her work, Bowen suggests that these are the only things women
are educated for and that war ideology crystallizes them in the role of wives
and mothers. Despite the conventionality and dullness of her life, however,
nothing in the text suggests that Mrs. Drover is so frustrated about her life as
to conjure up her former lover's ghost as the ultimate personification of her
"wanting to escape."[63]

Yet the escapist interpretation might be more profitably applied to other
stories in the book. Profoundly dissatisfied with her husband, who is not
"interested in anything but his work" and is only preoccupied with the war,[64]
the protagonist of "Pink May" seeks satisfaction in an adulterous relationship. At first, "this other man worked just as hard but *was* interested in [her],"
but then "he put [her] straight into a taxi and sent [her]—not took [her]—
home."[65] If this affair fails to rescue the woman from her paralyzed marriage,
a female ghost does succeed. She haunts the house that the couple moves into
during the Blitz, but she is just a projection of the protagonist's imagination.

Unable to break her marriage, the woman prefers to direct the responsibility for this separation away from herself, accusing the jealous ghost-woman.
Yet, she obliquely admits that she cannot be sure of the ghost's existence.

> *"But look, did you ever see it?"*
> "Well, not exactly. No, I can't say I *saw* it."
> *"You mean, you simply heard it?"*
> "Well, not exactly that . . ."
> *"You saw things move?"*
> "Well, I never turned round in time. I . . .
> "If you don't understand—I am sorry I ever told you the story! Not a ghost—
> when it ruined my whole life! Don't you see, can't you see there must have
> been something? Left to oneself, one doesn't ruin one's life!"[66]

The ghost might have never been actually there. Accused of having ruined
the protagonist's marriage, it ultimately turns out to be the fruit of her imagination and, in Bowen's words, "a saving hallucination."

Bowen makes only a few stories explicitly supernatural; in the postscript
to the collection, she states that only in "Green Holly" is the ghost "definite."[67] The reader here is forced to believe in the ghost's existence, because
the narration focuses on *her* point of view.[68] Actually, there is a ghostly
couple in this story, but only the female ghost is allowed to move and speak.
She even flirts with Mr. Winterslow, one of the people dealing with war
matters in the house, a member of a group of "Experts—in what the Censor
would not permit to say."[69] Accordingly, "they are accounted for by their

friends in London as 'being somewhere off in the country, nobody knows where, doing something frightfully hush-hush, nobody knows what.'"[70] Disappeared from London and ghostly figures themselves, they end up in a haunted house. The ironic tinge in this story recalls Virginia Woolf's ironic short story set in another house haunted by a ghostly couple.[71] Unlike Woolf's characters, Bowen's were not happy when they were alive. The ghostly woman complains about her marriage: "They should not have shut her up in the country. How could she not make hay while the sun shone? The year round, no man except her husband, his uninteresting jealousy, his dull passion. Then, at Christmas, so many men that one did not know where to turn. The ghost, leaning further over the gallery, pouted down at the suicide. She said: 'You should have let me explain.' The man made no answer: he never had."[72] It is not clear whether the woman had betrayed her husband, but it is quite plain that he did not let her talk. Only as a ghost can she speak and also communicate with the world of the living, while her husband, the very image of paralysis, "with the side of his head blown out lay as always, one foot just touching the lowest step of the stairs."[73]

In this story, the ghost herself undergoes a process of self-inquiry that leads her to question her identity and her desires: "It was not merely a matter of, how was she? but of, *was* she—tonight—at all? Death had left her to be her own mirror; for into no other was she able to see."[74] In this way, the ghost stages a process that turns women from objects of others' gaze (the mirror being an indirect way to look at themselves) into subjects of their own actions: "It is the haunted who haunt."[75]

BETWEEN LIFE AND DEATH

From what precedes, it should be clear that Bowen's representation of wartime London does not focus on ruins and corpses, but on the emotions of all-encompassing moments. This topic also fits the short form, which, in her words, "allows for what is crazy about humanity: obstinacies, inordinate heroisms, 'immortal longings.'"[76] The short story is "the *ideal* prose medium for war-time creative writing."[77] It can "render the great significance of a small event" and "register the emotional colour of a moment."[78]

Bowen rejects the conventional representation of war as a series of military actions and turns to the noncombatants' perception of the Blitz. To give a picture of a historical period—she argues in one of her critical works—one has to consider that "inseparable from happenings are the mood, temper and climate of the time," since "a picture presented in terms of the actualities *only* would be a false one."[79] As we have seen, she draws on different literary modes in order to represent what "psychic London"[80] was like in those years. Thus, Bowen's fiction is one of the best representations of those years. In

Bowen's view, art can serve memory better than history: "We must not shy at the fact that we cull the past from fiction rather than from history, and that art, out of the very necessity to compose a picture cannot but eliminate, edit and so, falsify. Raw history, in its implications, is unnerving; and, even so, it only chronicles the survivors."[81] In another work, she conflates history and myth; indeed, "history was fiction."[82] In her review of *The People's War* by Angus Calder, Bowen criticizes the rationalized way of representing history: "For the general run of us, existence during the war had a mythical intensity, heightened for dwellers in cities under attack,"[83] thence the psychic and the supernatural facet of her narrative. The ghost suffices for both, turning her wartime stories into ghost stories. It is a structural device that fulfills the aesthetics of the fragment ensuing from the war.

The war generates ghosts in Bowen's autobiographical writings as well as in her fiction. "London, 1940," for example, depicts the fragmentation of the city after a night of bombings. The city has a human aspect and resembles a wounded woman's body. London looks like a series of isolated villages. The broken urban space, as Italian literary critic Maria Stella suggests, coincides with the linguistic and stylistic construction of the work—this space is not a metaphor for the writing, but *is* the writing itself.[84] Different sections of the essay refer to different parts of the city and also use different registers. The ghost imagery significantly occurs in the passage about the writer's neighborhood: "Illicitly, leading the existence of ghosts, we overlook the locked park,"[85] and above all with regard to the evacuees, depicted as "risen dead in the doors of tombs."[86]

On the one hand, this death-in-life condition characterizes the survivors in most literature about World War II. The protagonist of "Ivy Gripped the Steps," for example, has "the face of somebody dead who was still there."[87] On the other hand, the dead still inhabit the city. As the narrator states in *The Heat of the Day*, "Most of all the dead, from mortuaries, from under cataracts of rubble, made their anonymous presence—not as today's dead but as yesterday's living—felt through London. Uncounted, they continued to move in shoals through the city day, pervading everything to be seen or heard or felt with their torn-off senses, drawing on this tomorrow they had expected—for death cannot be so sudden as all that."[88] In Bowen's fiction, war produces hallucinations as well as "real" ghosts, inasmuch as it blurs the distinction between life and death. Bowen's ghosts represent at the same time the survivors of the Blitz (alive only until the next bombing), hallucinations induced by air raids, and spirits from the past claiming a place among the living. The ghost, lingering in this liminal space, becomes an effective literary device in the representation of what people daily experienced in wartime London, where the categories of "certainty," "finality," and "reality" are repeatedly put into question.

NOTES

1. Elizabeth Bowen, *"The Demon Lover*, Postscript to First U.S. Edition," in *The Mulberry Tree: Writings of Elizabeth Bowen*, ed. Hermione Lee (London: Virago, 1986; reprint, New York: Vintage, 1999), 95. Hereafter this volume will be referred to as *MT*. If not otherwise specified the emphasis is in the original.

2. See, for example, William Heath, *Elizabeth Bowen: An Introduction to Her Novels* (Madison: University of Wisconsin Press, 1961); Harriet Blodget, *Patterns of Reality: Elizabeth Bowen 's Novels* (The Hague: Mouton, 1975).

3. Among others, see Declan Kiberd, *Inventing Ireland: The Literature of the Modern Nation* (London: Jonathan Cape, 1995); Gill Plain, *Women's Fiction of the Second World War: Gender, Power, and Resistance* (Edinburgh: Edinburgh University Press, 1996); Phyllis Lassner, *British Women Writers of World War II: Battleground of Their Own* (London: Macmillan, 1997); Andrew Bennet and Nicholas Royle, *Elizabeth Bowen and the Dissolution of the Novel* (London: Macmillan, 1995); Sinéad Mooney, "Unstable Compounds: Bowen's Beckettian Affinities," *Modern Fiction Studies* 53, no. 2 (2007): 238–55.

4. Robert L. Calder, "'A More Sinister Troth': Elizabeth Bowen's 'The Demon Lover' as Allegory," *Studies in Short Fiction* 31, no. 1 (1994): 91–98.

5. *MT*, 96.

6. See, for example, Douglas A. Hughes, "Cracks in the Psyche: Elizabeth Bowen's 'The Demon Lover,'" *Studies in Short Fiction* 10, no. 4 (1973): 411–13. Reacting against this psychological interpretation, Daniel V. Fraustino claims that the story must be understood as a mystery or murder story in his essay "Elizabeth Bowen's 'The Demon Lover': Psychosis or Seduction?" *Studies in Short Fiction* 17, no. 4 (1980): 483–87. Fraustino's reading is further questioned by Robert L. Calder (see note 4).

7. Neil Corcoran, *Elizabeth Bowen: The Enforced Return* (Oxford: Oxford University Press, 2004), 13.

8. Ibid.

9. Jacques Derrida, *Specters of Marx: The State of the Debt, the Work of Mourning, and the New International*, trans. Peggy Kamuf (New York: Routledge, 1994), xix.

10. "No justice . . . seems possible or thinkable beyond the principle of some *responsibility*, beyond all living present, within that which disjoins the living present, before the ghosts of those who are not yet born or who are already dead" (Ibid.).

11. Elizabeth Bowen, "In the Square," in *The Collected Stories of Elizabeth Bowen*, 609–15 (London: Jonathan Cape, 1980; reprint, London: Vintage, 1999), 609. Hereafter *CS*.

12. Ibid.

13. Ibid.

14. *MT*, 96.

15. The war prompted social transformation in two ways: The attack on the cities pushed the private space of the house into the public arena, and women gained self-determination power by doing war works and wartime activities. Many of Bowen's characters work as car drivers or ARP wardens, like the writer herself. See, for example, "Unwelcome Idea," "Pink May," and especially, *The Heat of the Day* .

16. *CS*, 610.

17. *CS*, 612.

18. *CS* , 615.

19. Elizabeth Bowen, *The Heat of the Day* (London: Jonathan Cape, 1949; reprint, London: Vintage, 1998), 195. Hereafter *HD*. The narrator also states: "The wall between the living and the living became less solid as the wall between the living and the dead thinned" (*HD*, 92).

20. *CS*, 615.

21. Elizabeth Bowen, "Mysterious Kôr," in *CS*, 728–40: 728.

22. First published in 1887, Haggard's *She: A History of Adventure* was extraordinarily popular in its time. The book affected Bowen's imagination from her childhood. See, for example, Bowen's broadcast "Rider Haggard: *She*," in *MT*, 246–50.

23. *CS*, 728.

24. *CS*, 730.

25. *MT*, 95.

26. *CS*, 730, 729.

27. *MT*, 96.

28. *MT*, 96. See also Victoria Glendinning, *Elizabeth Bowen: Portrait of a Writer* (New York: Avon, 1977), 145.

29. "The hallucinations are an unconscious, instinctive, saving resort on the part of the characters: life, mechanized by the controls of wartime, and emotionally torn and impoverished by changes, had to complete itself in *some* way. It is a fact that in Britain, and especially in London, in wartime many people had strange deep intense dreams" (*MT*, 96).

30. *MT*, 98.

31. Glendinning, *Elizabeth Bowen*, 143.

32. Elizabeth Bowen, "The Inherited Clock," in *CS*, 623–40: 639.

33. Ibid.

34. Elizabeth Bowen, "Summer Night," in *CS*, 583–608: 599.

35. Maud Ellmann, "The Shadowy Fifth," in *The Fiction of the 1940s: Stories of Survival*, eds. Rod Mengham and N. H. Reeve (New York: Palgrave, 2001), 11.

36. According to Derrida, a specter "is always a *revenant*. One cannot control his comings and goings because it begins by coming back." Derrida, *Specters of Marx*, 11.

37. *CS*, 627.

38. Ibid.

39. *CS*, 627, 635.

40. *CS*, 632.

41. Ibid.

42. *CS*, 631.

43. Derrida, *Specters of Marx*, xviii.

44. *MT*, 98.

45. *CS*, 611.

46. Elizabeth Bowen, *Bowen's Court* (London: Longmans, Green & Co., 1942), in *Bowen's Court and Seven Winters* (London: Virago, 1984), 454.

47. *HD*, 33.

48. Elizabeth Bowen "The Demon Lover," in *CS*, 661–66: 664.

49. *CS*, 661.

50. *CS*, 663.

51. *CS*, 665.

52. *CS*, 666.

53. Phyllis Lassner, *Elizabeth Bowen: A Study of the Short Fiction* (New York: Twayne, 1991), 66.

54. See *MT*, 98, where Bowen affirms that other "questionable" ghosts are those referred to in "Pink May" and "The Cheery Soul."

55. Tzvetan Todorov, *The Fantastic: A Structural Approach to a Literary Genre*, trans. Richard Howard (Ithaca, NY: Cornell University Press, 1975), 25.

56. Elizabeth Bowen, *Encounters* (London: Sidgwick & Jackson, 1923).

57. See Jeannette Ward Smith, "Being Incommensurable/Incommensurable Beings: Ghosts in Elizabeth Bowen's Short Stories," MA thesis, Georgia State University, 2006, at http://etd.gsu.edu/theses/available/etd-04282006-181909/unrestricted/ward_jeannette_w_200605_ma.pdf (accessed October 3, 2008).

58. Elizabeth Bowen, "The Happy Autumn Fields," in *CS*, 671–85: 677.

59. *CS*, 678.

60. See, for example, "Unwelcome Idea" (*CS*, 573–77), in which a man is said to blame women more than Hitler for having originated the war (576).

61. John Hildebidle, *Five Irish Writers: The Errand of Keeping Alive* (Cambridge, MA: Harvard University Press, 1989), 91.

62. Karen Schneider, *Loving Arms: British Women Writing the Second World War* (Lexington: University Press of Kentucky, 1997), 87.

63. As Daniel V. Fraustino suggests. See Fraustino, "Elizabeth Bowen's 'The Demon Lover,'" 485.

64. Elizabeth Bowen, "Pink May," in *CS*, 712–18: 716.

65. *CS*, 712, 718.

66. *CS*, 718.

67. *MT*, 98.

68. Ward Smith, "Being Incommensurable," 39.

69. Elizabeth Bowen, "Green Holly," in *CS*, 719–27: 719.

70. *CS*, 719.

71. Virginia Woolf, "A Haunted House," in *Monday or Tuesday* (London: Hogarth Press; New York: Harcourt, Brace, 1921); reprint, *A Haunted House. The Complete Shorter Fiction*, ed. Susan Dick (London: Vintage, 2003), 116–17.

72. *CS*, 723.

73. Ibid.

74. *CS*, 623.

75. Ibid.

76. Elizabeth Bowen, "Preface to *Stories by Elizabeth Bowen*" (1959), in *MT*, 126–30: 130.

77. Elizabeth Bowen, "The Short Story in England," in Lassner, *Elizabeth Bowen: A Study of The Short Fiction* (New York: Twayne, 1991), 138–43: 142.

78. Ibid.

79. Elizabeth Bowen, "*The People's War* by Angus Calder" (1969), in *MT*, 181–85: 183.

80. *HD*, 92.

81. Elizabeth Bowen, "The Bent Back" (1950), in *MT*, 54–60: 57.

82. Elizabeth Bowen, "Out of a Book" (1946), in *MT*, 48–53: 53.

83. Elizabeth Bowen, "*The People's War* by Angus Calder," in *MT*, 181–85: 182.

84. Maria Stella, "Territorio di guerra," in Elizabeth Bowen, *È morta Mabelle*, eds. Benedetta Bini and Maria Stella (Verona: Essedue Edizioni, 1986), 112.

85. Elizabeth Bowen, "London, 1940" (1950), in *MT*, 21–25: 24.

86. *MT*, 22.

87. Elizabeth Bowen, "Ivy Gripped the Steps," *CS*, 686–711: 711.

88. *HD*, 91.

Chapter Three

Those "Whose Deaths Were Not Remarked"

Ghostly Other Women in Henry James's
The Turn of the Screw,
Charlotte Perkins Gilman's
The Yellow Wallpaper,
and Marilynne Robinson's
Housekeeping

Jana M. Tigchelaar

Marilynne Robinson's 1980 novel *Housekeeping* ends with the novel's pro-tagonists, Sylvie and Ruth, living as drifters, riding the rails from town to town and taking odd jobs until "the imposture becomes burdensome, and obvious."[1] The two women have become more than just social outsiders; they are, essentially, ghosts. Robinson frames their transient life as a kind of haunting; not only do they drift from town to town, but they drift around the edges of society, the half-invisible specters on the fringes of "real" life. They are, as Ruth puts it, "not there. . . . We are nowhere."[2] Ruth and Sylvie's final path is a challenge to traditional ideas of conclusion. They resist closure and refuse to fall neatly into established categories of feminine identity. But is their existence as ghostly outsiders a conscious rejection of settled subjectiv-ity, or does their status communicate something about the identity of women who don't quite fit in?

The troubling, uncertain finish ties the novel to two other works well known for their puzzling conclusions: Henry James's *The Turn of the Screw* and Charlotte Perkins Gilman's *The Yellow Wallpaper*. But the similarities among these three works go beyond their analogous endings. *Housekeeping* and *The Turn of the Screw* feature parallel story lines in which potentially questionable women are put in charge of two orphaned children about whom the narratives also raise questions. *The Yellow Wallpaper* operates as the creative journal of one such problematic woman, who has been removed from the charge of her own child and is contained within a prison-like room. *The Turn of the Screw* and *The Yellow Wallpaper* are also recognized as works operating within the Gothic genre, and specifically as part of the Female Gothic.

When Ellen Moers coined the term "Female Gothic" in *Literary Women* in 1976, she wrote that the phrase was "easily defined: the work that women writers have done in the literary mode that, since the eighteenth century, we have called the Gothic."[3] Since that time, critics have expanded their analysis of Female Gothic to include works not only by women, but those centering on female characters. The tension surrounding female encounters with the corrupt patriarchal system lies at the root of the Female Gothic tradition. According to Juliann Fleenor, the Female Gothic "has been formed by dichotomies, the patriarchal dichotomy between the supposed complementary female and male, the feminist dichotomy between woman's prescribed role and her desire and hunger for change, and the dichotomies of good and evil projected by men upon women and consequently internalized by them."[4] This internalization is inherently linked to the challenges surrounding the formation of feminine subjectivity (by which I mean both a character's female identity and the way in which she as character presents herself).

Housekeeping, like *The Turn of the Screw* and *The Yellow Wallpaper*, revolves around the problems of femininity, and the establishment of feminine subjectivity works as the central anxiety in all three works. The primary female characters in each of these three works struggle to form subjectivity outside of the traditional confines of familial and social relationships, while wrestling with issues of insanity, instability, and status as "outsiders." In each story, the female characters (Sylvie and Ruth in *Housekeeping*, Miss Jessel in *The Turn of the Screw*, and the narrator and the woman/women in the wallpaper in *The Yellow Wallpaper*) are made ghostly by flaunting categorization—rejecting motherliness, transgressing social class, and refusing domestic boundaries. This failure to fit in leads to a crisis of identity because, for nearly all Gothic heroines, to be actualized requires some sort of residence within the father's house, the dominant patriarchal structure. By moving outside that structure, our heroines condemn themselves to a kind of social death, to a ghostly half-life as Others.

The patriarchal system frames and permeates *The Turn of the Screw*, which focuses on a household without a center, a home with no traditional family dynamic at work. Bly is a house full of Others: servants, orphaned children, and unmarried women. The governess, an Other herself, is placed in charge of Bly by the master, who, although he wants his orphaned niece and nephew raised appropriately, wants no part of the inconvenience of raising them himself. This situation reflects the traditional upper-class Victorian family dynamic in which the father, busy with his masculine duties outside of the domestic space, entrusts the mother with the tasks of parenting. In an interesting twist, the governess, who in genteel homes would work under the supervision of the mother, is herself the maternal figure.

The absent paternal figure, ruling from afar yet not actively involved in the child rearing, is also reflected in the patriarchal narrators that frame the tale. Before we even meet the governess, we are introduced to Douglas, the keeper of her tale, and—one more step removed—to the unnamed narrator of Douglas's tale. Douglas reveals that the reason the governess had long kept her story secret was not because of the horrible nature of her experience but because she was in love—and in love, it seems, with the master. It is this complication that establishes the governess's struggle for subjectivity. Because her role in the home is as a modified mother figure, the Victorian "angel in the house," her desire for the master is inappropriate, and, considering her instructions not to contact the master for anything at all, quite impossible.

This is where the dichotomy of subjectivity enters. Eugenia C. DeLamotte expands on this duality as she discusses

> the discovery of the Hidden Woman, a staple of women's Gothic that takes two different but related forms. One is the discovery . . . of a Good Other Woman, long-suffering and angelic, whose imprisonment and/or death was unmerited. The other is the discovery of an Evil Other Woman, who got no more than she deserved and is now either dead or sorry for her sins and about to die. The revelation of these sins usually implicates her as a bad (selfish) mother, a bad (undutiful) daughter, and/or a bad (sexual) woman.[5]

The governess herself is both the Good and the Evil Other Woman: good in her attempts to assume the role of angelic, asexual mother; evil in her forbidden desire to transgress her role and become her master's mistress. Priscilla Walton discusses the dangers of this feminine desire: "Patriarchy bars women both from subjectivity and the desire that is indicative of it. . . . Should she exhibit desire, and hence exhibit signs of subjectivity, she is derided, quelled, and dismissed."[6] Rather than suffer derision or face dismissal, the governess remains a divided subject at the risk of her sanity. Instead of struggling with and accepting the dual aspects of her nature, she "creates" the ghosts of Miss Jessel and Peter Quint as representatives of evil.

Throughout the story, we see the governess wrestling with her dual nature, letting feelings of infatuation and other emotions unbecoming of her position surface from time to time. First, she accepts the job, despite the fact that "it was a vision of serious duties and little company, of really great loneliness" because her passion "succumbed" to the "seduction exercised by the splendid young man,"[7] the master. The governess succumbs again to her passion in the book's pinnacle scene: catching Miles as he falls, the govern- ess "caught him, yes, I held him—it may be imagined with what a passion; but at the end of a minute I began to feel what it truly was that I held."[8] This passion is coupled with a sense of possession; the governess finds in Miles's "surrender of [Quint's] name . . . his tribute to my devotion," calling Miles "my own."[9] The governess's desire to claim Miles as her belonging reveals her equal desire to claim her status as mistress of the house.

Even more telling is the text's conflation of the governess and Miss Jessel, demonstrating that the governess and her predecessor are two of the same kind, practically interchangeable. When pressing Mrs. Grose, the housekeeper, for details about the former governess, the governess is told that she "was also young and pretty—almost as young and almost as pretty, miss, even as you." The governess then refers to Miss Jessel as a member of a collective in which she too has a part: "He seems to like *us* young and pretty."[10] The text establishes Miss Jessel as the Other Woman "who is at the same time the Heroine's double and her opposite."[11] According to Newman, Miss Jessel "monstrously exaggerates not only the governess's own social invisibility but also the unremitting surveillance that all governesses were expected to exercise, and . . . represents the temptation of refusing the bur- dens of domestic surveillance, and pursuing instead the recognition of one- self as a sexual being."[12] Miss Jessel pursued the latter, we are to understand, and the governess's visions of the former occupant of her post can be read as her struggles to find her own place within the Victorian duality. If Miss Jessel is the governess's dark double and, as I believe, Peter Quint is the same shadowy mirror of the master, then the governess's efforts to "prove" their ghostly appearances are really her attempts to deny the existence of her desire and passion, knowing as she does that those emotions are forbidden. Therefore the final scene, in which Miles speaks Peter Quint's name, iden- tifying the Other, serves as evidence that the governess is, indeed, the pure woman she is supposed to be, that she is not herself the Evil Other.

What is unusual in *The Turn of the Screw* is the discordant note that the story's ending strikes with what we "know" of the governess from Douglas's testimony in the prologue. We know that she continued to work as a govern- ess, serving as such for Douglas's sister some time after the events at Bly took place. How do we get from the ending of the tale to the beginning? If we see the information that we receive in the prologue as an "answer" to the questions that are raised in the ending, then we can assume that the governess succeeded in quashing the Evil Other Woman aspect of herself. She has, as Karen Stein puts it, put on the mask

to win social acceptance many women have sought . . . to be the virgin, the
angel, to hide or disown the traits which might be seen to threaten their accept-
ability. . . . At some point the mask is no longer a convenient defense but a
trap; the woman is then confronted with her own terrifying split between
"monstrous" inner drives and "nice" outward appearances. . . . If she continues
to wear the mask, she denies her own personhood.[13]

The governess has done just that. By donning the mask, she has returned to
the safety of her domestic role as a woman without subjectivity. In this way,
the governess is redeemed for her male narrators, becoming a safe object for
Douglas's desire, and, I believe, for James himself. The threat in *The Turn of
the Screw* is not the ghosts, but the terrifying prospect that a woman might
transgress her boundaries, might love outside of her class, might attempt to
unite the disparate duality of her chaste and corrupt selves. To do so would
create a new feminine subjectivity, one for which James and his readers were
not prepared.

Gilman's *The Yellow Wallpaper*, however, presents us with an alternative
to James's "redeemed" governess. In this tale, the unnamed narrator ultimately transgresses the boundaries of suitable femininity within the patriarchal system by casting off the mask of appearances and embracing her monstrous Other. The story's conclusion, which emphasizes the narrator's apparent descent into madness, demonstrates the limitations faced by women
whose duality labels them as outsiders and ultimately acts as a critique of the
system, but not a revision.

The tale begins with the narrator's impressions of her surroundings. She
and her husband, John, "mere ordinary people," have rented a house for the
summer, which the narrator describes as "ancestral halls . . . a colonial
mansion, a hereditary estate . . . a haunted house,"[14] the last with a bit of a
wink and a nod to the obvious Gothic overtones such a description reveals.
Like James's governess, the narrator of *The Yellow Wallpaper* is unnamed.
Her identity is completely subsumed by her status as wife and mother, and
because of this marginal position, she requires and receives no identifying
markers. Also like the governess, the narrator immediately senses something
awry with her surroundings. Although her knowledge of the house's "legal
trouble" between "heirs and co-heirs" spoils her idea of the home's "ghostliness," she still expresses an initial impression of something "off" with the
estate: "There is something strange about the house—I can feel it." Her
description of the house, with "hedges and walls and gates that lock" situated
"quite alone, standing well back from the road, quite three miles from the
village"[15] further establishes the unusual quality of the property and sets up
the idea of the home as a Gothic structure. By creating "a conventionally
Gothic setting," Gilman "has entered what the reader should understand as
recognizable territory for ghosts, hauntings, and possessions."[16]

Like James's Bly, Gilman's vacant ancestral home is the ideal setting for a traditional ghost story, and that perhaps may have been what Gilman's readers were expecting. For most of the twentieth century, *The Yellow Wallpaper* was anthologized among other Gothic and ghostly tales. And while contemporary critics now question the reality of Gilman's wallpaper-bound ghosts, there are still many who believe the tale to be one of an actual haunting.[17] This question is compounded when we examine the other Gothic conventions of the story. Within the structure is what Claire Kahane refers to as Gothic literature's secretive center space: the room with the yellow wallpaper.[18] And it becomes evident that the narrator is being confined by her husband, a doctor, primarily in this room (perhaps a former nursery, perhaps something more sinister) as treatment for postpartum depression. This therapy reflects the Victorian rest cure, developed by Dr. Weir Mitchell, which prescribed forced rest, abstinence from creative work, and excessive consumption of food as a cure for "hysteria." This knowledge raises questions about the story's narrator. Is she sane? Are the women whom she sees crawling around the grounds of the estate and trapped behind the wallpaper figments of her imagination, or are they actual ghosts?

The narrator's identity is further called into question in relationship to her creative writing. Her struggle for subjectivity between her dual roles as creative writer and good wife and mother reflects the protagonist's status as both potentially good, angelic woman and potentially evil, transgressive woman. The captive Other Woman within the narrator is expressed through her writing, which serves not only as a creative outlet but as "a great relief to [her] mind,"[19] a way to lessen the numbing monotony of the forced rest cure. The well-spoken heroine is a familiar trope in Gothic literature, and DeLamotte describes well this tension between eloquence and silence: "When they choose to speak, Gothic heroines can soar to rhetorical heights far beyond their enemies' range, but again and again they also choose to remain silent, even if it means remaining persecuted and misunderstood."[20] The protagonist hides her writing from her husband and sister-in-law, attempting to conform to their idea of a good woman, even to the point of expressing her dismay in her journal at her inability to be the Victorian angel: "I meant to be such a help to John, such a real rest and comfort, and here I am a comparative burden already!"[21] It is through her writing, conversely, that the narrator challenges the very framework through which she casts her identity. She dares only in her secret journal to challenge the imperative to stop writing: "Personally, I disagree with their ideas. . . . I believe that congenial work, with excitement and change, would do me good," and "I think sometimes that if I were only well enough to write a little it would relieve the press of ideas and rest me."[22] Because her journal is kept private, the narrator's potential voice remains silenced and marginalized, merely the outlet for her continued feelings of pain and persecution.

Constantly commanded by her husband to avoid her writing, the narrator creates her own Gothic mystery, focusing on the repetitive pattern in the room's wallpaper. According to DeLamotte, "her obsessive concentration on the wallpaper is both a desperate attempt to validate the ideology that limits women's proper sphere of knowledge to the mysteries of interior decorating and a way for her to inscribe her own mystery—the angry, Hidden Other Woman inside of her—on the walls of her domestic prison."[23] The heroine in her own fabricated tale, she invents a shadowy woman "trapped" behind the pattern in the yellow wallpaper. Locked within the inner room of the imprisoning Gothic structure, the narrator, like the governess in *The Turn of the Screw*, projects the dual aspects of her personality upon the offending wallpaper, "creating" the ghostly woman as a symbol of her "evil" side. Gilman's ghost woman (or women) appears to the narrator to make a sort of outcry against her situation, "creeping" publicly, rattling her bars and trying to break free. There is even a suggestion that some of the women behind the bars have committed suicide to escape. While the narrator continues to don the mask, her "ghosts" carry out the kind of activity she desires.

In contrast to *The Turn of the Screw*, the narrator soon gives up any attempts to "prove" the existence of her ghostly apparitions to her husband or sister-in-law, and thus does not strive as James's governess does to deny the existence of her creative desire. Instead, she seeks to identify and merge with the mysterious Other. In this way, *The Yellow Wallpaper* is not the conservative, cautionary tale that *The Turn of the Screw* proves to be. Instead of instructing her readers to idealize her "heroine's virtues, displace their own rebellious feelings with filial piety, their anger with fortitude, and their sexuality with sensibility,"[24] Gilman's protagonist looses her Hidden Other, valuing anger and rebellion over subjugation. In the story's penultimate scene, where the narrator works to remove the wallpaper, her cooperation with the Other Woman is the first step in her reunification of self: "As soon as it was moonlight and that poor thing began to crawl and shake the pattern, I got up and ran to help her. I pulled and she shook, I shook and she pulled, and before morning we had peeled off yards of that paper."[25] The exchange between the narrator and the ghostly woman of their respective tasks, shaking and pulling, demonstrates the breakdown of the boundary between the narrator's separated selves. This breakdown is complete in the final scene, where the narrator claims the Other as herself: "'I've got out at last,' said I, 'in spite of you and Jane. And I've pulled off most of the paper, so you can't put me back!'"[26]

This new subject is not, however, truly complete and whole. While Davison believes that the final scene demonstrates "a positive moment of union as opposed to fragmentation,"[27] I believe that we should instead read the conclusion as another example of division. The much-debated "Jane" to whom the narrator refers has been interpreted in a number of ways, including as being the narrator's third-person reference to herself. If this interpretation is correct, then instead of unifying her split subjectivity, the narrator has simply abandoned the "Good" for the "Evil." Her escape is ultimately limited. She achieves a visual victory in the end, taking a position of traditionally masculine authority as she crawls over her supine husband, who has fainted at the sight of his creeping wife. But this achievement is paradoxical, "obviously partial, destructive, and deeply ironic, even if we credit her present-tense narrative as a testament of survival. It is nonetheless escape to the only freedom available to her, and it functions as a scathing indictment of authority in the outside world."[28] The protagonist's repetitive creeping, obsessive attention to the room's décor, and final reluctance to be removed from her imprisoning domestic space are a grotesquely exaggerated presentation of the type of behavior to which the good woman was expected to subscribe. The narrator's unification with the ghostly Other Woman denies the "good," the third-person "Jane" she references. In this way, Gilman offers a critique of the patriarchal system, but creates no new subjectivity for her heroine, focusing instead on the dangers of fragmentation.

Nearly a century later, Robinson explores the same issues of fragmented identity and a new potential subjectivity for women in *Housekeeping*. In this text, the narrator, Ruth Stone, is abandoned by her father, orphaned by her mother, drifts from her sister, Lucille, and ultimately embraces a life of transience under the influence of her aunt, Sylvie. Sylvie, described as a drifter, a transient, and a migrant worker, tends to Ruth and Lucille in a strange, nontraditional way influenced by her years spent riding the rails. It is Sylvie's unwillingness (or perhaps inability) to provide a traditional, stable home that eventually separates Lucille and Ruth. Lucille leaves her aunt and sister to live a more traditional life with her home economics teacher in town, while Sylvie and Ruth abandon any pretense of a settled, domestic existence. Eventually, when the townspeople threaten to remove Ruth from Sylvie's care, the duo sets fire to the family home and escapes across the lake—the same lake in which Ruth's grandfather and mother both drowned.

It is difficult not to read Ruth and Sylvie's flight from Fingerbone as emblematic of a larger escape from the patriarchal domestic space. Additionally, by stepping outside the bounds of female behavior and living as transients, Ruth and Sylvie seem to be forging new ground for feminine identity—but Ruth's narrative troubles this straightforward reading. Throughout the text, Ruth is haunted by the trauma of her mother's death and influenced by her overpowering desire not to be abandoned again. Christine Caver questions any optimistic reading of *Housekeeping*'s conclusion, finding Ruth's narrative to be "deeply rooted in the trauma of abandonment."[29] There is, however, more than fear of abandonment driving Ruth's decisions in the novel. Her attempts to link her identity with her mother (and then, by extension, to Sylvie) demonstrate her desire to reunite the disparate halves of the female identity in a patriarchal society.

The memory of Helen, Ruth's mother, may then be read as a projection similar to the governess's of Miss Jessel, or Gilman's wallpaper woman. Helen, followed by Sylvie, comes to stand for the aspects of Ruth's potential subjectivity, which she fears and recognizes to be outside of the bounds of the patriarchal norm. For Kahane, this maternal Other takes on a ghostly form and acts as a representation of the difficulty inherent in achieving feminine subjectivity.[30] The text establishes the connection between Sylvie and Helen as maternal signifiers early on. As Ruth and Lucille await Sylvie's arrival in Fingerbone, they begin "to anticipate the appearance of our mother's sister. . . . She would be our mother's age, and might amaze us with her resemblance to our mother. . . . We began to hope, if unawares, that a substantial restitution was about to be made."[31] Ruth and Lucille believe that the arrival of their mysterious aunt might fill the gap left by their mother and explain, if not in some way make up for, their mother's troubling death. Before long, Ruth finds in Sylvie "such similarity, in fact, in the structure of cheek and chin, and the texture of hair, that Sylvie began to blur the memory of my mother, and then to displace it."[32] For Ruth, Sylvie may hold the potential for reconciliation and reunion with her mother, a return to wholeness that Ruth desires. For Lucille, however, Sylvie comes to represent a legacy of unreliable, potentially insane women. In Lucille's eyes, Helen's questionable death and Sylvie's transience and uncommon behavior serve to cast the sisters as outsiders. While Ruth desires to unite the disparate halves of her feminine self, Lucille continues to don the mask and reject full subjectivity.

As Lucille strives to fit in, she seeks to find a place within the patriarchal confines, a space that has no room for women like Helen and Sylvie, and, it seems, Ruth. Although the sisters had previously been so inseparable that Ruth referred to them collectively, Lucille now expresses a need for other friends and begins a program of improvement dedicated to making her fit in more with society.[33] Lucille, like the governess in *The Turn of the Screw*, recognizes that in order to be accepted into the social order, she needs to work against that part of herself that has no place in the patriarchy. Caver frames this as a failed attempt at agency on Lucille's part: "Given only two choices—to remain an outcast from the community as a member of Sylvie's dirty, cold, and disordered household or to embrace conventionality—Lucille chooses structure, the illusion of a self constructed of local values and appearances."[34] Ruth, in contrast, appears unwilling to reject Sylvie and Sylvie's way of life because she realizes that to do so is to eliminate any potential for full subjectivity.

After Lucille leaves, Sylvie decides that it is time to introduce Ruth to the mysterious place she had previously mentioned to the girls: an island in the center of Fingerbone Lake, a wild place that Sylvie believes to be populated with mysterious, ghostly children. Ruth and Sylvie's visit to the island is unsettling, as both Ruth and the reader are made privy to just how outside the norm Sylvie really is, how unearthly and ghostly. The abandoned homestead, built up next to cliffs, where Sylvie believes the children live, is cold and lifeless, so cold that Ruth insists on returning to the beach to build a fire and eat. Sylvie doesn't seem to feel the cold, nor does she seem to experience hunger, confessing that the crackers she keeps in her pocket are not for her own sustenance, but for the strange wild children.[35] With this, the "novel's occult subtext deepens, with increasing attention given to Sylvie's other-worldly nature, her preference for coldness and darkness, and her identification with the woods and the lake."[36] Like a ghost, Sylvie doesn't seem to require the formalities of human consumption and comfort.

Once the sun comes up, Sylvie and Ruth return to the homestead. The place is transformed, "as if the light had coaxed a flowering from the frost, which before seemed barren and parched as salt."[37] This rebirth leads Ruth to speculate that "to crave and to have are as like as a thing and its shadow. . . . For to wish for a hand on one's hair is all but to feel it. So whatever we may lose, very craving gives it back to us again. Though we dream and hardly know it, longing, like an angel, fosters us, smooths our hair, and brings us wild strawberries."[38] If this chill and sterile homestead can be reborn, then perhaps Ruth's mother too can return simply because of Ruth's desire for it to be so. Perhaps Sylvie herself is that return, the reconciliation that will make Ruth whole. This point is emphasized when Sylvie slips away while Ruth daydreams, and Ruth is left alone at the homestead:

> If I could see my mother, it would not have to be her eyes, her hair. I would not need to touch her sleeve. There was no more the stoop of her high shoulders. The lake had taken that, I knew. It was so very long since the dark had swum her hair, and there was nothing more to dream of, but often she almost slipped through any door I saw from the corner of my eye, and it was she, and not changed, and not perished. She was a music I no longer heard, that rang in my mind, itself and nothing else, lost to all sense, but not perished, not perished.[39]

After this expression of longing for her mother, it is Sylvie instead who returns, touching Ruth and comforting her, cementing Sylvie as the surrogate for the (m)other.

While critics have read Ruth's desire to identify with Sylvie as ultimately negative to her own subjectivity, I argue that Ruth's desire to "merge" with Sylvie actually demonstrates an acceptance of the duality of feminine nature.[40] Rather than attempting to destroy or overpower the Other or to create an illusion of self in the way Lucille does, Ruth tries to "merge" with Sylvie. Her doing so "can just as readily be seen as a challenge to the reader to consider the abjection of the mother as a dangerous cultural movement to exile a figure that unsettles cultural categories."[41] If Sylvie is the text's representation of the ghostly Other who transcends categorization, then Ruth's decision to align herself with Sylvie indicates a move toward whole-ness, a transformative subjectivity.

After her awakening at the abandoned homestead, Ruth's transformation is nearly complete. She and Sylvie spend the night out on the lake in the stolen boat, and Ruth imagines that the boat capsizes and she drowns, filling with water until she bursts: "Then, presumably, would come parturition in some form, though my first birth had hardly deserved that name, and why should I hope for more from the second? The only true birth would be a final one, which would free us from watery darkness."[42] This watery birth/death is what Ruth believes her mother desired when she drove off the cliff into the lake, an experience that would not end life but would, instead, bring about a reunification. Ruth herself imagines a reunification of a kind as she and Sylvie wait in the boat for the train to pass over the bridge: "The faceless shape in front of me could as well be Helen herself as Sylvie. I spoke to her by the name Sylvie, and she did not answer. Then how was one to know? And if she were Helen in my sight, how could she not be Helen in fact?"[43] It is, as Kaivola says, as though "on the lake she [Ruth] believes she can have what she wants and undo the irreparable loss of her mother's abandon-ment."[44]

But it is more than her mother's abandonment that Ruth, and *Housekeep-ing*, seeks to undo; it is the original tragedy, the abandonment of women's significance in a system that denies women their names and stories. After rowing ashore, Sylvie and Ruth hop in a train car to ride back across the bridge to Fingerbone. While crossing the lake on the train, Ruth imagines that

> Noah's wife, when she was old, found somewhere a remnant of the Deluge, she might have walked into it till her widow's dress floated above her head and the water loosened her plaited hair. And she would have left it to her sons to tell the tedious tale of generations. She was a nameless woman, and so at home among all those who were never found and never missed, who were uncom-memorated, whose deaths were not remarked, nor their begettings.[45]

What's implicit here is that Ruth's mother and her grandmother are among those "never found and never missed," the women whose "deaths were not remarked." The tragedy is not just Helen's death and the abandonment of her children, Sylvie's life as an outsider, Ruth's grandmother's unarticulated death, but the system that makes their stories unimportant. The lake can swallow up whole a train, a car, houses, families—much in the same way that a society can erase the existence of Others who are outside of it.

It stands to reason that Ruth and Sylvie must cross the bridge that spans this expanse, but in doing so they make a fateful choice to transgress society.

Heather Bohannan calls this a symbolic death, saying that "the drifters who wander through the town are ghosts to the townspeople, disembodied. And so it is in the eyes of a culture that can only accommodate and tolerate the enclosed body/spirit/woman that Sylvie and Ruth are passing between worlds when they finally cross the bridge."[46] It is not until society intervenes in Ruth and Sylvie's untraditional existence, though, that the duo decide to cross that bridge. After they return to town in the train, walking past the sideways glances of the town's scandalized residents, the citizens of Fingerbone begin to intercede. Bringing casseroles and concerned questions, the good house-wives drop in to visit regularly. Their fear, says Ruth, is that "my social graces were eroding away, and that soon I would feel ill at ease in a cleanly house with glass in its windows—I would be lost to ordinary society. I would be a ghost."[47]

The message is clear: To live as a transient is, to the public, a kind of social death, in the same way that to transgress social class like Miss Jessel or to desire creative freedom like Gilman's narrator is a death sentence. To abandon any pretense of living within the patriarchal confines is to abandon life itself. But in order for Ruth to fully realize personhood, she must em-brace that part of herself made manifest in Sylvie's strangeness, in her moth-er's dissenting death. What is problematic is Robinson's representation of Ruth's identity at the novel's end. Kaivola recognizes that difficulty: "But if *Housekeeping* is sympathetic to Ruth and Sylvie's escape from the control of the townspeople of Fingerbone, it is simultaneously uneasy about what that escape means."[48] To escape from the repression of patriarchy and commu-nity is to accept the loss of voice and identity in the social sphere. And I believe Robinson is suggesting that, as yet, there is no other sphere.

Paula Geyh asks, "Can the feminine subject ever really be thought beyond the structures of patriarchy, or is the transient subject finally only a specter, doomed to haunt the father's house forever?"[49] This is where the uncertain ending of *Housekeeping* finds us: with Ruth and Sylvie, ghostly Other-wom-en, haunting the perimeters of the patriarchal home. They have become like Miss Jessel and Peter Quint in *The Turn of the Screw* and Gilman's creeping narrator in *The Yellow Wallpaper*, outsiders whose decision to transgress their bounds has condemned them to ghostly half-life in the eyes of the patriarchy, forever peering in the windows or crawling around the attic of the ancestral home.

The final scenes return us to Fingerbone, where Ruth imagines Lucille living in the restored family home, and to Boston, where Ruth pictures an alternate existence for Lucille. At the old family home in Fingerbone, Ruth and Sylvie have "brought in leaves, and flung the curtains and tipped the bud vase, and somehow left the house again before she [Lucille] could run down-stairs, leaving behind us a strong smell of lake water."[50] In Boston, they are joined by a cast of the dead: "My mother, likewise, is not there, and my grandmother in her house slippers with her pigtail wagging. . . . We are nowhere in Boston. . . . [Lucille] does not watch, does not listen, does not wait, does not hope, and always for me and Sylvie."[51]

What haunts Ruth is not the actuality of her mother's death, but the inevitability of her death, and the death (both actual and figurative) of all women who, like her mother, did not fit comfortably into society's defined roles. And this is also what haunts Lucille at the story's end. No matter where Lucille searches, Ruth and Sylvie are not there. There is no place for them in Boston, in Fingerbone, in society. Robinson "elects the 'unnatural'—to characterize women's experience in its own right, thereby subverting the oppositional view of seeing and understanding women only or principally in relation to men."[52] But as of yet, Robinson indicates, there is no other way to see or understand in larger society. There is only the patriarchal sphere, and only the ghostly wilderness outside of it.

Housekeeping examines the lives of female characters who choose to live on society's margins and outside of the realm of patriarchal determination. This examination also considers, however, the implications of moving outside of this dominant sphere. A century ago, characters like Ruth and Sylvie would have been the unseen madwomen in the attic, the dangerous, concealed Others whose stories would either not have been told or would have been reabsorbed into the master narrative, suppressed like the governess's ghostly projections or locked away like Gilman's hysterical narrator. But Robinson "maps a shadowy territory between difference and sameness, preparing for us an existence predicated on hope and defined only by uncertainty."[53] Because *Housekeeping* focuses and clarifies the narrative of this "shadowy territory," the novel transcends the traditional categories of feminine subjectivity, but the story's return at its end to Lucille, the redeemed "good woman," demonstrates that until the system itself finds a place for women like Ruth and Sylvie, women who accept both the Evil Other and the Good facets of their identity, these women will remain marginal ghosts.

NOTES

1. Marilynne Robinson, *Housekeeping* (New York: Farrar, 1980), 214.

2. Ibid., 218.

3. Ellen Moers, *Literary Women* (Garden City, NY: Doubleday, 1976), 90.

4. Juliann E. Fleenor, "Introduction: The Female Gothic," in *The Female Gothic*, ed. Juliann E. Fleenor (Montreal: Eden Press, 1983), 28.

5. Eugenia C. DeLamotte, *Perils of the Night: A Feminist Study of Nineteenth-Century Gothic* (New York: Oxford University Press, 1990), 153.

6. Priscilla Walton, "'What Then on Earth Was I?': Feminine Subjectivity and *The Turn of the Screw*," in *The Turn of the Screw*, ed. Peter Beidler (Boston: Bedford-St. Martin's, 1995), 256.

7. Henry James, *The Turn of the Screw and Other Short Novels* (New York: Signet/Penguin, 1995), 297.

8. Ibid., 403.

9. Ibid., 297.

10. Ibid., 305 (emphasis mine).

11. Joanna Russ, "Somebody's Trying to Kill Me and I Think It's My Husband: The Modern Gothic," in Fleenor, *The Female Gothic*, 33.

12. Beth Newman, "Getting Fixed: Feminine Identity and Scopic Crisis in *The Turn of the Screw*," *Novel* 26, no. 1 (1992): 61.

13. Karen F. Stein, "Monsters and Madwomen: Changing Female Gothic," in Fleenor, *The Female Gothic*, 124–25.

14. Charlotte Perkins Gilman, *The Yellow Wallpaper: A Sourcebook and Critical Edition*, ed. Catherine J. Golden (New York: Routledge, 2004), 41.

15. Ibid., 42.

16. E. Suzanne Owens, "The Ghostly Double behind the Wallpaper in Charlotte Perkins Gilman's *The Yellow Wallpaper*," in *Haunting the House of Fiction: Feminist Perspectives on Ghost Stories by American Women*, ed. Lynette Carpenter and Wendy K. Kolmar (Knoxville: University of Tennessee Press, 1991), 70–71.

17. See Owens, "The Ghostly Double," for a more complete examination of the story's ambiguity.

18. Kahane, "The Gothic Mirror," in *The (M)other Tongue: Essays in Feminist Psychoanalytic Interpretation*, ed. Shirley Nelson Garner et al. (Ithaca, NY: Cornell University Press, 1985), 334.

19. Gilman, *The Yellow Wallpaper*, 41.

20. DeLamotte, *Perils of the Night*, 150.

21. Gilman, *The Yellow Wallpaper*, 44.

22. Ibid., 42, 46.

23. DeLamotte, *Perils of the Night*, 191.

24. Ibid., 154.

25. Gilman, *The Yellow Wallpaper*, 56.

26. Ibid., 58.

27. Carol Margaret Davison, "Haunted House/Haunted Heroine: Female Gothic Closets in *The Yellow Wallpaper*," *Women's Studies* 33 (2004): 66.

28. Michelle A. Masse, *In the Name of Love: Women, Masochism, and the Gothic* (Ithaca, NY: Cornell University Press, 1992), 38.

29. Christine Caver, "Nothing Left to Lose: *Housekeeping*'s Strange Freedoms," *American Literature* 68, no. 1 (1996): 113.

30. Kahane, "The Gothic Mirror," 336.

31. Robinson, *Housekeeping*, 41–42.

32. Ibid., 53.

33. Ibid., 131–33.

34. Caver, "Nothing Left to Lose," 123–24.

35. Robinson, *Housekeeping*, 148.

36. Caver, "Nothing Left to Lose," 126.

37. Robinson, *Housekeeping*, 152.

38. Ibid., 152–53.

39. Ibid., 159–60.

40. Karen Kaivola's reading of *Housekeeping* sees Ruth's desire to identify with Sylvie (and, by extension, with her dead mother), as a hindrance to Ruth's subjectivity. Caver supports Kaivola's interpretation, finding ultimately a fusion of identities rather than a new subjectivity. See Kaviola, "The Pleasures and Perils of Merging: Female Subjectivity in Marilynne Robinson's *Housekeeping*," *Contemporary Literature* 34, no. 4 (1993): 670–90.

41. Ruth Beinstock Anolik, "The Missing Mother: The Meanings of Maternal Absence in the Gothic Mode," *Modern Language Studies* 33, no. 1/2 (2003): 30.

42. Robinson, *Housekeeping*, 162.

43. Ibid., 166–67.

44. Kaivola, "The Pleasures and Perils of Merging," 687.

45. Robinson, *Housekeeping*, 172.

46. Heather Bohannon, "Quest-tioning Tradition: Spiritual Transformation Images in Women's Narratives and *Housekeeping*, by Marilynne Robinson," *Western Folklore* 51, no. 1 (1992): 73.

47. Robinson, *Housekeeping*, 183.

48. Kaivola, "The Pleasures and Perils of Merging," 671.

49. Paula E. Geyh, "Burning Down the House? Domestic Space and Feminine Subjectivity in Marilynne Robinson's *Housekeeping*," *Contemporary Literature* 34, no. 1 (1993): 119.

50. Robinson, *Housekeeping*, 218.

51. Ibid., 218–19.

52. Elizabeth Meese, *Crossing the Double-Cross: The Practice of Feminist Criticism* (Chapel Hill: University of North Carolina Press, 1986), 57–58.

53. Robinson, *Housekeeping*, 68.

II

Spectral Figures and Spectral Histories

Chapter Four

These Ghosts Will Be Lovers

*The "Cultural Haunting" of Class Consciousness in
Ian McEwan's* Atonement

Karley K. Adney

In Elizabeth Bowen's masterpiece *The Death of the Heart*, the narrator cautions readers to "Pity the selfishness of lovers: it is brief, a forlorn hope; it is impossible."[1] Bowen's work, published in 1938, reflects the disillusionment of the British—especially its upper class—during the interwar years. The story focuses on the orphan Portia Quayne, who becomes a ward of her well-to-do relatives. Portia, an awkward outsider, falls in love with an upper-class man, but rather than finding happiness, she finds her hope for love quashed by her unfeeling and dismissive relatives. Bowen's novel creates awareness of an attitude plaguing the contemporary upper-class British: Many seemed devoid of caring for anyone (especially those of a lower class) but themselves. Portia's plight, in many ways, resembles that of Robbie Turner's, one of the main characters in Ian McEwan's *Atonement*. The interactions between social classes portrayed in Bowen's work fittingly reflect the dynamics between the Tallises and the Turners, the two main families in McEwan's novel, since *Atonement* opens on a sweltering day in 1935, placing itself as contemporary to *The Death of the Heart*.[2] While many have treated McEwan's seminal work as an example of how one might deal with trauma by shifting and reshaping memories, few (if any) scholars have examined *Atonement* in light of the conventions of its most obvious genre: the ghost story. Undeniably, *Atonement* is a ghost story that explores the haunting ramifications of class consciousness in interwar Britain. McEwan's work—both the novel and film[3]—like any other "good" ghost story, unsettles its readers. In this case, the ghost story concerns the devastating effects of class

47

consciousness and the danger of judging an individual based solely on his or her social rank.

Classifying *Atonement* as a ghost story does require some explanation. *Atonement* serves as a fractured chronicle of the lives of Briony Tallis, Cecelia Tallis, and Robbie Turner. The Tallises, an upper-class family, employ Grace Turner as one of their servants; her son Robbie grows up in the Tallis household and receives assistance in his schooling from Mr. Tallis. A romance ignites between Cecelia and Robbie, but ends abruptly. Briony, the youngest Tallis sibling and a teenager longing to understand the complexities of the adult world, witnesses, reads, and misinterprets key exchanges between two couples: her older sister and Robbie, and her older cousin and a mysterious male figure. When someone rapes her cousin, Briony adamantly argues that Robbie committed the deed, when, in fact, he is innocent. Regardless, Robbie goes to jail and later serves as a soldier in World War II; Cecelia abandons the rich comforts always afforded her by her wealthy family after they blindly accept and then support Briony's accusations.

Leaving either by choice or force, Cecelia and Robbie become ghosts to their families. The war rips the lovers apart and makes them ghosts to one another. Readers remain in suspense for most of the novel: only near the end of the book do they witness Cecelia and Robbie reunited. Briony, now an adult, looks for atonement. She seeks out her sister, and although the meeting between the long-separated sisters is cold, the relationship between Robbie and Cecelia is warm and passionate. The two lovers share a kiss that seems to undo all the pain they have suffered in the past; for readers, the kiss grants relief. But this kiss never actually occurs. Briony, a talented writer since she was a child, reveals in a coda at the end that she wrote the novel readers just completed. She also informs readers that, sadly, Robbie and Cecelia both died in 1940: Robbie from injuries sustained in the war, and Cecelia during the bombing of London. Further, as part of atoning for her crime, Briony reveals that she refused to change the names of those in her story, including those who truly were guilty of the crimes Briony initially misinterpreted as a young woman. In the coda, Briony explains that *Atonement* could not be published until all those referred to by name in the narrative had died, including herself; this way she cannot be accused of slander. In turn, readers learn that the book they have just completed is, indeed, a ghost story. *Atonement*, then, has the first necessary characteristic for a ghost story: a ghost (or ghosts). The novel also fulfills the second requirement essential to qualify it as ghost story, which concerns the story's purpose. While it qualifies as fiction, the ghost story sets itself apart from other fiction because of its specific purpose to haunt and unsettle its readers, as McEwan's novel does. A ghost story resonates as a cautionary tale, whereas other fiction does not necessarily serve the same didactic purpose. Briony, by addressing the repressed trauma of her youth, yields ghosts that haunt both her and her readers. Similarly, the story unsettles its readers and reminds them of the dangers of class consciousness by imparting to them a moral, which, if observed, will keep readers from creating ghosts of their own if ever placed in a situation similar to that of McEwan's characters.

Critical work on ghosts and their function in literature provides context for why examining *Atonement* as a ghost story yields a dynamic exploration of class differentiation in 1930s Britain. In *Cultural Haunting: Ghosts and Ethnicity in Recent American Literature* (1998), Kathleen Brogan examines the role ghosts play in work by minority writers, claiming that ghosts capture their respective cultural identities and the problems faced by the ethnic group each ghost represents. Brogan says that these ghosts represent examples of "cultural hauntings," since "ghost stories reflect the increased emphasis on ethnic and racial differentiation in all social groups."[4] One of Brogan's prime examples of this "cultural haunting" concept is Toni Morrison's character of Sethe from her landmark novel *Beloved*. Based loosely on the case of Margaret Garner, Sethe escapes slavery with her children and would rather kill them herself than see them recaptured. Maria Margaronis appreciates the similarities between *Atonement* and *Beloved* as works of historical fiction, arguing that "both [novels] engage deeply with the purposes and processes of writing historical fiction, so that questions of authority, responsibility and authenticity are absorbed and expressed in their form."[5] More important, however, the novels both function as ghost stories that raise awareness. Morrison's work creates awareness about the devastating repercussions of American slavery. McEwan's novel, on the other hand, raises awareness about the danger of attempting to understand one's actions solely in relation to one's class status: Members of the upper class (the Tallises) inherently behave properly and morally, while lower-class citizens (the Turners) have the potential to behave inappropriately or criminally.

One of the purposes of *Atonement* is to explore the "cultural haunting" plaguing white Britain in the 1930s: class consciousness and the apathy of the upper class toward others, much like the situation portrayed in Bowen's *The Death of the Heart*. McEwan repeatedly emphasizes the "cultural haunting" of class consciousness throughout the novel via his narrator Briony. Since *Atonement* is Briony's view of events, she undoubtedly shapes her work to reflect what themes she remembers as most important to her. Consider that "memory, once viewed as important in anthropology because of its role in the maintenance of oral traditions, has returned to the fore, this time in recognition of memory's centrality to embodiment and the creation of meaning."[6] In creating her meaning, then, Briony (and inherently McEwan) pays careful attention to details regarding class and demonstrates the shaping force that class consciousness had on her as a young teenager in 1935. Critics also argue that "people filter memories according to what is important in the present."[7] If Briony continuously revisited *Two Figures by a Fountain* for over sixty years—and many of her memories concern the status of characters in the story—one could safely argue that the concerns over class conscious-ness were not only important to the adult Briony of the "present," but also remained important to her throughout her entire life.

Briony uses three primary methods to portray the "cultural haunting" of class consciousness affecting the interwar British: first, she emphasizes the Tallis estate; second, she portrays some of the characters in her story—including herself—as dominated by their own class snobbery; and third, she shapes her descriptions of the interactions between Cecelia and Robbie by stressing the haunting that eventually becomes the cause of their own ghost-ing. To begin, Briony repeatedly draws attention to the magnificence of the Tallis estate. The Tallises found wealth because of "Cecelia's grandfather, who grew up over an ironmonger's shop and made the family fortune with a series of patents on padlocks, bolts, latches, and hasps, [and] had imposed on the new house his taste for all things solid, secure, and functional"[8] ; the fact that the family fortune was made from such "solid, secure, and functional" products deserves attention. The locks and hasps—so cold, unfeeling, and unresponsive to anything but mechanics—clearly symbolize the Tallis family attitude, which echoes that of the upper-class interwar British. Because of the fortune, the Tallis property appears extraordinary. One of the first images indicative of the Tallis family wealth occurs during the description of the "half-scale reproduction of Bernini's *Triton* in the Piazza Barberini in Rome."[9] While this fountain had been constructed on the Tallis grounds years earlier, it still symbolizes the current family's concerns over status. The fountain chosen for their grounds is a copy of a masterful artwork stationed in Rome and is impressive in size as well. Such a structure boasts wealth and social rank. Similarly, Briony provides a detailed catalogue of only a section of the Tallis property to demonstrate the family's wealth. After Leon Tallis and Paul Marshall arrive at the estate, "Cecelia led [them] into the drawing room, through the French windows, past the roses toward the swimming pool, which was behind the stable block and was surrounded on four sides by a high thicket of bamboo."[10] This description testifies to the lavish grounds fit for, at the very least, members of the upper class. These details also provide a striking contrast to the modest bungalow in which Robbie and Grace Turner live. The bungalow is cramped: Robbie's room, bathroom, and bedroom are "squashed under the apex of the bungalow's roof," and most of the study is taken up by a "knife-scarred kitchen table," which provides an example quite contrary to any furniture found in the Tallis home.[11] The Turners clearly occupy only a liminal presence on the estate, no matter how often they visit or are welcomed into the Tallis home.

Briony also reflects the "cultural haunting" of obsession with class in her descriptions of various characters, including herself. At the start of the novel, Briony describes herself as "one of those children possessed by a desire to have the world just so,"[12] and as a girl with "a taste for the miniature."[13] Both of these descriptions reek of being accustomed to the luxuries of upper-class life. During the interwar years, only a child of a well-to-do family would expect for the world to be "just so." A "taste for the miniature" suggests that Briony desires control and power, as a member of the upper class would; indeed, Briony's obsession with miniatures and order portrays her as god-like—which, as a writer and the creator of a universe in every novel, she is. The film also emphasizes Briony's affinity for the miniature as well as her status. The film's opening scene occurs in Briony's room—a pan shot follows a parade of no less than fifty miniature animals, lined up "just so" along her bedroom floor. Perhaps her love for all things small hints at Briony's desire (and later, ability) to minimize characters, to award them no more than ghostly status, abilities that stem from her controlling nature and demonstrate themselves most obviously in the way she continually empha-sizes one's social rank. The film version of *Atonement* not only establishes Briony's power but emphasizes it heavily. During the first scene in which Briony and Robbie talk, the camera angles and composition of the ensuing shots establish her role as authority and his as servant. She stands in a doorway, still inside the house, while he stands at the bottom of a set of stairs leading up to the same door. He appears smaller than her, even though he clearly is the adult and she the child. The film then moves to a succession of shots alternating between Briony and Robbie. Only the first shot of Robbie shows him alone in the frame; Briony (or the manuscript in her hand) en-croach on each shot of Robbie thereafter, while each shot of Briony remains uninhabited by anyone but herself. These cinematic techniques in particu-lar—especially at the beginning of the film—stress the concept of class con-sciousness and the way in which it haunts and eventually transforms the characters in this piece into ghosts.

Briony stresses the problem of class consciousness even more forcefully in her descriptions of Paul Marshall, Leon's friend who comes to the Tallis estate, flirts with Briony's cousin Lola, and commits the rape for which officials—and most of the Tallises—wrongfully accuse and sentence Robbie. When Marshall, Leon, and Cecelia sit by the pool for some punch shortly after their arrival, Marshall "[takes] control of the conversation with a ten-minute monologue."[14] Much like Briony's desire for control, Marshall him-self assumes mastery of the situation, talking endlessly about himself without any respect for the interests of his hosts. During his monologue, Marshall chronicles his successes, mentioning how "he had bought a large house on Clapham Common and hardly had time to visit it."[15] Only someone with high social status could own a house in which he would barely spend any time because of his unrelenting business demands and success. But the most poignant example of Marshall's class snobbery occurs during his first con-versation with Briony's cousin Lola. When Lola tells Marshall that she likes his shoes, Marshall answers with the following: "Yes. Ducker's in the Turl. They make a wooden thingy of your foot and keep it on a shelf forever. Thousands of them down in a basement room, and most of the people are long dead" (57). This exchange exemplifies Marshall's lavish lifestyle, since shoes produced in this manner would surely present an extravagant cost. Further, the fact that his shoes are so tailored serves as yet another mark of his upper-class status. Interestingly enough, Marshall's own description dismisses ghosts; he mentions crudely that the mold of his foot sits among molds fashioned after men now dead. Unsurprisingly, Marshall does not appreciate the irony that someday he will join these ghosts. Rather, he exhibits the problematic attitude of the upper class: in a period in which resources are scarce, Marshall participates—guiltlessly and even happily—in wasting resources to satisfy his lavish taste. The wooden shoe models remain in storage long after those they were created for die. These relics to the rich clog a shoe shop basement, while the hundreds of pieces of wood could be put to much better use. In turn, McEwan provides readers with another powerful example of the mentality that kept Robbie and Cecelia from one another, allowing them only to become lovers when ghosts.

Even though she suffers as the victim of it, Cecelia herself also demonstrates and perpetuates the upper-class concern with rank by dismissing those who rank lower than herself. Unfortunately, then, she actively participates in the ghosting of herself, Robbie, and their relationship. When Briony first mentions her older sister by name in *Atonement*, she describes how Cecelia reacted to the stories Briony wrote as a young girl: "Cecelia's enthusiasm . . . seemed a little overstated, tainted with condescension perhaps, and intrusive too; her big sister wanted each bound story catalogued and placed on the library shelves."[16] Briony's description of Cecelia here explicitly addresses the possible condescension with which Cecelia reacts; while many older siblings may condescend to their younger brothers and sisters, the notion of Briony's stories being placed in the library demonstrates her class snobbery as well. Members of a lower class most likely would not suggest putting a child's works of fiction (after being bound, no less) in their own library, a luxury reserved for, and typically only to be afforded by, the wealthy. Initially representing Cecelia's ghost in this manner stresses her class and hints at the "cultural haunting" that will be her undoing.

Cecelia's class consciousness is demonstrated most powerfully by her passing thoughts about the servants in the Tallis home and her direct interactions with Robbie. When Cecelia walks through the Tallis home and pauses in the room where Marshall will stay, she thinks, "Mrs. Turner must have passed through that morning."[17] Just as Marshall dismisses the many ghosts of men whose molds haunt the basement of a shoe shop, Cecelia marginalizes Grace, the cleaning lady, quickly. More important, the description categorizes Grace as a ghost, since she merely "passed through" the room, as if she were a spirit. Similarly, in the film version a servant by the name of Danny Hardman carries in Leon and Marshall's bags when they arrive. The two visitors walk leisurely throughout the house while Hardman follows them diligently, even into the parlor, where the men begin to sip drinks with Cecelia. When she notices Hardman in the room with the suitcases, she exasperatedly states, "It's the big room next to the nursery." Hardman leaves and Cecelia and Leon look at one another, smilingly snobbishly at what they consider to be Hardman's stupidity; surely, the Tallis siblings suggest, Hardman's lower class accounts for the silly behavior and the man's lack of intelligence.

Cecelia's attitude toward the Tallis family's servants, dominated by the "cultural haunting" of class consciousness, is also clear when she talks with others about Robbie, or thinks about him. For instance, when Cecelia tells her older brother Leon that she wished he had not invited Robbie to join them at dinner that evening, Leon tells her that she only makes a fuss because she really believes that Robbie "can't hold a knife and fork."[18] Briony, writing from Cecelia's perspective, argues that Robbie "was always playacting the cleaning lady's son come to the big house on errand."[19] Cecelia recalls an earlier instance when Robbie comes to the house and ceremoniously removes his shoes and socks before entering the house to borrow a book; he actually makes this gesture out of respect to one of the other servants busy cleaning the floors, since he thinks his boots may be dirty. Cecelia reads the action as disrespectful, as if Robbie were making light of her status. This situation makes her wonder if Robbie was punishing her "for not having a charlady for a mother."[20] This "cultural haunting" of class consciousness—their difference in status—not only leads to their feeling uncomfortable around each other but creates many misunderstandings between the two as well. As Brian Finney argues, "The difference in social class accounts for the early misunderstanding between Robbie and Cecelia. She mistakes his removing his boots and socks before entering her house for an act of exaggerated deference. She has imbibed this sense of social difference from her class-conscious mother, Emily, who resents the fact that her husband has paid for Robbie's education."[21] The film adaptation of *Atonement* also draws special attention to Emily Tallis's influence over her daughters, and how Emily's obsession with class shapes the way in which her daughters react to members of lower classes. Emily's influence over Briony becomes especially evident in the film during the scene when police question Briony about what she saw on the grounds concerning Lola and her attacker. After Briony confirms that she saw Robbie with Lola, Emily emerges from the shadows behind her, squeezes Briony's shoulder approvingly, and says, "Well done, darling." McEwan does not include this scene in the novel; its inclusion in the movie stresses again the "cultural haunting" of class consciousness for viewers. This scene in the film also harks back to Bowen's *The Death of the Heart*, in which Portia is subjected to the class snobbishness of her own guardians. While some may argue that Briony is more intelligent and independent than Bowen's Portia, both girls are still subject to the influence of their guardians' beliefs and decisions.

The very attitudes perpetuated in the Tallis family concerning social rank rule Cecelia until her death (recall that she dies without reuniting with Briony to learn about Marshall's guilt). She assumes that Danny Hardman, another Tallis family servant, is guilty of raping her cousin. The possibility of Marshall's being the rapist never even occurs to her.[22] Cecelia links the foul act with a member of the lower class. In a letter she writes to Robbie, Cecelia tells him that she is "beginning to understand the snobbery that lay behind [her family's] stupidity. . . . When Hardman [Sr.] decided to cover for Danny, no one in my family wanted the police to ask him the obvious questions."[23] What is most important about this repeated acknowledgment and even stressing of class rests in exactly who draws attention to the problem; while Cecelia makes these comments, readers must account for the fact that Briony is, in fact, the one telling the story. More significantly, Briony was not present for any of the aforementioned scenes. As author of scenes with which she had no involvement, she transforms herself into a ghost whose function becomes to bear witness. She imagines the details with which she supplies her readers, and time and again, those details stress the concept of class. These details truly indicate the overwhelming haunting effect of class consciousness and its power to transform characters into nothing more than ghosts, hollow and wispy symbols associated only with their class, never with one who actually is.

The other primary method Briony uses to stress the haunting danger of class consciousness comes in the form of her shaping the direct interactions between Cecelia and Robbie by emphasizing their difference in social status. The first poignant example of Briony shaping the interactions between the two potential lovers occurs when Cecelia sees Robbie working on the Tallis property: "Robbie Turner was on his knees, weeding along a rugosa hedge, and she did not feel like getting into conversation with him. . . . There was talk of [his going to] medical college, which after a literature degree seemed rather pretentious. And presumptuous too, since it was her father who would have to pay."[24] Robbie's posturing here signifies clearly his lower social class. The description also makes readers privy to what Briony assumes her sister feels. Perhaps the slight condescension in Cecelia's suggestion to place Briony's bound manuscripts in the family library among the leagues of literary giants remains with Briony and causes her to consistently portray her sister as snobbish and unfeeling toward others. When Cecelia questions Robbie about pursuing a medical degree, Robbie answers first by saying, "Look, I've agreed to pay your father back. That's the arrangement," a statement that strikes a nerve with Cecelia: "She was surprised that he should think she was raising the question of money. That was ungenerous of him. Her father had subsidized Robbie's education all his life. Had anyone ever objected?"[25] Besides the basic plot Briony addresses, which demonstrates the difference in class between Cecelia and Robbie, the diction in this passage is especially effective in stressing their respective statuses. The use of "ungenerous" highlights Cecelia's disgust, since Robbie should respond in no manner but with gratitude. Even more effective, however, is the use of "subsidized," a term resonating with formality and business, denoting Robbie as a charity case rather than a young man looking for assistance and support because he has no father of his own to support him. Similarly, Briony casts herself into Robbie's ghost, imagining how he both reacted to and addressed the difference between his social status and that of his patrons. He imagines that when Cecelia crossed paths with him at Cambridge "she always seemed to find it awkward—That's our cleaning lady's son, she might have been whispering to her friends as she walked on. He liked people to know he didn't care. There goes my mother's employer's daughter, he once said to a friend."[26] Robbie's comments here demonstrate precisely that he cares about Cecelia being a member of the upper class and he of the lower because he draws attention to the difference. Since Briony gives life to these ghosts, one must observe, yet again, that class consciousness also presents a concern to her.

Readers may assume that when Robbie and Cecelia finally express their romantic feelings for one another (literally within hours of the exchange examined above and at the root of the tension between their recent interactions), their difference in class no longer carries any importance. When they reveal their feelings, one might hope that all else falls away and what comes to matter most is the lovers' happiness, regardless of their stations. Indeed, when Briony first describes the two ghosts as they become physically intimate, Robbie and Cecelia become "strangers, their pasts . . . forgotten."[27] But this description conversely and simultaneously demonstrates the significance of their pasts, depending most on their social rank. Even their first sexual meeting, in which they connect not only physically but also emotionally by telling each other they love one another, suffers domination from class consciousness. While they make love, Briony refers to the lovers in several ways, including "childhood friends" and "university acquaintances," but first and foremost she describes them as "the son of Grace and Ernest Turner, the daughter of Emily and Jack Tallis."[28] Even the ghosts who become lovers remain defined in terms of the social classes that haunt their entire lives.

Avery F. Gordon, in *Ghostly Matters: Haunting and the Sociological Imagination*, addresses the concept of "complex personhood"; she explains that the concept "means that the stories people tell about themselves, about their troubles, about their social worlds, and about their society's problems are entangled and weave between what is immediately available as a story and what their imaginations are reaching toward."[29] Briony undoubtedly demonstrates "complex personhood," focusing on the troubling issues of class consciousness as, perhaps, the most significant issue in her social world. Many critics disregard the main problem in *Atonement*: Briony's youth and her misunderstanding of the exchange between Cecelia and Robbie does not represent the catalyst for this ghost story. Instead, Briony as an adult and likewise her audience realize that the child Briony's fundamental mistake lies in accepting and then acting in support of the dominant ideologies associated with class consciousness. The film version makes this problem explicit when Robbie confronts Briony at the close of the story after she arrives at the flat he now shares with Cecelia. Robbie thunders, "You assume that for all my education I was *still* little better than a servant, *still* not to be trusted" (emphases added to represent James McAvoy's tone). Robbie's accusation here does not appear anywhere in the novel; thus it provides yet another effective example of how the film version seeks to stress the problem of—and dangers inherent to—class consciousness for its viewers.

Guilt should not only be assigned to Briony for this crime, but also to Cecelia for assuming Danny Hardman's guilt, and especially to Emily Tallis for perpetuating the cycle of socialization in which her daughters learn to view and treat members of the lower class as, in many cases, ghosts. Simply because Robbie functions as a servant, Briony (and Emily Tallis, among others) assume he not only can but *has* raped Lola, Briony's cousin. When the police question Briony on how certain she is that she indeed saw Robbie assaulting Lola, she answers not only with "I saw him," but even more tellingly, "I've known him my whole life."[30] To Briony, Robbie represents a man she admits having been in love with as a child, a man who saved her from drowning as a girl; but fundamentally, he represents a member of the marginalized lower class—a servant. As such, she considers him to be capable of committing the foul act of rape or sending Cecelia a letter in which he tells her he imagines making love to her all day long and "kiss[ing] her sweet wet cunt"[31] ; surely no member of the upper class Briony knows would think or write such inappropriate thoughts.

After considering Briony's crimes, Elke D'Hoker poses the following questions:

> How to end a confession? How to achieve atonement . . . ? Briony claims quite simply that it is an impossible aim. Yet, she adds that what matters is not so much the outcome . . . as the attempt. . . . By analogy one could argue that even if the truth of the self simply cannot be reached in confession, what matters is the attempt . . . which generates and reveals a true story.[32]

Likewise, one could argue that even though Briony's novel reflects and perpetuates the problems associated with class consciousness, she raises awareness in her readers of the problem. David Jays offers, "*Atonement* insists on the moral purpose of fiction—its ability to see from another's perspective while offering the shivery possibilities of reading wrongly."[33] Similarly, one can argue, as I have, that Briony's primary mistake is being dominated by the "cultural haunting" of class consciousness that leads her to "read wrongly," to assume that she knows Robbie simply based on his marginalized status as a servant. Briony could have performed more, or less, revision. She might have supplied readers with even more detail about the happiness her lovers finally found, or she might have kept from informing her audience that Robbie and Cecelia, among others, actually died and were merely ghosts all along. But then by what would her readers be haunted? Much like Bowen's readers of *The Death of the Heart* as a love story in which the lovers do not find happiness together, *Atonement*'s readers may feel sad and angry. As a ghost story in which the characters become destroyed by the "cultural haunting" of class consciousness, however, readers will feel how a truly good ghost story should make them feel: unsettled by what they have just read, or frightened that the situation may occur again.

NOTES

1. Elizabeth Bowen, *The Death of the Heart* (New York: Alfred Knopf, 1938), 220.

2. An interesting connection exists between Bowen and *Atonement*. When Briony receives a feedback letter about an early manuscript of *Atonement* (known then as *Two Figures by a Fountain*), the editor writes, "It may interest you [Briony] to know that one of your avid readers was Mrs. Elizabeth Bowen." Ian McEwan, *Atonement* (New York; Anchor Books, 2001), 296. Bowen's taking special interest in Briony's work links the women in terms of literary tradition.

3. I include the film version of *Atonement* as McEwan's work as well, since he was an executive producer. He explained to Deborah Solomon of the *New York Times* that it was very important for him to "stay involved" with the making of the film. See Deborah Solomon, "A Sinner's Tale," *New York Times*, December 2, 2007, at http://www nytimes.com/2007/12/02/magazine/02wwln-Q4-t html?_r=1 (accessed August 4, 2012), 15.

4. Kathleen Brogan, *Cultural Haunting: Ghosts and Ethnicity in Recent American Literature* (Charlottesville: University Press of Virginia, 1998), 4.

5. Maria Margaronis, "The Anxiety of Authenticity: Writing Historical Fiction at the End of the Twentieth Century," *History Workshop Journal* 65 (2008): 140.

6. Gay Becker, Yewoubdar Beyene, and Pauline Ken, "Memory, Trauma, and Embodied Distress: The Management of Disruption in the Stories of Cambodians in Exile," *Ethos* 28, no. 3 (2000): 320.

7. Ibid., 320–21.

8. McEwan, *Atonement*, 18.

9. Ibid., 17.

10. Ibid., 46.

11. Ibid., 76.

12. Ibid., 4.

13. Ibid., 5.

14. Ibid., 46.

15. Ibid.

16. Ibid., 7.

17. Ibid., 43. Briony presents her readers with Grace's perspective of the situation as well. When Robbie mentions he will join the Turners and their special guest Marshall for dinner,

Grace realizes Marshall's importance with her comment to Robbie: "Oh, and there was me all afternoon, on the silver. And doing out his room." Ibid., 84.

18. Ibid., 50.

19. Ibid., 26.

20. Ibid.

21. Brian Finney, "Briony's Stand against Oblivion: The Making of Fiction in Ian McEwan's *Atonement*," *Journal of Modern Literature* 27, no. 3 (2004): 76.

22. See Finney (note 21) for a similar observation.

23. McEwan, *Atonement*, 196.

24. Ibid., 18.

25. Ibid., 25, 25–26.

26. Ibid., 74.

27. Ibid., 127.

28. Ibid., 128.

29. Avery Gordon, *Ghostly Matters: Haunting and the Sociological Imagination* (Minneapolis: University of Minnesota Press, 1997), 4.

30. McEwan, *Atonement*, 157.

31. Ibid., 80.

32. Elke D'Hoker, "Confession and Atonement in Contemporary Fiction: J. M. Coetzee, John Banville, and Ian McEwan," *Critique: Studies in Contemporary Fiction* 48, no. 1 (2006): 41.

33. David Jays, "First Love, Last Rites," *Sight and Sound* 17, no. 10 (2007): 34.

Chapter Five

The Spectral Queerness of White Supremacy

Helen Oyeyemi's White Is for Witching

Amy K. King

If people are what they eat, then the same applies to societies at large, because the "dietary desires" of economic and political systems reflect the essences of those systems. Once imperial societies find "the food" they prefer—cheap labor forced out of "minority" bodies—they "stuff" themselves, and such societies have not suffered from a lack of such food. In Helen Oyeyemi's novel *White Is for Witching* (2009), the body of the teenage protagonist Miranda Silver bears the weight of such British (neo)imperial tastes in the late twentieth century as the extreme ideals of whiteness supernaturally take over her body and mind. Miranda develops the eating disorder pica when her family moves from London to her mother's inherited house in Dover—a sentient house possessed by the ideals and tastes of white British supremacy. As the Dover house molds Miranda's appetites and thus her physical body, she essentially becomes a hungry ghost that acts as an agent of racist ideology and haunts a multiethnic Britain.

Throughout Oyeyemi's national allegory, Miranda's hunger for nonfood items escalates into a desire that is more menacing and telling about her society's appetites. Initially, Miranda believes she eats "exactly what she like[s], and she [does not] like the usual things."[1] What she "likes" to eat at the beginning of the novel are chalk, spatulas, and other organic and man-made items. Regularly eating things without nutritional value takes a toll on Miranda's body, and she becomes emaciated. In a Gothic twist to the story, Miranda starts to crave something else to eat: human flesh. Why Miranda's dietary desires regress from nutritious food, to nonnutritious organic and man-made matter, to human flesh is central to the way the novel portrays the idealization of white Britishness. Through depicting whiteness as a sterile, consumptive ideal, *White Is for Witching* puts forth the thesis that although the "Motherland," Great Britain, is now populated by immigrants from all over the globe, the specter of white racial purity and superiority still lingers beneath—and sometimes above—the surface of the "multicultural" space. The novel portrays the symbolic "queerness" of this British ideal of whiteness through desires that are characterized by consumption, not production— such as pica, incest, and vampirism.

Perfected in imperialism, the idea that "white" Britishness is superior to other ethnicities and races is a surprisingly modern phenomenon dating back approximately 300 years. According to Gary Taylor, "After 1700 Anglos *remembered* that they were white and *forgot* that whiteness was a recent invention,"[2] and "by 1704, when Newton published his *Optics* . . . , the British had bought—lock, stock, and gun barrel—the metaphor that told them they were white, and that their generic whiteness was a sign of their superiority to all other peoples."[3] This supposed racial superiority that, as Warren Montag says, means "all (others) are inferior, having fallen short of the universal [ideal of whiteness] and therefore of humanity,"[4] is unfounded, of course. Ashley Dawson's work argues against a historically homogeneous British population even in the early eighteenth century,[5] although "whiteness" and "Britishness" had by this time become synonymous in popular consciousness.

Therefore, even when the British debated the end of the transatlantic slave trade, the issue was one of a "white" Britain freeing a "black" Other elsewhere. According to Linda Colley, the de jure end of the British slave trade and widespread antislavery sentiments in the nineteenth century "supplied the British with an epic stage upon which they could strut in an overwhelmingly attractive guise"[6] of altruism, because "slaves, in short, did not threaten, at least as far as the British at home were concerned. Bestowing freedom upon them seemed therefore purely an act of humanity and will, an achievement that would be to Great Britain's economic detriment, perhaps, but would have few other domestic consequences."[7] Although white Britain could remove itself from the slave trade in the 1800s partially because it did not have contact with slaves at home, the end of the British Empire after World War II had a much different effect, as immigrants from former British colonies came to the "Motherland" in search of security and opportunities.

Modern Britain's diverse population due to people immigrating there from around the world—whether by choice or necessity—solidifies its status as "multicultural." Yet this space is not free from extreme racism. Paul Gilroy claims that in Britain the "new racism" attempts to keep Others out by using exclusionist tactics.

Language of war and invasion is the clearest illustration of the way in which the discourses which together constitute "race" direct attention to national boundaries, focusing attention on the entry and exit of blacks. The new racism is primarily concerned with mechanisms of inclusion and exclusion. It specifies who may legitimately belong to the national community and simultaneously advances reasons for the segregation or banishment of those whose "origin, sentiment, or citizenship," assigns them elsewhere. [8]

Along these lines, Dawson puts forth that "long after Britain lost its colonies, it retained its insular sense of cultural superiority" and that "the more potency they lost on the global stage after the eclipse of imperialism, the harder some Britons clung to the illusory status symbol that covered their bodies— their white skin—and the immutable cultural difference that it seemed to signify." [9] Therefore, even in recent cultural memory, "Britishness" has been equated with "whiteness." This ideal is severely scrutinized in Oyeyemi's *White Is for Witching* through the novel's depiction of a barren white ideal that believes it can protect the "key to England," Dover. [10]

Women's bodies in Oyeyemi's novel bear important allegorical significance according to the ideals of white supremacy. While white women's bodies would undoubtedly be exalted for their role in producing more members of the white race, the bodies of white women in *White Is for Witching* suffer from emaciation—they do not have matronly bodies. Miranda's great-grandmother, grandmother, and mother have all experienced the pica eating disorder that Miranda undergoes, although Miranda undergoes pica more fully than the other women. This matrilineal line of starvation is crucial to the way the novel portrays whiteness. According to Radhika Mohanram, Richard Dyer claims in his 1997 text *White* that at the height of empire in the Victorian Era, "white women [were] whiter than white men" as they were "the distillation of white attributes such as morality, ideals, the angelic, the spiritual, and the ethereal." [11] However, Mohanram asserts that the very principles that were thought to show how white British middle-class women were the embodiment of Britishness actually reveal "a hysteria" of the time, as women's sexuality "was a matter to be policed because [they] could dilute the ethnic/racial group." [12] She states,

What made the British woman the innermost, the purest, was precisely that *she was also the boundary*, the space of dilution, making the outer into the inner. At the very moment the British woman played the role of the essential and constitutive of Britishness, she undermined it by showing her potential/ability to contaminate it. Thus, contamination was at the very heart, the very core of white Britishness. [13]

"Mother" Britain and the "Angel in the House" were connected via a fragile lie that attempted to ensure the so-called "purity" of Britishness, and the

faults of this lie are evident in Oyeyemi's novel as Miranda finds herself
conforming to the desires of 29 Barton Road.

In what should be a domestic, wholesome space according to Victorian
ideals, the house at 29 Barton Road creates a hostile environment for all
unwelcome people—black guests.[14] The Dover house is an allegoric manifestation of the ideals of white Britishness. Throughout the novel, the reader
gathers bits of information directly from the house's point of view, and its
perspective always reflects the same preoccupation with the purity of its
women, the Silver women. For example, when Miranda's mother dies on a
trip in Haiti, the house wonders, "Why do people go to these places, these
places that are not for them? It must be that they believe in their night vision.
They believe themselves able to draw images up out of the dark. But black
wells only yield black water."[15] This depiction of Haiti as a "black well"
stretches as far back as the slave revolts there, which earned freedom for
slaves in Haiti long before Britain emancipated its slaves. As a place that
symbolized the fear of slave uprisings, Haiti was a "dark" neighbor to the
United States and to other Caribbean islands, as slave owners were terrified
of the same thing happening on their plantations. Later, motions in the United States to "send . . . blacks to Haiti" and afterward "to protect or even
annex Haiti in the interests of property" shows the "tangled plot of economic
greed and racial prejudice" that has influenced other countries' interactions
with Haiti since nationhood.[16]

Just as the Dover house believes black and white people have their respective places where they should remain, so has U.S. policy attempted to
dictate people's correct "places" based on skin color. Mimi Sheller adds
another layer to this depiction of Haiti: "As the oft-repeated 'poorest country
in the Western hemisphere' Haiti has become a 'poster child' for the ills of
poverty, disease, ecological crisis, and political catastrophe. However real
these concerns might be, they also fit into an established pattern of patholo-
gising Haiti."[17] The Dover house's depiction of Haiti as one of the "black
wells" in the world is significant, for the novel plays off of the gross misper-
ceptions people have held about Haiti throughout time. The house thus ob-
sesses over blackness, for it deems itself and Britain not to be a "black well,"
and any contact it has with the Other becomes an instance of contamination,
first through the house's interactions with the black workers and guests who
stay at the house, then through the house's interactions with refugees and
immigrants in Dover. The house says of itself and the Silver women, "We are
on the inside, and we have to stay together, and we absolutely cannot have
anyone else."[18] Like the hysteria concerning the purity of white British wom-
en, the Dover house's insistence on preserving the Silver women—literally,
as it keeps their bodies—at any cost reveals the nature of white supremacy.
The depiction of 29 Barton Road as a destructive British domestic space
shows the irony of the ideals of whiteness, for they turn a physical house that

should provide shelter into a house haunted by the violent legacy of British whiteness, and this house will stop at nothing to "cleanse" itself.

Thus, the pica eating disorder represents the Dover house's will to have "its women" remain "pure" (i.e., very white and very thin, with a child/ fashion model–like physicality). As stated earlier, the disease pica, which is "an appetite for non-food items, things that don't nourish," enters Miranda's life when her family comes to live in Dover.[19] On the first day at the house, Miranda's twin brother Eliot notices that she "f[inds] something on the floor of that room she . . . pick[s] as hers," which is chalk that she begins to nibble on.[20] While Miranda may appear to embrace pica when she relishes in her thinness, her desires are controlled by a force she cannot initially identify: "Scarecrow girl. She felt proud and nauseous, chosen and moulded by hands that froze."[21] The "hands" that "freeze" Miranda belong to something that has affected the women in her mother's family for generations: Anna Good Silver—Miranda's great-grandmother—started eating acorn husks, leaves, and pebbles when she was about to move into the house in Dover;[22] Jennifer Silver—Miranda's grandmother—ate her "tiny replica of a yew tree" and later "branches from the garden;"[23] Lily Silver—Miranda's mother—ate "ladybirds and things."[24] Every Silver woman feasts on items that do not nourish her body, and this anorexic behavior begins when she makes contact with the house in Dover.

As a symbol of the destructive nature of white supremacy, the Dover house is crucial to the Silver women's development of pica and the vampiric desires that form after pica drains their bodies. During the house's narration, it explains that Anna Good experienced pica before she was alone in the house with "the thing that asked her to let it out."[25] Likewise, before Miranda is sent away for therapy, she stands in the house and wonders, "Who was it that needed to talk to her, that she needed to talk to?"[26] The same "thing"—a desire that goes nameless during most of the novel—speaks to both Anna and Miranda, yet the evil desires of the house affect Miranda more than they did her grandmother or mother, as Miranda later physically transforms into a vampiric being. Why the house so favors Miranda to act on the ideals of whiteness speaks to her symbolic importance in the novel. Miranda's birth in 1982 establishes her as an allegoric representation of Britain, as the Falklands War waged during the year of her birth marked Britain's last-ditch effort to hang on to its empire. Her birth year also calls to mind the at-home violent upheavals of the race "riots" in Britain during the late 1970s and 1980s, which showed how poorly the government addressed racial tensions. Therefore, Miranda and post-imperial Britain age together. To recall one of Ashley Dawson's quotations, when the empire fell, some white Britons held tighter to their claim of racial superiority. As *White Is for Witching* shows, though, this illusory belief of superiority extends to the present, with a child of the empire's last stand becoming the hideous physical manifestation of white British ideals. Thus, these ideals are damaging to the victims of racist violence as well as to Britain as a whole.

One facet of Miranda's grotesque allegorical representation of idealized whiteness is the incestuous undertones that appear in the relationship between Miranda and her twin brother, Eliot. Although Eliot and Miranda do not consummate their desires for each other—indeed, the novel rarely articulates the desire—each twin's longing for the other is still present in the novel. Miranda knows Eliot is "her knight,"[27] and Eliot verbalizes the common perception that the male twin is "the prince at the foot of Rapunzel's tower before the tower is even built."[28] Although Eliot does not want to acknowledge the desire he has toward his sister, he ends his neurotic ruminations about other people's perceptions of him and Miranda with the following: "The question is, were they born in love with each other, these twins, or did it blossom? At any rate it's already happened, the onlookers agree. It must have. Ask them when they fell. The brother and sister say no, no, it's nothing like that, but what they mean is they can't remember when."[29] Although the novel does not provide Miranda's view of the matter, Eliot's thoughts here establish that he believes they are connected beyond a platonic relationship. Additionally, Eliot and Miranda clearly have a degree of sexual tension between them as teenagers because when they fight they try, "for some reason, to hold each other flat in the shadows."[30] In a telling scene, Eliot's feelings for Miranda get in the way of his relationship with his long-term girlfriend Emma, with whom he wants to end his relationship, but he decides he cannot "blank [her] altogether, because that would look weird," and he does not want to "risk her saying anything to any of [their] other friends."[31] Eliot realizes their society would not accept his feelings for his sister, yet the emphasis on white "purity" as a crucial means of preserving Britishness essentially uplifts incest as an ideal means of procreation.

Incest and miscegenation are theoretically diametrically opposed, as one reproduces sameness and the other produces difference. John T. Irwin writes about the incest trope in William Faulkner's fiction that "the temporal aspects of doubling and incest evoke the way in which the circle of the self-enclosed repeats itself through time as a cycle, the way that the inability to break out of the ring of the self and the family becomes the inability of successive generations to break out of the cyclic repetition of self-enclosure."[32] Therefore, in Faulkner's body of work, incest operates as a "symbol . . . of the state of the South after the Civil War, [a] symbol . . . of a region turned in upon itself."[33] In the same way, *White Is for Witching* uses incest as a symbol to critique white Britain as a culture "turned in upon itself." The *sameness* of Miranda and Eliot is evident in the novel, as they have identical dark hair and white skin that does not "tan in the slightest."[34] With their very white skin as a primary characteristic between them, Miranda and Eliot's relationship calls to mind how, according to Richard H. King, "the incest taboo forbids the identity relationship based upon repetition, while the prohibition of miscegenation forbids the relationship between the 'different.'"[35] Late in the novel, Eliot ponders why he cannot write to Miranda when she is studying at Cambridge University and he is putatively in South Africa. He wonders why, specifically, he cannot tell her "I love you": "It wasn't safe to say something like that without [our mother] Lily between us. Lily was always very careful to pull us apart, to make Miri and I understand that we were not each other, that my pressing my lips to Miri's nine-year-old heartbeat was not the same as feeling the blood move in myself."[36] Thus, while Eliot and Miranda keep their relationship at a certain distance throughout the novel, there is some danger that they will in effect become the same person through having offspring of their own.

If Eliot and Miranda did have a sexual relationship that produced offspring, the child would be a replica of them: white and British. Their child would be a symbol of the homogeneity privileged by a white British ideal, an ideal that puts sameness above creative heterogeneity, and the potentially deformed offspring of an incestuous relationship would signify the distorted views of a racist society. The brother and sister do not have this kind of relationship in the course of the novel, but readers are led to believe that they *could* have consummated their desires eventually. What intercedes in their relationship is the house in Dover, which thinks the two are "better off apart" once the house ingests Miranda at the end of the novel.[37] Although the house does favor white Britishness, the house gets in the way of any possible reproduction between the brother and sister and, symbolically, ends its own family line of whiteness. Instead of letting Eliot and Miranda be together and possibly produce another Silver girl to carry out the will of the house/white Britain, the house destroys its chances at using and consuming another Silver woman after Miranda. Even though Eliot could presumably go outside of the house to find a suitable white British mate with which to have children, his actions after Miranda disappears at the end of the novel reflect a truly inert, unproductive existence that shows the sterility of whiteness in the novel. Waiting for Miranda to return, Eliot compulsively cleans out her shoes, which mysteriously fill with thick, red rosewater. He believes he is "chained to the shoes" and will not get rid of them.[38] Like a tortured soul in a Gothic tale, Eliot will probably waste away in his obsession: in his longing for his sister, all he can do is remain in the house, and the red water that he empties out of the shoes is just like the vitality that will gradually pour out of him. Eliot's fruitless end signals a warning to Britons about the dangers of allowing such racist views to go unchecked, for Oyeyemi's allegorical tale points toward a bleak future if the ideals of white supremacy triumph.

Also complicating the house's chances at having more Silver women is that Miranda enters into a lesbian relationship. While the thesis of this paper is that the white British ideal is essentially flawed in its inherent sterility, readers cannot avoid the fact that Miranda's relationship with Ore would not yield children and, in the traditional sense, would not be "productive." Their lesbian relationship does not suggest sterility, however, as Miranda and Ore do find some, albeit brief, pleasure in each other's company. Also, because their relationship goes against the conventions of white British superiority, Miranda and Ore reveal that perhaps the younger generation of Britons is more willing to embrace flexible ethnicities, sexualities, and gender roles as opposed to Britons in the past. Ore, as a young woman of color, is despised by the Dover house. When Miranda tells the house she is "in love" with Ore, the house pictures what "Ore" means: "The squashed nose, the pillow lips, fist-sized breasts, the reek of fluids from the seam between her legs. The skin. The skin."[39] Although the house mostly dwells on Ore's skin color in its depiction of the young woman, the house is also occupied with the aspects of Ore's anatomy that would signal that she has a reproductive body: her breasts and vaginal fluids. Even though Miranda and Ore cannot procreate together, and the threat of miscegenation does not apply, the house views Ore as a very real menace to the "purity" of the house, Miranda, and—thus— whiteness.

Lee Edelman's discussion in *No Future* about how homosexual desire indicates no futurity is essential here. In his book, Edelman puts forth that the universal "Child remains the perpetual horizon of every acknowledged poli- tics, the fantasmatic beneficiary of every political intervention."[40] Conse- quently, queerness "names the side of those *not* 'fighting for the children,' the side outside the consensus by which all politics confirms the absolute value of reproductive futurism."[41] Societies, then, depend on the image of the Child for their futurity, as everything must be done to ensure that a society's beliefs and practices are passed down from generation to generation. The fact that Miranda is involved in a lesbian relationship, in contrast, means she is "both freed and excluded from normative societal expectations."[42] "If the notion of reproduction is removed from the timeline of life, if the present no longer pivots around the past and future," says Rebecca Fine Romanow, "then the subject lives in 'queer time.'"[43] The fact that Miranda goes against white British societal expectations and exists in "queer time" is clear when she begins her romantic involvement with Ore; Miranda will not contribute more white British children for the house, or society at large, to use and consume. Because of her "stubborn" nature,[44] according to 29 Barton Road, Miranda must be "save[d] even if [the house] ha[s] to break her."[45] Her choice *not* to reproduce leaves Miranda at the mercy of the house's anger, even though the house has starved Miranda to the point that she is likely too emaciated to conceive a child.

While the house is molding Miranda to its purposes, it shows her a glimpse of a "perfect person," someone whom Miranda believes looks like her "but perfect" to spark the desire that consumes her after pica.[46] Miranda sees this perfect person face-to-face when eating plastic does not satisfy her hunger and she gorges herself on beef stew in the kitchen.[47] This person is like one of Lily's childhood drawings Miranda found: "She was not quite three dimensional, this girl. And so white. There couldn't be any blood in her. She was perfect. Miranda but perfect. She was purer than crystal."[48] Thus, the girl's incredible skinniness and the "purity" of her skin appeal to Miranda and, as the reader can assume, to the house as well. While the girl's thinness and whiteness make her "perfect" to Miranda, what Miranda notices first are the girl's jagged teeth. The fact that Miranda eats nutritional food is notable and that she eats the *meat* on the plate is important, for Miranda is searching for what will satisfy her hunger, and the girl's sharp, vampire-like teeth provide a hint for what kind of food Miranda desires now—human flesh.

Later in the novel, when Miranda returns to the Dover house after she cannot bear being away from it in Cambridge, 29 Barton Road remarks on the "beauty" of Miranda's emaciated appearance: "My Miranda came home from college and her change had almost come full circle. She looked so beautiful. Tiny. Immaculately carved; an ivory wand."[49] Like the "perfect" person Miranda sees at the dinner table, Miranda has been transformed into an "ivory wand," a startlingly white and thin version of herself that is an exaggerated replication of a "Western" ideal of beauty. Now, Miranda may be used by the house. Readers piece together that the "perfect person" with the sharp teeth who looks like Miranda—but goes by the name "Anna" like her great-grandmother[50] —has been brutally stabbing immigrant youths in Dover. Like the mythical soucouyant that Ore describes in the novel as a female demon who feasts on the souls of people at night, the "perfect person" roams under the cover of darkness and looks for "newcomers"—immigrants—to harm.

Soucouyant myths exist in numerous cultures and usually entail that the soucouyant lives in the form of a woman by day and sheds her skin by night to feast on the bodies/souls of her victims. Destroying or identifying a soucouyant involves sprinkling salt on her discarded skin so she will perish or be easily recognized because of her intense pain and wailing. This mythos traditionally entails that the soucouyant is an evil female being that, according to C. R. Ottley's *Tall Tales of Trinidad and Tobago*, comes from "a long line of ancestral soucouyants."[51] Therefore, Giselle Anatol summarizes the significance of gender in the colonial contexts of these soucouyant tales:

> It is clear that the evil and corruption must be passed on through the mother, and only through the mother, because all soucouyants are female . . . [as] there is no male soucouyant in most versions of the tale. The history of slavery in the attitudes of Caribbean and British slave owners towards the reproduction of "property" are thus subtly referenced: soucouyant children follow in the line

of the mother, much as the status of children was determined by that of their mother during slavery. In other words, the soucouyant tale holds important reminders about the intertwining of gender and colonialism.[52]

Anatol points to the specific role the matrilineal line of the soucouyant plays in the framework of slavery; the lineage of the soucouyant serves as a reminder of the very system that oppressed so many people. Likewise, in *White Is for Witching*, Ore describes the soucouyant as "the wicked old woman who flies from her body and at night consumes her food, the souls of others."[53] As previously stated, the matrilineal line of vampirism in Miranda's family is important as it shows the faulty, but persistent, logic that white British "purity" must be upheld through white womenfolk. Using this soucouyant myth to describe Miranda's vampirism thus employs the colonial mythos in a different way, as it reflects the consumptive nature of the empire back to itself. As Ore realizes, there is a "double danger" with a soucouyant: "There is the danger of meeting her, and the danger of becoming her."[54] While Ore does not change into a soucouyant, Miranda knows by the end of the novel that she and the house together are a soucouyant-like being called "the good-lady"[55] —a title that plays on her great-grandmother's maiden name "Good"—which, in reality, is definitely not "good." Instead, Anna Good first stirred the house and "gave" the house its "task" when she vehemently proclaimed, "I hate them. . . . Blackies, Germans, killers, dirty . . . dirty killers."[56] Anna Good, who was "afraid to wear white" because she had the "feeling that she was not clean,"[57] embodies the paranoia and (self-)hatred inherent in white supremacist ideals, and the house passes an incarnation of these emotions—via the soucouyant, vampire form—down Anna Good's matrilineal line. For Miranda, transforming into the "goodlady," a soucouyant-like being, begins when she encounters the "perfect girl" with the sharp teeth.

The "perfect" girl's seemingly impossible attribute of not having blood is important here considering the girl's—and the house's—plan for Miranda to become a vampiric being. Without blood of her own, the girl must presumably take the blood of others to survive, and this could be viewed as a representation of stagnant white Britain's insatiable hunger for the "blood" of immigrants—a relationship classified by both hunger and repulsion. While the "perfect person" does her nightly work, she apprentices Miranda to do the same by giving her the desire to consume immigrants, beginning with the teenager Jalil, whom Miranda impulsively kissed one night in a pub. In a nightmarish sequence of events that is probably a hallucination, Miranda is led into a room of the house where GrandAnna, Jennifer, and Lily are standing around a table that holds a feast. Even though many different kinds of food are available there, including the chalk Miranda would usually prefer, "all [the food] d[oes] [i]s make Miranda hungrier for what [i]s not there, so hungry that she release[s] her mother's hand and h[olds] her own throat and gag[s]. Her hunger harden[s] her stomach, gr[ows] new teeth inside her."[58] As she wonders what she wants to eat, Miranda notices fingers sticking through some holes in the wall: They are the lifeless fingers of Jalil. Horrified, Miranda believes "she ha[s] done this" to Jalil "in a period of inattention," signaling that she believes she performs soucouyant-like acts at night when she is unaware.[59] Miranda now understands that the "unspeakable" thing she craves to eat is human flesh. Thus, the house plainly reveals its evil intentions to Miranda as it wishes to use her to bring about the slaughter of young immigrants in Dover.

As Mimi Sheller's project indicates, the consumption of bodies in "the imagery of cannibals, vampires, and zombies" can help people "question the eating of others not only in terms of symbolic forms of commodity consumption, but also in terms of the actual material relations through which bodies in one place unethically touch bodies in another place."[60] Therefore, *White Is for Witching* shows the very real destruction and absorption of humans into Britain as the harsh ideals of white British supremacy dominate them. As Miranda's desires to consume immigrants later include Ore, who was born to a black Nigerian mother and adopted by a white Kentish couple, her "tastes" for "others" grows more refined. At one point, Miranda actually contemplates removing Ore's heart while she sleeps,[61] thus desiring to "eat the Other," as bell hooks describes. According to hooks, "In ancient religious practices among so called 'primitive' people, the heart of a person may be ripped out and eaten so that one can embody that person's spirit or special characteristics."[62] Because she desires to eat the Other, Miranda has the desire to incorporate the Other into her self, like the soucouyant does, and just as Britain does to its immigrant population. What the Dover house and therefore Britain as a whole do not realize is that consuming the Other inevitably integrates characteristics of the Other into the fabric of society. Although the idea of Otherness repulses the white British ideal, the very fabric of British society requires the labor of "Others," and their Otherness unavoidably becomes a part of British culture. Regardless of Miranda's intentions and efforts not to act on her vampiric urges—"Ore is not food. I think I am a monster"[63] —her relationship with Ore is consumptive. As Miranda causes Ore to lose weight (Ore "had never eaten so much, [she] had never wanted to eat so much. But [her] clothes kept getting looser"[64]) and Miranda even sucks the very breath out of Ore's body ("As we kissed I became aware of something leaving me. . . . I tried hard to breathe, harder than I have ever tried at anything. . . . But I couldn't"[65]), the reader sees Miranda as a symbol (albeit unwilling) of white Britishness that can only consume the Other.

As Miranda takes on vampire-like qualities—her teeth eventually grow jagged like the "perfect person's"—she serves as a representation of the vampire in postcolonial literatures. As John Allen Stevenson indicates, the Victorian vampire tale *Dracula* "insistently—indeed, obsessively—defines the vampire . . . as a foreigner, as someone who threatens and terrifies precisely because he is an outsider. In other words, it may be fruitful to consider Stoker's compelling and frequently retold story in terms of inter*racial* sexual competition."[66] This particular telling of the vampire myth thus depicts Victorian fears of miscegenation and infiltration. However, as with the soucouyant legend, *White Is for Witching* switches the roles of "predator" and "prey" commonly seen in the mythos influenced by *Dracula*. As Miranda grows vampire-like teeth, she *has* become the vampire;[67] she is the Other to be feared. According to Gerry Turcotte, when a vampire appears in a colonial/postcolonial setting, "the vampire is European culture, which descends upon and feeds off Indiginous peoples (neatly reversing the cannibalism stereotype)."[68] While the setting of *White Is for Witching* is in the Motherland, not the colony, the novel's representation of the idealization of British whiteness as a vampiric, cannibalistic force is powerfully evocative. Because the house desires that Miranda consume immigrants in order to expel them from Britain, its craving reflects what Dean MacCamell sees in his essay "Cannibalism Today" as the very relevant application of cannibalism to the current state of political and economic structures around the world: "Cannibalism in the political-economic register is the production of social totalities by the literal *incorporation* of otherness. It deals with human difference in the most direct way, not merely by doing away with it, but by taking it in completely, metabolizing it, transforming it into shit, and eliminating it."[69] Because the house takes in black "others," puts them to work, uses them up, then expels them with its cold racism—"White is for witching, a colour to be worn so that all other colours can enter you, so that you may use them"[70] —MacCamell's depiction of cannibalism illustrates how the house operates as an agent of the nation at large. White Britain, according to the novel, knows only how to consume—and if this continues, *White Is for Witching* suggests, Britain will consume itself.

Ultimately, the novel depicts the vampirism of the white British ideal as a self-destructing force. The house points out that Miranda's great-grandmother is related to a woman who "slash[ed] at her own flesh," then drank "off her blood, then bit . . . and suck[ed] at the bobbled stubs of her meat" because "her appetite was only for herself."[71] Likewise, Anna Good Silver is sent to an asylum because she acts like "the heraldic pelican . . . the bird that pecks itself to death to feed its children" when she tries to feed her blood to the very young Eliot and Miranda.[72] Importantly, Miranda's last vampiric desire is to attack and feed off of Eliot—to "strip him down to true red."[73] Although Miranda feels empowered by the harm she could presumably inflict on Eliot, her desire to "see red," to consume her own brother's blood and life, confirms the ungovernable destruction that white British supremacy entails for the entire culture. The novel shows that the idealization of whiteness ultimately leads to a self-cannibalizing urge that removes the ideal altogether. Even though the house in Dover may be "still fighting" as the "key to a locked gate" of white Britishness,[74] the house is "storing its collapse" after World War II and the passing of empire.[75] After all, Miranda is the last of the Silver matrilineal line, and the house literally consumes her in order to "save" her.[76] The tropes of pica, incest, and vampirism in the novel all illustrate how nonproductive and, ultimately, destructive the ideal of white Britishness can be. As *White Is for Witching* reveals, the haunted house of white superiority is built on very shoddy foundations that do not stand up to scrutiny.

NOTES

1. Helen Oyeyemi, *White Is for Witching* (New York: Doubleday, 2009), 31.
2. Gary Taylor, *Buying Whiteness: Race, Culture, and Identity from Columbus to Hip Hop* (New York: Palgrave Macmillan, 2005), 7.
3. Ibid., 341.
4. Warren Montag, "The Universalization of Whiteness," in *Whiteness: A Critical Reader*, ed. Mike Hill (New York: New York University Press, 1997), 292.
5. Ashley Dawson, *Mongrel Nation: Diasporic Culture and the Making of Postcolonial Britain* (Ann Arbor: The University of Michigan Press, 2007), 6.
6. Linda Colley, *Britons: Forging the Nation 1707–1837*, rev. ed. (New Haven, CT: Yale University Press, 2009), 366.
7. Ibid., 362–63.
8. Paul Gilroy, *"There Ain't No Black in the Union Jack": The Cultural Politics of Race and Nation* (Chicago: University of Chicago Press, 1991), 45.
9. Ibid., 6.
10. Oyeyemi, *White*, 100.
11. Radhika Mohanram, *Imperial White: Race, Diaspora, and the British Empire* (Minneapolis: University of Minnesota Press, 2007), 30.
12. Ibid., 34.
13. Ibid.
14. Oyeyemi, *White*, 129.
15. Ibid., 8.
16. Joan Dayan, "'A Receptacle for That Race of Men': Blood, Boundaries, and Mutations of Theory," *American Literature* 67, no. 4 (1995): 803.
17. Mimi Sheller, *Consuming the Caribbean: From Arawaks to Zombies* (New York: Routledge, 2003), 168.
18. Oyeyemi, *White*, 109.
19. Ibid., 20.
20. Ibid., 18.
21. Ibid., 34.
22. Ibid., 21.
23. Ibid., 78.
24. Ibid., 150.
25. Ibid., 21.
26. Ibid., 24.
27. Ibid., 26.
28. Ibid., 41.
29. Ibid.

30. Ibid., 43.
31. Ibid., 41.
32. John T. Irwin, *Doubling and Incest / Repetition and Revenge: A Speculative Reading of Faulkner*, expanded ed. (Baltimore: Johns Hopkins University Press, 1996), 59.
33. Ibid.
34. Oyeyemi, *White*, 111.
35. Richard H. King, *A Southern Renaissance: The Cultural Awakening of the American South, 1930–1955* (Oxford: Oxford University Press, 1980), 126–27.
36. Oyeyemi, *White*, 172.
37. Ibid., 210.
38. Ibid., 226.
39. Ibid., 179.
40. Lee Edelman, *No Future: Queer Theory and the Death Drive* (Durham, NC: Duke University Press, 2004), 3.
41. Ibid.
42. Rebecca Fine Romanow, *The Postcolonial Body in Queer Space and Time* (Newcastle upon Tyne, UK: Cambridge Scholars Publishing, 2008), 6.
43. Ibid.
44. Oyeyemi, *White*, 109.
45. Ibid., 180.
46. Ibid., 45.
47. Ibid., 70.
48. Ibid., 73.
49. Ibid., 178.
50. Ibid., 105.
51. Carlton Robert Ottley, *Tall Tales of Trinidad and Tobago* (Port-of-Spain, Trinidad: Horsford Printerie, 1972), quoted in Giselle Anatol, "Transforming the Skin-Shedding Soucouyant: Using Folklore to Reclaim Female Agency in Caribbean Literature," *Small Axe* 7 (2000): 50.
52. Giselle Anatol, "Transforming the Skin-Shedding Soucouyant," 50–51.
53. Oyeyemi, *White*, 137.
54. Ibid., 144.
55. Ibid., 203.
56. Ibid., 109.
57. Ibid., 107.
58. Ibid., 118.
59. Ibid., 119.
60. Sheller, *Consuming the Caribbean*, 147–48.
61. Oyeyemi, *White*, 177.
62. bell hooks, "Eating the Other: Desire and Resistance," in *Media and Cultural Studies: KeyWorks*, ed. Meenakshi Gigi Durham and Douglas M. Kellner (Malden, MA: Blackwell, 2001), 432.
63. Oyeyemi, *White*, 177.
64. Ibid., 172.
65. Ibid., 198.
66. John Allen Stevenson, "A Vampire in the Mirror: The Sexuality of *Dracula*," *PMLA* 103, no. 2 (1988): 139.
67. Oyeyemi, *White*, 219.
68. Gerry Turcotte, "Vampiric Decolonization: Fanon, 'Terrorism,' and Mudrooroo's Vampire Trilogy," in *Postcolonial Whiteness: A Critical Reader on Race and Empire*, ed. Alfred J. López (Albany: State University of New York Press, 2005), 109.
69. Dean MacCannell, *Empty Meeting Grounds: The Tourist Papers* (New York: Routledge, 1992), 66.
70. Oyeyemi, *White*, 108.
71. Ibid., 22.
72. Ibid., 67.

73. Ibid., 221.
74. Ibid., 100.
75. Ibid., 53.
76. Ibid., 180.

Chapter Six

In the Spirit of Reconciliation

Migrating Spirits and Australian Postcolonial Multiculturalism in Hoa Pham's Vixen

Jessica Carniel

Australia remains haunted by a complex colonial past marked by Indigenous dispossession, cultural genocide, and racial inequality, later further compli-cated by stringent immigration controls on the basis of race. This past is the subject of an ongoing discussion: How, it is asked, do we remember this past, and how can contemporary Australian society, which has largely been built on postwar immigration, progress into the future when haunted by the memo-ries of these dark beginnings? As one of the characters in Hoa Pham's *Vixen* says, "Spirits come and go. But we're still here. The land is still here."[1] This quotation forms part of the most important exchange in Pham's novel, a "historical fantasy"[2] about migrant and Indigenous Australian spirits. These words are spoken by a ningaui, an Aboriginal Australian spirit, sometimes known as a bunyip, to comfort a Vietnamese fox fairy (a mythical creature who is able to take the form of a woman) who mourns the death of her friend, a fox fairy from China. It is a moment of mutual respect and recognition, and, simultaneously, an articulation of Indigenous custodianship of and belonging to the land. It is a gesture of hospitality to the migrating spirits. *Vixen* is, as mentioned above, what Pham calls a "historical fantasy"; she deliberately plays with mythologies from various cultures against a historical backdrop that makes no claims to accuracy. Nonetheless, Pham captures a truth in this moment and others like it in the novel. This is a moment of recognition between historically marginalized groups in Australian society, namely mi-grant and Indigenous Australians, and a motion toward reconciliation, which is an ongoing process of negotiation and mutual respect that seeks to unite

Indigenous and non-Indigenous Australians socially, culturally, and political-
ly in light of their shared past. Pham's fictional exchange between the ningaui and the fox fairy is also a moment in which complex histories of colonialism and migration converge and are tentatively negotiated within discourses of postcolonialism and multiculturalism. It is not a moment of complete resolution (before disappearing, the ningaui invites the fox fairy to
return another time, signaling a desire for an ongoing interaction), because
reconciliation in Australia is an ongoing process and the relationship between
the Indigenous and the nonsettler (nonwhite) migrant is particularly new.
Literary critic and critical multiculturalist Sneja Gunew argues that the Australian state has failed its multicultural subjects—its migrants—as much as it
has failed its Indigenous subjects.[3] Pham's novel, in a sense, attempts to
respond to this suggestion as well as to propose a solution: The encounter
between the fox fairy and the Aboriginal spirit is a moment of negotiation
between Indigenous and multicultural subjects under the broader rubric of
postcolonialism. The use of spirit forms allows Pham to draw upon the
collective experiences and memories of these particular subject positions, as
well as to explore the multifarious ways in which postcolonial and multicultural nations are haunted by both their past and the pasts of the nations left by
its migrant subjects.

Pham's historical fantasy is ambitious and not limited to this imagined
negotiation between Indigenous and multicultural subjects in Australia; *Vix-
en* offers an allegorical commentary on twentieth-century history, with its
particular focus on the shared histories of Vietnam and Australia. Various
historical, political, and cultural subject positions are represented in *Vixen* by
various mythical creatures who interact in various symbolic ways. In the
novel, after defeating a French vampire and losing her human lover to a
conflict with emerging northern communists, the unnamed Vietnamese fox
fairy flees Vietnam as it falls to these twin pressures of decolonization and
communism. Taking on the identity of a woman killed by the communists,
she migrates to Australia, where she befriends Chen, a Chinese fox fairy
living in the Australian countryside, who migrated from China during the
gold rushes of the 1850s. Here in the countryside she also encounters the
ningaui, with whom Chen is also acquainted. Eventually the fox fairy returns
to Vietnam, where she meets with a young dragon and finds an orphaned fox
kitten. The novel ends with the fox fairy choosing to remain in Vietnam with
her newly adopted kitten, who will now learn to be a fox fairy too.

There are three key encounters of concern in this essay that can be roughly categorized respectively as the colonial encounter, the multicultural encounter, and the postcolonial encounter. The colonial encounter occurs between the Vietnamese fox fairy and the French vampire. As a critique of the
effects of French colonization on Vietnam, the colonial encounter suggests
that colonial powers can be parasitic and so weaken the political and cultural

climate of a nation. In the multicultural encounter between the Vietnamese and Chinese fox fairies, Pham explores the possibility of intercultural dialogue within the multicultural state, which emphasizes the importance of migrant pasts in creating and enriching understandings of Australia as multicultural. Finally, the postcolonial encounters that occur between the fox fairies and the ningaui are used to imagine the political and cultural possibilities of conversations between multicultural and Indigenous subjects in a postcolonial and multicultural Australia. In particular, the shared experience of colonialism by the Vietnamese fox fairy and the ningaui opens up an even more interesting transnational dialogue that, I argue, gestures toward a form of what Appiah calls "rooted cosmopolitanism."[4] These various mythical creatures are utilized by Pham as a means of exploring historical experiences and imagining the possibilities of new intercultural interactions and negotiations.

Pham's use of spiritual beings deviates somewhat from the norm in ethnic literatures and allows her to provide a commentary on the intersections of Australian and Vietnamese histories. Ghosts are a common feature of much migrant or multicultural writing, as well as Indigenous writing in Australia and other settler societies, such as the United States, Canada, and New Zealand. In her study of ghosts in contemporary American ethnic literature, Kathleen Brogan argues that ghosts function "to re-create ethnic identity through imaginative recuperation of the past into the service of the present."[5] More important, she argues that these ghosts "lead us to the heart of [America's] discourse about multiculturalism and ethnic identity. . . . They reveal much about the dynamics of social and literary revisionism in response to cross-cultural encounters."[6] In Brogan's sample texts, the ghosts are usually ancestral, related in some way to the haunted protagonists, who, in their turn, are coming to terms with their ethnic heritage. Pham's spiritual beings, conversely, are creatures drawn from traditional Vietnamese, European, and Australian mythologies; they are not ordinary "ghosts," as such, and are not related to the other migrant characters found in the novel. These creatures are more allegorical in that they represent a group's collective history as living and dynamic, subject to change and interpretation. The fox fairy in *Vixen* becomes, therefore, an embodiment of Vietnamese ethnicity, if one understands this term to mean the collective histories, experiences, and traditions of a group. But she does not haunt a protagonist: Ethnicity itself, in a sense, is the protagonist.

More so than even the ancestral ghost, the various spirits that inhabit Pham's novel serve to highlight the relationship between the past and present because they are witnesses to both.[7] They represent memory and history, and they are testimony. This representation highlights the importance of history and tradition for ethnicity and the process of ethnic identification. Ken Gelder and Jane Jacobs observe that "the past is always ghostly"[8] in Australia.

The ephemeral quality that the "ghostliness" of the past suggests belies its very real and constant politicized presence in Australian culture and society. Pham's spirits are immortal (as long as they choose to be, as demonstrated by Chen's voluntary death), but they are also corporeal (again, in the case of the ningaui at least, if they choose to be). But reading the corporeality of the fox fairies as an indication of the very "realness" of the migrant presence in Australia complicates the ningaui's mutability and her reclusiveness; there is a danger of inferring from this that the Indigenous presence in Australia is also changeable, reclusive, and, as the fox fairy herself once wonders, indifferent: "The English took over everything. Like in America. I did not understand. Why did not the Australian people rebel, like the Vietcong?"[9] This is a question eventually answered in the postcolonial encounter, an answer found in the Indigenous relationship to land.

THE COLONIAL ENCOUNTER

The Indigenous past is pale and ghostly even in this tale of spirits, referenced only in Chen's account of her experiences in Australia and interactions with the ningaui. The nature and process of colonization is instead depicted within the Vietnamese context, embodied by the French vampire, Chloe. As Ken Gelder states, "Vampirization is colonization,"[10] and Chloe quite literally sucks the lifeblood out of Vietnam by preying on its emperor. Graham Huggan, drawing on Gelder, teases out the ambiguities of the vampire as a manifestation of colonialism:

> On one level, the vampire represents a destructive meeting of extremes, in which civilizational excess (often framed as decadence) becomes interchangeable with barbarity; on another, it represents the blurring of all ontological categories, so that vampires not only constitute a threat to specific personal/ cultural identities, but also demonstrates that identity, however produced or protected, will always be foreign to itself.[11]

Chloe is depicted in lush terms of excess: "She spills out of a beautiful green silk dress and teeters in spiky black heels. . . . [The emperor] says that she is France—elegant, graceful and rich."[12] There is something seductive about colonization, the novel daringly suggests, even for its object, but its essence is parasitic. While the emperor is enchanted by Chloe, he also is enchanted by the colonial presence of the French. Although the fox fairy does not immediately recognize Chloe's true nature, she is suspicious of this encroachment on her territory and mentally attacks Chloe's physical otherness, which is further accentuated when she dons an *ao dai*. The traditional Vietnamese dress, the fox fairy observes, "makes her breasts look like udders,"[13] and she is unimpressed that Chloe "thinks it's amusing to look like one of us."[14]

Chloe's ill-fitting *ao dai* and her broken Vietnamese mark her failure to create a secure sense of belonging as the colonizer within the colonized state, largely because of the lack of respect that she affords her hosts and their culture, and so signals the inevitable demise of the French occupation of Vietnam. Another attempt to adhere to local custom is similarly marked by disrespect. She presents the fox fairy with a ruby ring, believing that the small trinket will buy the protecting fox fairy's permission to colonize, a process represented by her feeding on the emperor. Both the giver and the receiver misinterpret this gift exchange: Chloe thinks that the ring buys permission to stay unequivocally, whereas the fox fairy asserts that it granted her audience with the emperor but not the right to feed. Angered by her disrespect and greed, the fox fairy poisons Chloe by lacing her white rice pudding with silver, a metal typically considered lethal to vampires and werewolves in European traditions. This action results in the fox fairy's flight from the court to escape imprisonment for murder. Chloe's greedy consumption of the poisoned rice pudding encapsulates Huggan's further characterization of vampires as "symbols of an overweening 'West' that, driven by a greed far beyond nourishment, is eventually condemned to turn in on, and consume, itself."[15]

While Chloe represents France and its colonial power, the meaning of the fox fairy is more elusive. As discussed above, she does not act to revive Vietnamese ethnicity in others in the same way as the visitations of ancestral ghosts of other ethnic fictions. In such fictions, the ghosts usually bring about the ethnic catharsis of the protagonist by reminding her of the ethnic past. By contrast, the fox fairy's meaning is complicated because she does not haunt the protagonist, nor is she a traditional ethnic protagonist herself. As discussed by Brogan, ghosts in ethnic literature usually serve to recreate or revive ethnic identity through recollection of the past. The fox fairy does not need to be reminded of her ethnicity, nor does she remind others of theirs—although, as will be discussed later, her survival does depend on the ethnic identification of others. Rather, the fox fairy, displaying a certain territorial concern for Vietnam, plays witness to historical events and, subsequently, is shaped by those national historical forces. This reading sees the fox fairy's role as an embodiment of Vietnamese ethnicity as a dynamic, living thing with an important relationship to history, memory, and the past. This is further reinforced by the fox fairy's duty to ghosts in Asian traditions.[16] These other ghosts and spirits perform the traditional role of ghosts in ethnic literature, representing a lost past. When the fox fairy summons the spirit of her dead lover, Han, for the last time, she notices details that indicate his immunity to historical change: "His accent is now archaic, untouched by European vowels."[17] Han is also unable to remember information she has given him in other visits, and he admits, "I do not remember much. You summon me and I come. Otherwise I just drift from place to place. I mostly guard the tomb of the Emperor. But when I'm with you I'm alive."[18] Trapped as he is in the moment of his death and expecting to see her each time as when he last left her, the fox fairy comes to realize that Han cannot love her for what she is—as the embodiment of a broader, living Vietnamese ethnicity, she is subject to change: "Han never understood the way Vietnam was, the way Vietnam is. He never went beyond the Inner Citadel."[19]

THE MULTICULTURAL ENCOUNTER

Viewing the fox fairy as this embodiment of Vietnamese history and tradition is not challenged by her departure from that land. As she states at the beginning of the novel, "There are many myths and stories about fox fairies. But the only ones I can tell are mine."[20] Even within a single nation, there can be multiple histories, and through the processes of migration and diaspora these histories are arguably further fragmented. This fox fairy embodies the particular trajectory of history that led many Vietnamese to migrate to Australia and is witness to these historical experiences of Vietnamese Australians. Her migration therefore challenges understandings of history as static and localized and shows the ways in which the histories of the places where migrants come from intersect with the histories of their destinations. This recalls, somewhat obliquely, the creative tension between "where you're from" and "where you're at" that Ien Ang argues allows for a "productive, creative syncretism"[21] in diasporic cultures and that, I argue, is also necessary in multicultural sites.

In coming to Australia, the fox fairy inevitably brings the Vietnamese past with her. Through her migration, she comes to represent the intersection of its histories and traditions with those of Australia and to form the Vietnamese Australian present. Her survival in Australia is, however, dependent upon the continued ethnic identification of other Vietnamese migrants. The fox fairy is also frustrated to find that the Vietnamese in Australia gradually abandon the practice of honoring their spirits, which weakens her: "With no one to worship me I lost my sense of self. . . . Living as Hong's sister, I was like a ghost. I affected no one and no one treated me as was my due."[22] The Chinese fox fairy chooses to die rather than continue to live unworshipped in Australia. Her death symbolizes the gradual "death" of ethnic groups as they are absorbed into the Australian mainstream culture over time, indicated also by the ease with which she wore Australian clothes as a human. Pham does not suggest that assimilation (along with the dissolution of ethnic identity that can result) is inevitable but rather a possibility. Again, this reaffirms the reading of the fox fairy as a dynamic and living embodiment of Vietnamese history and tradition; she must be honored and remembered or else she will fade and die. It also rests upon a particular understanding of the relationship between ethnicity, history, and memory. As Brogan argues, "Memory is the mirror that reflects ethnicity: to be Cuban, Irish, or Jewish is, to a degree, to remember oneself as such, a memory of connectedness that carries with it certain privileges and responsibilities."[23] Unlike traditional ethnic spirits, the fox fairy's presence does not revive the ethnic identification of those with whom she interacts. In contrast, her sense of self—*her* identity—is dependent upon the ethnic identification of others: there can be no ethnicity without those who identify with it. The relationship between ethnicity and history is presented as symbiotic, and memory is central to both.

As Amritjit Singh, Joseph T. Skerrett Jr., and Robert E. Hogan argue, memory "interrupts linear conventional narratives in order to make room for multiple voices and perspective. . . . This use of multiple voices [in ethnic literatures becomes] . . . a means of creating community as part of the dialectic between the past and the present in moving toward the future."[24] Chen, the Chinese fox fairy, plays a similar role to that of the Vietnamese fox fairy; she migrates to Australia during the gold rush of the 1850s and is witness to the racism and violence against the Chinese in the goldfields. The Vietnamese fox fairy appears either ignorant of or indifferent to the history of exclusion and racism pertaining to Asian migration to Australia, and she is relatively oblivious to the few instances that she witnesses in the city. Chen's recollection of the violence of the goldfields highlights the problematic history of Asians and Asianness in Australia and the different historical experiences that can be encompassed by this category. Chen also warns the Vietnamese fox fairy about the dangers of forgetting such exclusions: "You cannot forget. If you forget it will happen again."[25] It is important to remember, therefore, that Asians were historically excluded from Australia for much of the twentieth century by what has come to be known as the "White Australia policy." The Vietnamese fox fairy, migrating to Australia in the mid-1960s, arrives at the point when Australian immigration policy was slowly being reformed to allow nonwhite immigration. This reform resulted largely from growing international pressure regarding the inherent racism of Australia's immigration policy and escalating tensions in the Asia-Pacific region, such as the Vietnam War, that were producing large numbers of Indochinese refugees; pressure mounted for Australia to "take in its fair share."[26] The fox fairy's apparent obliviousness to the particular race relations prevalent in Australia throughout her stay (she returns to Vietnam around the 1990s) is problematic, particularly given her sensitivity to the political tensions in Vietnam. It perhaps indicates her difficulty in creating a meaningful connection to Australia and Australians. In a sense, her relationship with Chen, and the recollection of Chen's story in the narrative, is necessary to awaken in her a historicized race consciousness.

The friendship that develops between Chen and the Vietnamese fox fairy also represents the tentative alliance that is formed between migrant groups—particularly those assigned the same race category, in this case "Asian"—in response to the host society. "Fox fairy" here comes to symbolize "Asian," but by emphasizing the differences between the two fairies, Pham effectively critiques this problematic category, which is commonly imagined as homogenous despite the diverse cultural groups it encompasses;[27] they might share a "race" but are differentiated by the specific Chinese and Vietnamese ethnic histories they represent. The shared Asian mythology from which the fox fairies derive, together with the Vietnamese fox fairy's Sino features in woman form, also refer to the old cultural ties between China and Vietnam and serve to strengthen the relationship between the two fairies. Their apparent sameness is, however, initially cause for suspicion, given the territoriality of fox fairies. When she first encounters Chen on her initial journey into the Australian countryside, the Vietnamese fox fairy necessarily shows deference to the older Chinese spirit and respect for her ownership of the land. As spirits that honor ghosts and embody histories and traditions, they have respect for the rules that necessarily govern their interactions and intersections. Pham does not set up a hierarchy of migration histories in doing so, but merely establishes a relationship between Chinese and Vietnamese histories that converges in the Australian context on the shared basis of race. The Vietnamese fox fairy must learn about the Chinese past in Australia in order to understand the tenuous position of Asians in Australian society. This creates, to paraphrase Singh et al., community within the dialectic between the migrant past(s) and the multicultural present. Their friendship represents the possibilities of multicultural encounters and the necessary intersections of histories that must occur within a multicultural state.

THE POSTCOLONIAL ENCOUNTER

The fox fairies' interactions with the ningaui must also be seen as a necessary encounter that brings together Australia's migrant and Indigenous histories to create a new multicultural and postcolonial dialogue. Consequently, the intersection between postcolonialism and multiculturalism is key to understanding Pham's novel and the historical fantasy that she is attempting to imagine for contemporary Australia. As Sneja Gunew observes at the beginning of *Haunted Nations: The Colonial Dimensions of Multiculturalism*, "The relationship between multiculturalism and postcolonialism is an uneasy one."[28] Nonetheless, there *is* a relationship, which is drawn out effectively in Gunew's comparison: "Multiculturalism deals with theories of difference but unlike postcolonialism, which to a great extent is perceived to be defined retroactively by specific historical legacies, multiculturalism deals with the often compromised management of contemporary geopolitical diversity in former imperial centres as well as in their ex-colonies."[29] Multiculturalism is, in a historical and often physical or geographical sense, quite literally postcolonial. It does not, however, always comfortably encompass the specific historical legacy, as Gunew terms it, of colonialism, particularly within the Australian context. Indigenous thinkers and leaders have deliberately distanced themselves from Australian discourses of multiculturalism because of the importance of recognizing that their special rights as dispossessed peoples are different and distinct from the needs of migrants and their children, which the policy of multiculturalism first sought to address.[30] Nevertheless, various critical multiculturalists, such as Gunew, Ghassan Hage, and Bob Hodge and John O'Carroll, seek to explore the necessary relationship between those managed by colonialism and those managed by multiculturalism.

This notion of cultural "management" derives from the work of Ghassan Hage, who argues that migration is a continuation of the colonization process and so finds an even more causal relationship between colonialism and multiculturalism, which in turn affects multiculturalism's relationship with postcolonialism. In his exploration of Australia's often-racist immigration history, Hage discerns what he calls a "White colonial paranoia"—the "fear and loss of Europeanness or whiteness and of the lifestyle and privileges that are seen to emanate directly from that."[31] The various policies of the twentieth century that restricted nonwhite immigration, which have come to be known historically as the White Australia policy, have been, Hage argues, manifestations of this colonial uneasiness that still plays out today through multiculturalism. White colonial paranoia highlights the tenuousness of colonial power and the need to establish institutions and structures that maintain this power in order to manage interaction with and between society's Others. Multiculturalism, Hage argues, is the management of the diversity that resulted from largely postwar waves of immigration to Australia by the white core established at the center of Australian society through colonization.[32]

What occurs in Australia is a situation wherein the Indigenous and the multicultural negotiate only with this white core and rarely with each other. Peta Stephenson argues that the "continuing cleavage of 'the immigrant' and 'the Indigenous' in contemporary paradigms of reconciliation provides little space for discussion on the potential role and contribution of migrant Australians to the reconciliation process."[33] Stephenson challenges the artificiality of this cleavage by highlighting the various historical and cultural encounters between Indigenous and Asian Australians over time. She does not argue that all of these encounters result in positive resolutions but merely uses them to develop a "clearer understanding of the related histories of struggle of oppressed and exploited minorities against the homogenising tendencies of nationalist imaginaries."[34] The possibility of dialogue between the Indigenous subject and the multicultural subject offers a potential challenge to the power of Hage's white core; it does not exclude the core from the dialogue but rather challenges the intermediary role it has played historically.

Pham's novel rather bravely imagines this dialogue through the fox fairies' encounters with the ningaui. Interestingly, however, the Australian white core is given no ghostly or spiritual presence in Pham's novel, unlike Chloe's representation of French colonialism in Vietnam. In Australia, the spiritual encounters occur between multicultural subjects (the Vietnamese and the Chinese fox fairies) and between these subjects and the Indigenous subject (the ningaui). The concept of colonization is not entirely absent but simply not given a direct spiritual presence in Australia, which raises interesting questions as to how the novel depicts the colonization of Australia. The white core is thus effectively excluded from *Vixen*, which leads the novel away from the traditional binary structure of postcolonial and multicultural dialogues.

This is not to say that these dialogues occur easily and without miscommunication. What matters, though, is that they occur. When Chen first encounters the ningaui in her search for a safe place to look for gold, she is necessarily wary of the Aboriginal spirit because her only terms of reference are the behaviors of spirits in China: "I frowned. It was the spirit's territory and spirits usually get angry when they are disturbed. No one survives who steals the treasure of a fox fairy."[35] To Chen's surprise, the ninguai is courteous and permits Chen and her human husband to pan for gold in her river, "Since you ask."[36] The fact that Chen asks for permission is vital, as it shows respect for the ningaui, and in showing respect for her, Chen is also paying respect to the land. It is important to note that the Indigenous Australian relationship to land is not one based on ownership of the land but on belonging to it. The ningaui does not feel it is necessary to be territorial because the land will defend itself against the white man. When the white gold miners do disrupt the ninguai and damage the riverbed where she resides, darkness falls and they are massacred by shadowy presences.

The ningaui's river had been the site of a massacre of blacks by whites and is overwritten by the massacre of the miners by the Aboriginal ghosts. It is both what Maria Tumarkin terms a "traumascape," a place "marked by traumatic legacies of violence, suffering and loss,"[37] and what Ross Gibson terms a "badland," a site where the often violent legacy of colonialism can be simultaneously acknowledged and ignored.[38] Such massacre sites as the ningaui's river are unfortunately plentiful throughout Australia, and a violent massacre of Chinese miners did occur on the Australian goldfields. Pham conflates the site of such violent events for, as Tumarkin argues, traumascapes are places where "the past is never quite over"[39] and Pham's spirits are living witnesses to the ongoing histories of places and peoples. In a similar vein, Tony Birch argues that "the land itself is the repository of historical memory,"[40] particularly in Indigenous culture. A particular relationship is thus created between the ningaui and the land, based upon the significance of the land in Indigenous Australian cultures and the dispossession of Indigenous peoples from their lands. If the ningaui is, like the fox fairy, a spiritual embodiment of history and tradition, and the land itself is likewise a repository of historical memory, then the distinction between the land and the ningaui becomes blurred.

To reiterate, the Indigenous relationship to land is not one based upon ownership *of* the land but of belonging *to* it. As Richard Broome asserts, "Aboriginal people traditionally had a peculiarly intense and symbiotic relationship with particular country of which they were spiritually a part, to which they were bound by totems and by their responsibility as custodians. Land, people and the great ancestors were fused together."[41] The ningaui embodies that spiritual connection to land and is at once the land, its people, and its memory. Upon meeting the ningaui, the fox fairy finally receives her answer to the question of why the Australians did not fight against British colonization: "This is her land and she does not even need to threaten me. The ningaui is more friendly than Chen or myself."[42] This is not to suggest that Indigenous Australians passively acquiesced to British occupation but that the Indigenous relationship to land is not easily severed. It is the ningaui who says to reassure the fox fairy, "Spirits come and go. But we're still here. The land is still here."

Australian colonization as an act of dispossession, to play on words, is not about exorcizing the spirit from the land but rather about disrupting, often violently and irrevocably, the people's connection to it. The ningaui is, however, confident of the spiritual connection that she holds to the land; she and the Indigenous people will still exist as long as the land does, and the memory of colonization permeates the landscape. As Gelder and Jacob argue, "the postcolonial ghost story speaks not so much about possession as (dis)possession, coming as it does *after* the fact of settlement."[43] They utilize Freud's concept of the "uncanny" to read the unease with the landscape that results from Australia's problematic past, the discomfort of having dispossessed an Other. When the Vietnamese fox fairy finally encounters the ningaui herself after the voluntary death of Chen, the Indigenous spirit is initially suspicious, fearing that the Vietnamese fox fairy is a possessed fox,[44] until the fox fairy insists that she is not there to desecrate but to respect. The ningaui understands this: In postcolonial Australia, the uneasiness with the colonial act of dispossession—whether termed the uncanny or white colonial paranoia—is in itself a form of respect that keeps the ningaui and her memories of colonization alive. In the act of dispossession, the colonizers enable and ensure Indigenous haunting.

This recalls an earlier quote from Gelder and Jacobs: "The past is always ghostly here [in Australia]."[45] The process of reconciliation in particular, they argue, "bring[s] the nation into contact with the ghosts of its past, restructuring a nation's sense of itself by returning the grim truth of colonization to the story of Australia's being-in-the-world. But it is not surprising that, rather than laying things to rest, these ghosts . . . in fact set a whole range of things into motion."[46] The Australian ghost story, they assert, "confronts these issues directly."[47] Indeed, the encounters between the spirits in *Vixen* involve a direct confrontation of issues emerging from postcolonialism and multiculturalism that are rarely imagined in other forums. As discussed above, Indigenous and migrant dialogues are rarely imagined and encouraged still less despite the potential contribution that could be made to the processes of reconciliation.

There is, however, debate about what relationships migrants should have to this past.[48] John Howard, the Australian prime minister between 1996 and 2007, once controversially stated, "Australians of this generation should not be required to accept guilt and blame for past actions and policies over which they had no control."[49] This generation of Australians is culturally diverse; more than half of Australia's population has either immigrated or has at least one parent born overseas. Their relationship to Australia's colonial past and its policies is, some might argue, even more complex, as they are personally more distant from these past policies and practices than those Australians descended from the generations who were present and responsible. As Tumarkin poignantly reflects, "New urban immigrants, like my family, arriving in Australia in the 1990s, could spend decades, sometimes lifetimes, not once coming face to face with the reality of the continent-wide death which has served as a foundation of this country in its present form. *We are new here. It's OK.*"[50] Tumarkin highlights the ethical conflict faced by migrants in their search for belonging: that by belonging to a culture and society that has been built on such actions, if we seek to imagine ourselves as part of that culture and society, then we must also imagine ourselves within its historical narrative and accept responsibility for both the good and the bad.

Birch, in his essay "Returning to Country," draws a vital connection between Indigenous Australians and refugees, as a large number of Vietnamese Australians were, as dispossessed peoples. There is a need, he concludes, "to welcome . . . refugees to Aboriginal Australia"[51] based upon a shared understanding of the loss of homeland. When the Vietnamese fox fairy finally encounters the ningaui after the voluntary death of Chen, it is, as I argued above, a moment of recognition, similar to the welcome and recognition that Birch offers refugees. Initially suspicious, as Chen also once was, the ningaui thinks that the Vietnamese fox fairy is a possessed fox, until the fox fairy insists that she is not there to desecrate but to respect. The ningaui understands this: "You have to be respected to exist, mate. And they don't respect us until they're out bush and there ain't no one else."[52] As the conversation continues, the ningaui expresses curiosity about the fox fairy's homeland and whether she misses it, to which the fox fairy responds, "Yes. But it would be different now. There was a war there."[53] This particular exchange between the Vietnamese and the Indigenous Australian spirits is more complex and interesting than even the encounters between Chen and the ningaui, because both Australia and Vietnam are sites with colonial pasts and legacies of internal and external displacement.

The question then arises of why the fox fairy returns to Vietnam and the consequences this has for Vietnamese, or migrants, remaining in Australia. The fox fairy's return to Vietnam does not disrupt Vietnamese Australians' belonging to Australia; in a sense, they have inscribed their own belonging to Australia through their complicity with the very type of multiculturalism that Hage critiques. In returning to Vietnam, I argue, the fox fairy effectively reclaims—or repossesses—her land and creates a transnational connection and sense of belonging between Australia and Vietnam. Gelder and Jacobs argue that "Australian ghost stories generally do not respect the 'localness' of their sites; they are by no means constrained in this sense."[54] While Pham's spirits generally emphasize the importance of place, history, and memory, particularly within the postcolonial context, the fox fairy uncovers a form of "rooted cosmopolitanism,"[55] wherein the intersection of multiculturalism and postcolonialism has created a "morally and emotionally significant commnit[y]"[56] among the ningaui and the fox fairy, and effectively among Indigenous and multicultural Australians. The possibilities of the exchange between the fox fairy and the ningaui therefore go beyond national boundaries, gesturing toward the possibility of transnational understandings based upon historical sympathy.

As Hsu-Ming Teo observes of the spiritual encounters in *Vixen*, "Australian stories, Australian histories, thus become entangled with those of other nations."[57] A novel like *Vixen*, Teo argues, "throw[s] open the window to new, previously disregarded historical vistas, suggesting that Australian history is rooted in more than just a British past."[58] It also throws open the window to new intercultural and transnational dialogues and the cultural, social, and political possibilities that such conversations open up. Pham's use of spirits to enact these conversations in her novel does not lessen the significance of their interactions. As historical fantasy, *Vixen* is allegorical: It is a critical reflection upon the intersecting historical pasts of Australia and Vietnam, a critique of colonization and assimilation, and more optimistically, a hopeful projection of the possibilities held for new cultural dialogues.

Conversations about reconciliation and immigration can be particularly difficult to have in Australia. Although Australian Prime Minister Kevin Rudd took an important step forward with his apology in February 2008 to those generations affected by the policy of forcible removal of Indigenous children, known as the Stolen Generations, this immense symbolic act was but another step in the ongoing process of reconciliation. Significantly, this gesture was immensely popular among Australians; it perhaps signified that Australians' relationship to the past was and remains strong, haunted as they are by the colonial past, which remains present in the very mechanics of their society and its national ideologies. Although Australia and other lands may be haunted by their pasts, it does not necessarily follow that these spirits are unfriendly to the people who have come to live there; all they ask for is to be remembered and respected.

NOTES

1. Hoa Pham, *Vixen* (Sydney: Hodder Headline, 2000), 187–88.
2. Ibid., vii.
3. Sneja Gunew, *Haunted Nations: The Colonial Dimensions of Multiculturalism* (London: Routledge, 2004), 44.
4. Kwame Anthony Appiah, "Cosmopolitan Patriots," in *Cosmopolitics: Thinking and Feeling beyond the Nation*, ed. Pheng Cheah and Bruce Robbins (Minneapolis: University of Minnesota Press, 1998), 91.
5. Kathleen Brogan, *Cultural Haunting: Ghosts and Ethnicity in Recent American Literature* (Charlottesville: University Press of Virginia, 1998), 4.
6. Ibid.
7. In *Haunted Earth*, Peter Read suggests that Pham's fox fairy is capable of traveling back and forth in time. There is, however, no evidence to suggest this in the narrative. The fox fairy's relationship with time is linear; she simply witnesses and remembers the past, and she can reflect upon it more easily in the present than a human. See Read, *Haunted Earth* (Sydney: UNSW Press, 2003), 112.
8. Ken Gelder and Jane Jacobs, *Uncanny Australia: Sacredness and Identity in a Postcolonial Nation* (Carlton: Melbourne University Press, 1998), 30.
9. Pham, *Vixen*, 93.
10. Ken Gelder, *Reading the Vampire* (London: Routledge, 1994), 12.
11. Graham Huggan, "Vampires, Again," *Southerly* 66, no. 3 (2006): 193.
12. Pham, *Vixen*, 30–31.
13. Ibid., 34.
14. Ibid., 35.
15. Huggan, "Vampires, Again," 193.
16. E. T. C. Werner, *Myths and Legends of China* (Singapore: Graham Brash, 1991), 370.
17. Pham, *Vixen*, 240.
18. Ibid., 242.
19. Ibid., 244.
20. Ibid., 1.
21. Ien Ang, *On Not Speaking Chinese: Living between Asia and the West* (London: Routledge, 2001), 35.
22. Pham, *Vixen*, 190.
23. Brogan, *Cultural Haunting*, 130.
24. Amritjit Singh, Joseph T. Skerrett Jr., and Robert E. Hogan, "Introduction," in *Memory, Narrative, and Identity: New Essays in Ethnic American Literatures* , ed. Amritjit Singh, Joseph T. Skerrett Jr., and Robert E. Hogan (Boston: Northeastern University Press, 1994), 18.
25. Pham, *Vixen*, 142.
26. Ang, *On Not Speaking Chinese*, 119.
27. For a discussion of this with particular reference to the Australian context, see Ang, *On Not Speaking Chinese*, 112–25.

28. Gunew, *Haunted Nations*, 15.

29. Ibid.

30. See, for example, Bob Hodge and John O'Carroll's discussion of Aboriginal poet Oodgeroo Noonuccal's objections to multiculturalism in *Borderwork in Multicultural Australia* (Crows Nest, NSW: Allen & Unwin, 2006), 110–13.

31. Ghassan Hage, *Against Paranoid Nationalism: Searching for Hope in a Shrinking Society* (Annandale, NSW: Pluto Press, 2003).

32. Ghassan Hage, *White Nation: Fantasies of White Supremacy in a Multicultural Society* (Sydney: Pluto Press, 1998).

33. Peta Stephenson, "New Cultural Scripts: Exploring Dialogue between Indigenous and 'Asian' Australians," *Journal of Australian Studies* 77 (2003): 66.

34. Ibid., 67.

35. Pham, *Vixen*, 148.

36. Ibid., 149.

37. Maria Tumarkin, *Traumascapes: The Power and Fate of Places Transformed by Tragedy* (Carlton: Melbourne University Publishing, 2005), 12.

38. Ross Gibson, *Seven Versions of an Australian Badland* (St Lucia: University of Queensland Press, 2002), 13–15.

39. Tumarkin, *Traumascapes*, 12.

40. Tony Birch, "Surveillance, Identity, and Historical Memory in Ivan Sen's *Beneath Clouds*," in *Empires, Ruins + Networks: The Transcultural Agenda in Art*, ed. Scott McQuire and Nikos Papastergiadis (Melbourne: Melbourne University Press, 2005), 198.

41. Richard Broome, *Aboriginal Victorians: A History since 1800* (Crows Nest, NSW: Allen & Unwin, 2005), 379.

42. Pham, *Vixen*, 188.

43. Gelder and Jacobs, *Uncanny Australia*, 32.

44. Importantly, the fox is an introduced species in Australia that affected native wildlife populations.

45. Gelder and Jacobs, *Uncanny Australia*, 30.

46. Ibid.

47. Ibid.

48. See, for example, Gelder and Jacobs, *Uncanny Australia*, 24, and Ghassan Hage, "Polluting Memories: Migration and Colonial Responsibility in Australia," in *"Race" Panic and the Memory of Migration*, ed. Meaghan Morris and Brett de Bary (Hong Kong: Hong Kong University Press, 2001), 333–62.

49. John Howard, Opening Address to the Australian Reconciliation Convention, Melbourne, May 26, 1997, at http://www.austlii.edu.au/other/IndigLRes/car/1997/4/pmspoken html (accessed August 4, 2012).

50. Tumarkin, *Traumascapes*, 166.

51. Tony Birch, "Returning to Country," in *A Museum for the People: A History of Museum Victoria and Its Predecessors 1854–2000*, ed. Carolyn Rasmaussen (Melbourne: Scribe, 2001), 400.

52. Pham, *Vixen*, 186.

53. Ibid., 188.

54. Gelder and Jacobs, *Uncanny Australia*, 31.

55. Appiah, "Cosmopolitan Patriots," 91.

56. Pnina Werbner, "Vernacular Cosmopolitanism," *Theory, Culture, and Society* 23, nos. 2–3 (March–May 2006): 497.

57. Hsu-Ming Teo, "Future Fusions and a Taste for the Past: Literature, History, and the Imagination of Australianness," *Australian Historical Studies* 33, no. 118 (2002): 137.

58. Ibid.

Chapter Seven

Haunting Mothers

Alternative Modes of Communication in
Geographies of Home *and* Soledad

Betsy A. Sandlin

Two contemporary Dominican-American novels, *Geographies of Home* (1999) by Loida Maritza Pérez and *Soledad* (2001) by Angie Cruz, feature young Dominican women in the process of discovering who they are and who they want to be. Yet it is the mothers who occupy a central role in both narratives. I argue that the mothers metaphorically "haunt" their daughters in an attempt to communicate with them about and despite social systems that threaten their emerging identities. Although both of the mothers are physically alive, I use the term "haunting" because these women blur the boundaries between presence and absence in order to influence their daughters psychically. "Haunting" thus serves as a metaphor for the way in which the mothers communicate with their daughters, in the sense that Avery Gordon forwards in *Ghostly Matters: Haunting and the Sociological Imagination*: "Being haunted draws us affectively, sometimes against our will and always a bit magically, into the structure of feeling of a reality we come to experience, not as cold knowledge, but as a transformative recognition."[1] It is this "transformative recognition" that takes place between mother and daughter that I explore in these novels by Pérez and Cruz. The young protagonists in both works have left home in search of their own paths, and yet they are drawn back by their mothers. As "spectral" figures who have learned to conjure and wield power from a marginalized position, I posit that the mothers in *Soledad* and *Geographies* employ alternative communication strategies—including silence, "madness," telepathy, voodoo, and the exorcism of their own ghosts—in order to challenge their daughters and to warn them about patriarchal oppression.

In Pérez's novel, home is a hostile environment represented by a physical decay that symbolizes the state of life inside, which is marked by Seventh-Day Adventist conservatism and an ultra-strict father, one sister's mental illness, another's repeated physical abuse at the hands of her husband, economic struggles, and other sources of unease. Iliana, the young protagonist, attempts to "escape" this environment by enrolling in a prestigious college in upstate New York, five hours away from her family in Brooklyn. Similarly, the title character of Cruz's *Soledad* is also a young woman who has recently left home—Washington Heights—for a more independent life in the arts scene of Manhattan. For Soledad, "home" is marred by a strained relationship with her mother, who is still haunted by the ghost of her dead husband. In addition, Soledad feels that she doesn't belong in her extended Dominican family, because of what she sees as their old-fashioned values.

In both *Soledad* and *Geographies of Home*, the young women are drawn back home by their mothers. Iliana is forced to leave school and return home to help deal with various family situations, including her mentally ill sister. She contemplates what this change means for her: "Only by leaving home had she, on occasion, acquired the confidence to express her opinions, and she feared that by returning she would fall silent once again."[2] For Iliana, the loss of voice is equivalent to the loss of her new identity and her independence. Likewise, in *Soledad*, family members implore the protagonist to return home in order to help her mother, who appears to be suffering from a mental and emotional breakdown. The opening sentence of *Soledad* reveals how, like Iliana in *Geographies*, Soledad is also reluctant to return: "It's always like that: just when I think I don't give a shit about what my family thinks, they find a way to drag me back home."[3] Like Iliana, Soledad initially sees home as an obstacle, an idea that is symbolized once again by the inability to speak/communicate. When trying to talk to her mother once Soledad has returned to her side, the daughter is described as "stutter[ing]" as if "hold[ing] something back."[4] In both novels, then, identity is intimately linked to the concept of having a "voice," being able to speak for oneself.

When communication breaks down, the mother in each book must find alternative modes of reaching her daughter. The ability to motivate their daughters' return demonstrates a type of power that is yielded by the mothers in both novels. Yet it is not what they are able to do, but rather how they do it, that illustrates the strategies they have developed from a position of seeming powerlessness. While both are physically alive, the mothers in *Soledad* and *Geographies* are metaphorically spectral in that they "haunt" their daughters from afar, if we understand the act of haunting as Avery Gordon describes it: "That which appears to be not there is often a seething presence, acting on and often meddling with taken-for-granted realities."[5] The mothers are certainly "meddling" in their daughters' lives, as we see from the first few pages of both works, whereas on the surface, it seems that Soledad's mother (Olivia) and Iliana's mother (Aurelia) have been silenced and made "absent" by the patriarchal forces in their lives, particularly their domineering husbands. As Kathleen Brogan reminds us, "As an absence made present, the ghost can give expression to the ways in which women are rendered invisible in the public sphere."[6] Again, while not literal ghosts, both mothers become a "seething presence" in their daughters' lives, albeit in a positive sense, an ability that highlights the (in this case, metaphorical) ghost's "double-sided figuration as powerlessness and power."[7]

Despite, or perhaps because, they exist in society's margins, the spectral mothers are able to safely yet subversively act, while going relatively unnoticed except by those whom they choose to haunt (in this case, their daughters). Thus, as the women in *Geographies* and *Soledad* illustrate, while spectrality may appear to be a frightening or confusing state, it can be a powerful one as well. In the words of Erica Johnson, "Ghosts mediate cultural, historical, and psychological spaces that they alone can traverse."[8] Brogan has also discussed this persistent and potentially positive trait of ghosts: "They figure prominently wherever people must reconceive a fragmented, partially obliterated history, looking to a newly imagined past to redefine themselves for the future."[9] In the case of *Geographies* and *Soledad*, it is not just ethnic history that is being reconceived, but matrilineal history as well, focusing specifically on the transmission of personal and familial stories and knowledge from mothers to daughters. That is, in these novels by Pérez and Cruz, the mothers are not only engaged in their own redefinition, as we will see, but also in the reconfiguration of their daughters' identities and futures. As specters, they are able to tap into various unorthodox modes of communicating with their daughters: Olivia employs silence, her body, and madness to get her daughter's attention, while Aurelia communicates telepathically and through a magical kind of singing, while also effecting change with voodoo.

At first glance, Olivia appears to be what Mickey Pearlman calls a "missing mother," physically present but emotionally absent.[10] When *Soledad* begins, Olivia has retreated from society and her family and withdrawn to her room and into her own world. In a telling turn of phrase, her brother refers to Olivia as "the family's living ghost."[11] Her silence is, in part, a reaction to a lifetime of trauma and abuse. In the Dominican Republic, Olivia became a prostitute at the age of fifteen in order to escape poverty and a forced marriage to a family friend, whom she did not know. She became pregnant and married a client named Manolo; although Soledad calls him her father, it is implied that he most likely is not. Manolo physically and verbally abused Olivia, controlling her in every way, including her voice and her body: "He was very strict with her. He didn't let her speak in public. He said she didn't know about certain things like ordering food. . . . He told Olivia how to wear her hair, the color to paint her nails, the way to swing her hips."[12] Manolo's death occurred during a violent argument in which Olivia pushed him out of an open window in an uncharacteristic moment of defiance and self-defense.[13] As the novel begins, however, Olivia has retreated into silence and appears to be suffering from a mental breakdown.

While Elena Stone discusses silence as a typical reaction to trauma and abuse, as well as a sign and symptom of repression, she also acknowledges the difference between "being silenced" by outside forces and choosing silence as a form of defiance. While racism, classism, sexism, and social stigma can keep women from talking about their experiences and speaking for themselves, Stone argues that for some women, silence can be a form of resistance, what she calls "returning to 'the root called quietness,' reclaiming silence as a source of healing and replenishment."[14] Audre Lorde has also written about silence as a potential site and source for creativity, power, and transformation.[15] In Debra Castillo's groundbreaking study *Talking Back: Toward a Latin American Feminist Literary Criticism*, she also posits that while historically, women have found themselves relegated to a silent position, silence may be employed strategically and transgressively: "The revolutionary response to silencing is resemanticization: to use silence as a weapon."[16] In this way, the mother in *Soledad* actively chooses silence, a subversive mode as characterized by Castillo: "A woman who is neither passive nor accepting may yet preserve the advantages of distance and silence for her own reasons, using distance to her advantage, using the mask of silence to slip away."[17] In Cruz's novel, the mother "slips away," but she does so in order to pull her daughter back home, and thus, silence becomes not only a strategy of self-protection, but also a way of reaching out to her daughter, an ironically effective mode of communication.

Although Olivia is physically silent in the fictional world of the story and the other characters are never privy to her thoughts, her internal "voice" is accessible to the reader as it is presented in the text with italics. Through her own perspective, Olivia's withdrawal, which her sister Gorda calls "dream walking," is portrayed as a more active state than what other family members refer to as simply "resting." During her "dream walks," Olivia is frequently naked: "Olivia is standing by the window naked. . . . She is standing on the corner of the fire escape, leaning back on the brick wall, with her arms spread open as if she's about to fly. . . . Olivia is smiling, glowing in the moonlight like a firefly."[18] Her apparent sense of joy is cut short, however, when her brother (Victor) brings her back to "reality": "He throws a sheet around Olivia and pulls her fragile body inside. With the sound of his voice Olivia folds over into a fetal position covering her head."[19] Here, the absent female voice is replaced by the fully present, joyful, and unrestrained female body, represented by her preflight pose, nakedness, and the light provided by the traditionally female archetype of the moon. Yet when the male voice—a symbol of patriarchy—disrupts her powerful moment, she reverts to a position of self-protection.

"Madness" here is reconfigured as freedom (flight), and Olivia in her silent state is not a victim but rather someone who has seized control of her own agency, albeit temporarily. In Olivia's words, *"When I close my eyes I become invisible and can do anything with my time. . . . I can do anything I want."*[20] Silence and dreams, or "dream walking," become alternative modes of survival and, most importantly, ways of communicating and reconnecting with her daughter. Dream walking itself is a sort of spectral activity—floating in and out of consciousness as well as in and out of physical spaces, a state of being both (physically) present and (emotionally) absent.

Olivia's withdrawal is a way to get her daughter's attention, not in a selfish sense (as Soledad suspects in one moment of anger),[21] but because she wants to warn Soledad of potential dangers to her as she attempts to become more independent. This is what Olivia wishes her mother had done for her: *"In my dreams, me and my mother have long conversations. I ask her if she desired my father, or did he just take her when he pleased? Did she ever say no to him? And if she did, did he hit her, like Manolo hit me?"*[22] Since her mother never taught her these life lessons, and could not serve as a model for combating patriarchal oppression, Olivia becomes more and more adamant about communicating with her own daughter as the novel progresses: *"My body fights to get out of bed. I need to see Soledad. I have to tell her I love her. Tell her about her father. . . . She doesn't have much time before Manolo gets to her too. . . . I squeeze the mattress. The fitted sheets pop off. They bunch up around me. I've made a mess. A mess is good. Soledad will come faster that way."*[23] Olivia's first step in closing the gap between herself and her daughter, then, is to force Soledad to come home. In a sense, Olivia has followed her own advice, which she gave to her niece, Flaca: "Talking don't do anybody any good. It's all about doing."[24]

For the mothers in both novels, Aurelia and Olivia, connecting to and acknowledging past experiences plays a vital role not only in their own sense of self but also in what they perceive as important lessons to pass on to their daughters. In *Soledad*, it is the revelation of Olivia's past—something that she has worked to keep a secret—that ultimately brings mother and daughter closer together. While Olivia is called the family's "living ghost" by her brother, there are literal ghosts in the novel as well. Soledad, at first, does not believe in spirits and instead calls her mom crazy for claiming to be bothered by Manolo's ghost. Her attitude changes, though, when her aunt Gorda reveals that Manolo has been haunting her, too: "All those times I thought she was crazy when I would listen to her yelling, breaking things, falling on the floor when she was supposed to be all alone in her room sleeping, she was fighting. Fighting my father. All those years she told me that she used to see him, I dismissed her because I couldn't see him myself."[25] Soledad has always resided more firmly in the realm of "logic" and "reason," discrediting her mother's experiences that challenged so-called reality.

In a symbolic role reversal, though, Soledad soon discovers that she can play a crucial part in her mother's rebirth: "When I look at my mother, I realize that the more I discover about her and the more time I spend with her, the freer she becomes."[26] The act of learning about her mother culminates in her discovery of a very long list of names that holds the key to unlocking Olivia's past:

- Mayo 17 el griego, super borracho
- Mayo 18 el suizo bello pero pequeño
- Mayo 19 el suizo otra vez
- *Mayo 20 alemán gordo con olor de cigarillo*[27]

The list continues until she arrives at "*Junio 14 Manolo*. June 14 Manolo. My father, Manolo."[28] As Soledad reads the list aloud, the men magically materialize in front of her, lounging around her mother's apartment, signaling that "finally, my mother's secret is out."[29] Just as Olivia stands freely naked in her "dream walks," the men from the list are also naked as her once-silenced past is disclosed.

The solution to Olivia's ghost problem in *Soledad* is to return to the mother('s)land, the Dominican Republic, to destroy the list of lovers. As Olivia contemplates, "*I want to erase all those years I lived with Manolo. I want my ears to catch the wind and carry my dreams into the clouds and let them rain over me so I can cleanse my spirit and start again.*"[30] Such a ritualistic cleansing is exactly what takes place at the conclusion of the novel. With Dominican relatives serving as guides, Soledad and Olivia climb onto a raft in a wet cave, where they throw old photographs, one by one, into the water: "The photographs of those that need to be cleansed from all the trappings in life will dip and then float. When we see them float we know they will be OK."[31] Soledad wants to keep her mother's list because she thinks that it may provide some clues about who her real father is. But as she pulls it out of her pocket, her mother grabs it, burning it and tossing it into the water, symbolically regaining control of her identity by purging this painful memory.[32] As the list disappears, so too do the ghosts in Olivia's New York apartment.

As Kathleen Brogan points out, "Frightening ghosts . . . can sometimes be put to rest, not in the sense of being forever banished, but in the sense of being transformed into memories that usefully guide, rather than overwhelm, the present."[33] In this way, once her own past is cleansed, Olivia can now take a more active part in her daughter's future. As Avery Gordon notes regarding the exorcism of a negative ghost, "What it represents is usually a loss, sometimes of life, sometimes of a path not taken. From a certain vantage point the ghost also simultaneously represents a future possibility, a hope."[34] Therefore, the recognition of Olivia's "path not taken" and the loss and recuperation of her own identity and life can now help her regain her own voice, and with it, the ability to communicate with her daughter. As she places Soledad's picture into the water, however, it begins to sink. Against the warnings of her family, Soledad jumps into the water to try to retrieve her photo. As Soledad struggles to stay afloat, we see the scene from Olivia's perspective: *"I want to help Soledad find a way out. . . . She doesn't know I am here for her. I tell her she's an angel, born in my dreams. And when I see Soledad surrender, I scream."*[35] This sense of Soledad's physical danger, symbolic of potential dangers to be faced in the world beyond the cave/homeland as an independent woman in the United States, is the catalyst for Olivia's decision to break her strategic silence so that Soledad will *not* surrender. The novel ends with Soledad safely lying with her head in her mother's lap and Olivia finally speaking, a moment described by Soledad in this way: ". . . as if all this time she has been listening, reading my mind, waiting to tell me the things I want to hear. She tells me about the day I was born, how when she first looked down at me, so tiny and vulnerable, she named me Soledad. My name means loneliness in Spanish, the language my mother speaks and dreams in."[36] The novel, which began with Soledad's resentful, angry voice, ends with the once-silent mother, Olivia, now reclaiming her voice so that she may explain the past to Soledad and, thus, make her daughter stronger, a better survivor. Once spectral herself, Olivia is able to exorcise her ghosts so that she may rejoin the living and help her daughter. In this way, spectrality is a temporary, self-imposed and self-determined state from which Olivia is able to exert a positive impact on her daughter's life.

While Soledad's mother, Olivia, is voiceless and employs her body, supposed madness, and silence to reach her daughter, Iliana's mother in *Geographies of Home* is just the opposite. Rather than a voiceless body, she is described as a "disembodied voice" that is able to speak telepathically and across great distances to her daughter. When the novel opens, Iliana is packing to return home "because a voice had been waking her with news of what was taking place at home."[37] The voice is that of her mother, Aurelia, "authoritative but hinting mischief as when she had taught her to dance merengue on a Sabbath morning while the rest of the family attended church."[38] Aurelia's telepathic communication with her daughter is akin to an unwelcome haunting. Like Olivia in *Soledad*, Aurelia in *Geographies* presents a subversive challenge to patriarchal dominance; in this case, that of her religiously zealous husband, who has raised the family under strict surveillance and Seventh-Day Adventist conservatism: "Everything Iliana had been brought up to believe denounced the voice as evil. Yet her instincts persuaded her it wasn't so."[39]

The power of Aurelia's voice to reach and influence her daughter, despite the strict teachings of the father, is further revealed as Iliana later spies on her mother singing in the kitchen: "Listening to those sounds, Iliana believed in magic. . . . She even felt it flickering within her, awakening a knowledge of things she'd never seen and lives she'd never lived. Her spirit soared toward her mother's. Gratefully, she embraced her with the strength of all the affection she had grown too embarrassed to express."[40] As she absorbs her mother's magical/spectral voice, Iliana begins to recall that she too once had access to such special power or knowledge: "Aurelia had taught [her and her brother Tico] to speak a wordless language. Re-creating and inventing sounds, they had tapped into their emotions and conveyed them purely, unhindered by words that limited or defined."[41] Iliana's recollection is reminiscent of Julia Kristeva's notion of the semiotic, the pre-Oedipal realm of communication between mother and child through instinct and sound before separation and entrance into the realm of the symbolic, the Law of the Father.[42] Iliana admits, in fact, that she has separated from her mother and attempted to gain access to the symbolic, suppressing the special language that her mother had taught her as a child: "Iliana's tongue had since lost that magic. It rested heavy, burdened by a need to speak like others, trapped by an education which had early on impressed upon her the need for clarity. As if life itself were clear. As if anything in this world were delineated and easily discernible."[43]

Unlike the mother in *Soledad* who employs silence as a strategy, it is Aurelia's ability to act and, most significantly, communicate through what Toni Morrison has called "discredited knowledge"[44] that serves as her method for challenging patriarchy. In addition to her powerful voice, she questions and blurs the boundaries between reality and magic and taps into her supernatural powers to secretly change the fate of another daughter, Rebecca, who has suffered years of physical and emotional abuse by her husband, Pasión. As she prepares a feast for the family, on the surface remaining firmly ensconced in an acceptable gender role in the kitchen, defined by patriarchy as a "feminine" space, Aurelia is able to conjure her secret powers in order to kill her son-in-law. As she plucks the chicken's feathers in her kitchen, Pasión's own chickens, which he has been raising inside his apartment across town, begin to attack him: "They lashed out at Pasión, pecking his face, his hands, his wrists, and any other bits of skin exposed as he crawled from the room to collapse on the third-floor landing. Even then, Aurelia felt no remorse. Even then, she persuaded herself that nothing short of his death would make up for his crimes."[45] Like her telepathic communication, Aurelia's violent act of revenge against her son-in-law is another nonverbal way of protecting her daughters through alternative means. Significantly, we learn that Aurelia's powers were passed down to her by her mother, Bienvenida. However, Aurelia too had rejected her mother's teaching initially: "So many lessons she had refused to learn because they had been taught to her by her mother."[46]

Years later, in the hospital with yet another daughter, Marina, who has just attempted suicide, Aurelia makes a vow: "She would no longer depend on anyone else to do for her or her children what she should have taken it upon herself to do."[47] For her, the decision to empower herself and utilize her special abilities, rather than ignoring them or hiding them because of her husband's religious beliefs, is also tied to her sense of place. That is, as Aurelia accepts her abilities, she also becomes comfortable with the notion that "here," New York, can be reconfigured as "home":

> Aurelia for the first time granted herself permission to sprout roots past concrete into soil. Throughout more than fifteen years of moving from apartment to apartment, she had dreamed, not of returning, but of going home. Of going home to a place not located on any map but nonetheless preventing her from settling in any other. Only now did she understand that her soul had yearned not for a geographical site but for a frame of mind able to accommodate any place as home.[48]

The ability to put down roots and yet to see "home" as a frame of mind, rather than as a geographical location, is what Aurelia achieves through taking control of her destiny and, by extension, that of her children, regardless of her husband's powerful presence in the family.

Despite her mother's decision to accept "here" as "home," as the novel ends, Iliana has decided to leave her family's home once again, in a symbolic gesture of distancing herself from the law of the (literal and metaphorical) father, after being raped twice by her mentally ill sister, Marina, and having several disagreements with her domineering father: "Everything she had experienced; everything she continued to feel for those whose lives would be inextricably bound with hers; everything she had inherited from her parents and had gleaned from her siblings would aid her in her passage through the world. She would leave no memories behind. All of them were her self. All of them were home."[49] Iliana has rejected the father's teaching, internalized the once-taboo lessons learned from her mother, and gained strength from her new understandings of "self" and "home" as subjective states of mind over which she now has control. As María Luisa Ochoa Fernández argues, for Iliana, speaking out and expressing her opinions, educating herself, and "rejecting the house as a patriarchal domain and finding a space of [her] own" are all active modes of rebellion against patriarchy demonstrated in the novel.[50]

In *Soledad* by Angie Cruz and *Geographies of Home* by Loida Maritza Pérez, spectrality is a metaphorical state from which the mothers are able to communicate with their daughters from a marginalized position. "Dream walking," madness, telepathy, silence, and voodoo, for instance, are portrayed as modes of specifically female resistance that pose alternatives to both dominant U.S. and Latino (male) ways of knowing and communicating. Although the relationships are strained at first, the daughters eventually learn to value their mothers' experiences and special forms of knowledge, even though they may be deemed "irrational" or "crazy" or simply dismissed, by dominant society. This slow process may be understood as an example of the "transformative recognition" discussed by Avery Gordon in relation to the experience of being haunted. By the end of the novels, the daughters are themselves transformed as they "recognize" their mothers' wisdom, acknowledging and accepting it as useful. Yet in another interpretation of the term, the young women also "re-cognize" their mothers in that they reconsider and rethink the validity of their mothers' experiences and/or advice. The conclusions of both works suggest that, through this recognition, the daughters will be able to better confront social obstacles, such as the patriarchal oppression once suffered by their mothers. As Soledad and Iliana search for their own voice in the process of constructing their identity, their mothers haunt them, in a positive manner, forcing them to return home. Indeed, these novels could suggest that the cycle will continue and that these young daughters will carry on their mothers' legacy, serving as helpful specters to their own daughters, should they have any. Or, perhaps the hope is that such communication from a spectral position will no longer be necessary once Soledad and Iliana are able to find and assert their own voice.

NOTES

1. Avery Gordon, *Ghostly Matters: Haunting and the Sociological Imagination* (Minneapolis: University of Minnesota Press, 1997), 8.
2. Loida Maritza Pérez, *Geographies of Home* (New York: Penguin, 1999), 10.
3. Angie Cruz, *Soledad* (New York: Scribner, 2001), 1.
4. Ibid., 69.
5. Gordon, *Ghostly Matters*, 8.
6. Kathleen Brogan, *Cultural Haunting: Ghosts and Ethnicity in Recent American Literature* (Charlottesville: University Press of Virginia, 1998), 25.
7. Ibid.
8. Erica Johnson, "Giving Up the Ghost: National and Literary Haunting in *Orlando*," *Modern Fiction Studies* 50, no.1 (2004): 111.
9. Brogan, *Cultural Haunting*, 29.
10. Mickey Pearlman, "Introduction," in *Mother Puzzles: Daughters and Mothers in Contemporary American Literature*, ed. Mickey Pearlman (New York: Greenwood Press, 1989), 1.
11. Cruz, *Soledad*, 177.
12. Ibid., 50.
13. Ibid., 136.
14. Elena Stone, *Rising from Deep Places: Women's Lives and the Ecology of Voice and Silence*, vol. 2 of *Feminism and the Social Sciences* (New York: Peter Lang, 2000), 20.
15. See Audre Lorde, *Sister Outsider* (Freedom, CA: Crossing Press, 1984), referenced in Stone, *Deep Places*, 36–37.
16. Debra Castillo, *Talking Back: Toward a Latin American Feminist Literary Criticism* (Ithaca, NY: Cornell University Press, 1992), 38–39.

17. Ibid., 40.
18. Cruz, *Soledad*, 45.
19. Ibid., 45.
20. Ibid., 165.
21. Ibid., 82.
22. Ibid., 120.
23. Ibid., 154.
24. Ibid., 113.
25. Ibid., 155.
26. Ibid., 169.
27. Ibid., 193–94.
28. Ibid., 195.
29. Ibid., 195.
30. Ibid.
31. Ibid., 223.
32. Ibid., 224.
33. Brogan, *Cultural Haunting*, 19.
34. Gordon, *Ghostly Matters*, 63–64.
35. Cruz, *Soledad*, 226.
36. Ibid., 227.
37. Pérez, *Geographies*, 1–2.
38. Ibid., 2.
39. Ibid., 4.
40. Ibid., 88.
41. Ibid.
42. See Julia Kristeva, *Revolution in Poetic Language*, trans. Margaret Waller (New York: Columbia University Press, 1984).
43. Pérez, *Geographies*, 89.
44. Emilia Ippolito notes as a characteristic of Caribbean women's writing "the multiplicity of voices and perspectives within a text." She argues that "stylistically, this facilitates the representations of a world of fluid boundaries between self/other; living/dead; mad/sane; dream/reality. This fluidity is implicit in the use of the trope of spirit possession as a metaphor for the recovery of African cultural values in the black 'diaspora,' and suggests that a re-valorization of such 'discredited knowledge'—in the sense of the term used by Toni Morrison—is a major project in much female-centered fictional writing." Emilia Ippolito, *Caribbean Women Writers: Identity and Gender* (Rochester, NY: Camden House, 2000), 8. While spirit possession per se does not appear in *Soledad* or *Geographies of Home*, other forms of "discredited knowledge" are present, as I have illustrated.
45. Pérez, *Geographies*, 256.
46. Ibid., 135.
47. Ibid., 137.
48. Ibid.
49. Ibid., 321.
50. María Luisa Ochoa Fernández, "Family as the Patriarchal Confinement of Women in Sandra Cisneros' *The House on Mango Street* and Loida M. Pérez's *Geographies of Home*," in *Evolving Origins, Transplanting Cultures: Literary Legacies of the New Americans*, ed. Laura P. Alonso Gallo and Antonia Domínguez Miguela (Huelva, Spain: Universidad de Huelva, 2002), 126.

III

Spectral Projections

Chapter Eight

Aesthetics of Haunting as Diasporic Sensibility

Julie Dash's Daughters of the Dust

Yu-yen Liu

In 2004, Julie Dash's groundbreaking film, *Daughters of the Dust*, was added to the National Film Registry in the Library of Congress, an honor that recognizes the film's cultural, historical, and aesthetic significance. Released in 1991, *Daughters of the Dust* narrates the reunion of an extended black family on Ibo Landing the day before most of the family members will depart for the American mainland. "Our Ellis Island"[1] is what Dash calls the Sea Islands off the coast of Georgia and South Carolina, where Ibo Landing is located.[2] Africans living on the island mainly grow rice and work indigo, using the unique skill of blue dye manufacturing brought from West Africa. After the abolition of slavery, many Africans set up home on this hinterland. Because of the relative isolation of the island life, a distinct culture of African diaspora developed and is preserved there—the Gullah.[3] As film-maker, director, and writer, Dash draws on diverse sources of the Gullah culture and weaves a magical sense of the place into the very texture of the film. The success of *Daughters of the Dust* puts the black woman independent filmmaker on the cinematic map,[4] marking a paradigm shift in black film for its distinctive subject matter. As the first feature-length film by a black woman director to go into national theatrical release in the United States, *Daughters of the Dust* received largely positive reviews, most of which acclaimed its remarkable achievement. The film has therefore been considered one of the most important films on the culture of the African Diaspora. In 1999, it was given an award as one of the best African American films of the twentieth century.

Daughters of the Dust is concerned primarily with the dilemma of migration. Most of the central characters in the film are torn between the ancestral land of the small island and the lure of the New World, the American mainland. The migration plot that underwrites the story demonstrates the intricate anxieties involved in moving across these boundaries. Adroitly, the film dwells on the ambivalence of migration to articulate the complicated existence of the African diaspora. The Unborn Child, the name of the spectral figure in this film, comes not from the past but from the future. She has, as she tells us, been sent back in time by the old souls. She appears as a five-year-old girl in this poetic and spiritual film, serving as one of the film's two narrators (the other is her great-grandmother, Nana Peazant). Unlike the "ghost" figures in other literary works, who stick around one place either unwilling or unable to leave, the Unborn Child is a liminal figure, a being in transition, living between worlds, and traveling in time to "intervene" in the past events. She is both the heir to Nana Peazant and the force that will eventually be able to carry the past into the future and to transmit cultural memories through generations.

Through this transgenerational figure, the traces of cultural continuity become even more inspiring and empowering. In a sense, *Daughters of the Dust* resonates intertextually with Toni Morrison's *Beloved* (1987). While Morrison's use of the spectral figure, Beloved, is a fruitful and necessary mode for envisioning the past and restructuring a future, Dash's Unborn Child seems to promise more cultural resuscitation in its emphasis on the concept of "connection" embodied in the hybrid spirit girl. Dash incorporates spectral presences into her film in order to bear witness to histories of the African American diasporic dislocation.

Daughters of the Dust deepens and diversifies the representation of ethnicity and black diaspora through its specifying the "spectral figure" that eludes easy categorization—a central point of my argument. By negotiating the powerful presence of the Unborn Child in *Daughters of the Dust*, the film presents a divergent and fresh meditation on "spectral identities" in relation to the issues of cultural identity and the negotiation of history through aesthetics.

THE SPECTRAL FIGURE AND FEMALE GENEALOGY

On August 18, 1902, on the beautiful pure white beach next to the bush, the Peazants in their Sunday best are preparing for a feast before the migration the next day. Nana's daughter, Yellow Mary (Barbara-O), in her lacy veil and Victorian long dress, comes back home with her friend Trula. Though deemed a "ruint" woman, Yellow Mary appears self-confident, elegant, and beautiful, contrary to what the other family members believe her to be. Yellow Mary's cousin Viola (Cherly Lynn Bruce), a reformed Christian, who has established her life in the North, also returns to the island for what could be the last family reunion. Viola brings Mr. Snead, a photographer, who will document the memorable event. Unlike Yellow Mary, Viola is a respectable woman and already "Westernized." To flaunt her status as a well-educated woman, when commenting on the family's migration, she recites Shakespeare: "What's past is prologue. . . . I see this day as their first steps towards progress, an engraved invitation, you might say, to the culture, education and wealth of the mainland."[5] "What's past is prologue," a fleeting remark from Viola, infiltrates insinuatingly all of the threads of the plot, leading to the crux of the story—what is past is the prologue of the new life in the North. These two women return to renew their lives, making fresh steps toward their futures. Being returnees, these two women show, however, different outcomes of migrating outside the island. While Viola, a missionary, returns to document her family's exodus, Yellow Mary, once a prostitute, returns to reshape her life—to terminate her miserable experiences in the North and in Cuba. There is, understandably, some tension between them.

In fact, Nana and Yellow Mary's dour sister-in-law Haagar (Kaycee Moore) are in conflict, the latter eager to discard the past, considering the "Geechee" ways to be backward.[6] Nana's great-grandson Eli (Adisa Anderson) and his wife Eula (Alva Rogers) are also in a strained situation; Eula is pregnant, possibly the result of being raped by a white plantation owner, but she will not reveal who raped her, for fear that her husband might be lynched because of her. As such, the seemingly fragmented narratives are intertwined through these tensions. Taking central roles, women characters in the movie are then thematically more important.

As Manthia Diawara puts it, the main plot incidents of the film "are narrativized from black women's points of view."[7] Varied women are foregrounded in *Daughters of the Dust*, and it is Eula's unborn child, the spectral figure, that envisions a female genealogy in the film. To begin with, Haagar and Eula, Nana's daughters-in-law, suggest two different kinds of black women. Haagar seems to be a good mother; she has the best interests of her daughters in mind. To provide a better future for her children, she is eager to jettison everything related to what she sees as the old, backward ways of life on the island that Nana seeks to preserve. In one scene, she declares eloquently and definitively, "I might not have been born into this family, but I'm here now. And I say let Nana Peazant stay behind, that's what she wants. We're moving into a new day. She's too much a part of the past."[8] A tough and radical woman, Haagar is obviously fond of making cynical remarks and is always ready to stand up against the "moral decay" embodied in Yellow Mary. Unlike Haagar, Eula adheres to the Gullah heritage, even though she marries Nana's grandson, Eli, and does not have any blood link to this ethnic culture. In due time, it is Eula who urges the female kin to be what they actually could be:

> There going be all kind of road to take in life. . . . Let's not be afraid to take them. We deserve them, because we all good women. Do you . . . do you understand . . . who we are, and what we have become? We're daughters of those old dusty things Nana carries around in her tin can. . . . (pausing) We carry too many scars from the past. Our past owns us. We wear our scars like armor . . . for protection. Our mother's scars, our sister's scars, our daughter's scars. . . . Thick, ugly scars that no one can pass through to ever hurt us again. Let's live our lives without living in the fold of old wounds. [9]

Indeed, black women in diaspora are multiply victimized and bearing numerous ugly traumatic scars. These wounds, suggestive of a sorrowful past, turn out to be obstinate shields that guard the women from being vulnerable again. Eula's announcement best elucidates how the black women in the film are empowered. Apparently a far cry from Haagar, Eula is positive and eager to protect the ethnic legacy.

Like Haagar, Yellow Mary is tough, but in a very different sense. She is "charismatic."[10] Before strolling along the beautiful long beach with Trula and Eula, Yellow Mary tells one of her stories. On the mainland, she saw a luxurious music box. At that time, she had a troubled life, and she wanted to lock up all of her sorrow in that song:

> Once, I saw a pink satin case for jewelry, for rich women, in a store window. And it had a thing on the side and you turned it and music came out. I couldn't afford that case for myself, and I didn't ask anybody to buy it for me. But in my mind, I put all those bad memories in that case and I locked them there. So I could take them out, look at them when I'd feel like it, and figure it out, you know. But I didn't want them inside of me. I don't let nothing in that case or nobody outside that case tell me who I am or how I should feel about me. [11]

From this memory, we know how she asserts herself on the mainland. She learns to be self-aware through sensation, perception, maturity, and self-determination. Another bitter story that she shares is about her stillborn baby. Without compassion for her misery, the white family she worked for forced her to wet-nurse their children. She ends her doleful story with an uncompromising remark: "I wanted to come home, but they wouldn't let me. I tied up my breasts. They let me go."[12] In these two episodes, Yellow Mary illustrates her rebellious tendencies, yet in a subtle way. The first story shows how she asserts herself in the face of hardship and fetish temptation in the urban North; in the second, she refuses to be a nurturing black mother as categorized in American popular culture. Eventually, Yellow Mary's stories establish her as a distinctive black woman who defies the image of stereotypical black woman and defines resistance as being self-determined.

Nana, the matriarch, is undoubtedly another central figure. As the Peazant family celebrates this last day together, Nana, who will not leave the ancestral land, tells stories of the arrival of slaves on the shores and how they survived the old bitter days. Nana's narrative of the ethnic past serves as a bridge, connecting the stories of African capture and enslavement to their subsequent years of staying on the small island. In a climactic moment of the film, Nana struggles to assemble various items from her tin box—a lock of hair that her mother cut from her head and gave to her before being sold off to another owner; a lock of her own hair; and other bits and pieces of her life—into an "amulet," a hybrid of different religious icons. Twining the scraps together with a Bible, Nana says:

> When I was a child, my mother cut this from her hair before she was sold away from us. Now I'm adding my own hair. There must be a bond . . . a connection, between those that go up North, and those who across [*sic*] the sea. A connection! We are as two people in one body. The last of the old, and the first of the new. We will always live this double life, you know, because we're from the sea. We came here in chains, and we must survive. We must survive. There's salt-water in our blood. [13]

For Nana, the mingling of locks of hair symbolizes the enduring bond among the family members. In this episode, we find that symbols and religious practices coming from varied sources contribute to the cultures of African diaspora. *Daughters of the Dust* articulates the complicated existence of the African diaspora, informing the ambivalence with moods, music, tones of voice, and the spectacular view of the expanding sea. Particularly, the images of women's hair that conceptualize cultural remembrance and connection are emphasized. A female genealogy is thus suggested. To redirect typical Hollywood images of African American women, Dash views her women as conduits of cultural memories, figures of rebellion, and the reminders of the strength that needs to be honored. The "return" of the spirit girl from the future is therefore of utmost significance to the central theme of the film.

Though the film has two narrators, it is the narration of the unnamed spirit girl that has special bearing on the plot. It is her voice-over that initiates the film: "My story begins on the eve of my family's migration North. My story begins before I was born. My great Nana Peazant, saw the family coming apart. Her flowers to bloom in a distant frontier. . . . And then there was my ma and daddy's problem."[14] She foreshadows the film's primary conflicts: the breakup of the family through migration and the trouble between her parents over her paternity. As a spectral figure invisible to the other characters, Unborn Child flits across the screen every now and then. While sitting among other little girls on the beach, she at times looks through a stereoscopic viewer and sees black-and-white moving pictures of New York City in the early twentieth century, "in which trolley cars and pedestrians bustle through crowded streets"; [15] at other times, she views the pictures of commodites in a catalog of the future world. To the photographer's surprise, she once mysteriously shows up in his compositions and disappears suddenly. The use of a preborn spirit-figure as a major character highlights the point that Dash seeks in her historical narrative to reassemble fragments of African American history in a unique way that links the past to the future generation. [16]

THE SPECTRAL FIGURE AND TEMPORALITY

Set in 1902, *Daughters of the Dust* engages a critical juncture in U.S. history. At the turn of the twentieth century, the Peazants are in the midst of great changes. They are in the tumult of postslavery migration to the urban North, to the West (e.g., the Oklahoma project), or back to Africa, in the wake of the activism of Ida B. Wells, a decade before the Niagara/NAACP merger, and roughly one generation away from the Garvey and the New Negro movement. In 1902, there were also race riots in New Orleans. Set during this grand period of change for African Americans, *Daughters of the Dust* significantly encodes a defining moment in black history in which the aforementioned events were beginning to transform the lives of the black diaspora for good.

Even though it is grounded in a specific time, the film reframes and complicates its "temporality." By adding the Unborn Child to the family saga, Dash implicates the linkage of ethnic culture from the past to the future. Through the film's seemingly disconnected yet sequential images and the spectral girl's illustration of a concurrency of the present, the past, and the future, a peculiar sense of time is being established. To begin with, in order to open up a real dialogue between past, present, and future, Dash has Eula narrate the legend of Ibo Landing to the Unborn Child inside her body at the turning point of the film. As such, the child from the future learns her ethnic past, which is then connected through her to the future. Standing before the "African warrior," the wooden prow from an old slave ship floating on the inlet for years, Eula narrates:

> The minute those Ibo were brought ashore, they just stopped, and took a look around . . . not saying a word, just studying the place real good. And they saw things that day that you and I don't have the power to see. Well, they saw just about everything that was to happen around here . . . The slavery time, the war my grandmother always talks about . . . Those Ibo didn't miss a thing. They even saw you and I standing here talking." [17]

In a motherly gesture, Eula kindly tells her unborn baby their ancestors' story; her account of Ibo Landing mythologizes the slave revolt.

Before Eula's story, we see Unborn Child in the figure of a little girl run toward her; she enters "the billowing folds of Eula's voluminous skirt and fades back into her mother."[18] In the meantime, Eli, in a trance-like state, walks on the waters and pays libation to the wooden African figure floating on the inlet. It takes his epiphany—a conversation with the mysterious, shackled African warrior—to teach Eli the message from the informed landscape. At this moment, when he walks on the water in the presence of the Ibo icon, Eli comes to understand what his ancestors are trying to inspire in him. The category of "time" seems to merge into the category of "space" at the moment of epiphany. Prodded by the Unborn Child, Eli achieves an epiphanic understanding of the truths lying beyond the physical domain that he is the Unborn Child's biological father, and that his ethnic people will thrive in the future since their ethnic identity has been inscribed in eternal time. Ibo Landing not only forms a peculiar cinematographic space but also registers on the screen a mythic return, from which the filmic narration expands into alternate dimensions.[19] At the moment when the Peazants are about to leave the island, Unborn Child casts an eye on the family graveyard. She narrates, "(remembering) In this quiet place, years ago, my family knelt down and caught a glimpse of the eternal."[20] The "epiphany" and "a glimpse of the eternal" are both suggestive of the film's elaboration and cultivation of a special sense of "temporality." While Morrison's spectral figure is set to acknowledge the discontinuous presence of a past that can never be fully reclaimed, Dash's spectral figure facilitates historical narration through a fascinating vision of how the spirit girl intervenes into the "past" to herald a future. Unborn Child desires to traverse the temporal gap, and her presence suggests a recovery of histories threatened by erasure or fragmentation.

In a sense, Dash adopts the spirit girl to call into question certain aspects that our contemporary literary discourses fail to address: When the spectral figure comes from the future, what difference does it make? Here, a special sense of "temporality" is also ushered in by the spirit girl narrator, who often begins her voice-over with "I remember," "recollecting," or "remembering," which suggests that what is going to happen, or is happening, has already been in the collective memory. One example occurs when Unborn Child plays with a stereoscope viewer "with black and white moving pictures of the overcrowded cities of the North"; she narrates, "(recollecting) It was an age of beginning, a time of promises. The newspaper said it was a time for everyone, the rich and the poor, the powerful and the powerless."[21] As elsewhere in the film, Unborn Child uses the past tense to narrate events that are supposed to happen in the film's temporal future, but have already unfolded in her past. In this way, the preborn spirit acts as an agent and a central character—an unborn child intervenes in the events of the past. In the film, the spirit girl provides the viewer with a perspective to follow her in approaching the ethnic histories of the Gullah people. The arrangement of an unborn child and her great grandmother as joint narrators of the ethnic story entails, moreover, a shifting of viewpoint as well as a sense of the reoccurrence of time, interweaving the encounters of the past, the present, and the future. The dual narration cradles the filmic plots and events. The shifting of time as embodied in the duet of the two narrators becomes a remarkable feature of the film. As Toni Cade Bambara notes, "The duet also prepares us for the film's multiple perspectives."[22] Unborn Child heralds the advent of the future as if the very future has been past, while Nana connects the present to a past rooted both on the island and in Africa.

True to Dash's intent to tell a different story of displaced African Americans, *Daughters of the Dust* negotiates historical facts through myth, symbol, and re-molded temporality. The film is organized around what Bambara calls "multilayered unfolding" in the context of "dual narration, multiple-point-of-view camerawork," and "shared space (wide-angled and deep-focus shots in which no one becomes backdrop to anyone else's drama)."[23] Triggered by the spirit girl from the future generation, the film creates a reflexive mode in a rhythmic cycle. In a 1995 interview, Dash said that her goal "was to tell the story with an unfolding, like women's weaving," in the manner of a West African *griot*, or storyteller, "the way an old relative would retell it, not linear but *always coming back around*"[24] (italics added). While Bambara asserts that the story is "scripted on an arrival–departure grid,"[25] Caroline Brown remarks that *Daughters of the Dust* is a film "referring to a return to the past."[26] With such a rhythmic pattern, *Daughters of the Dust* elaborates on a "return," a different sense of "haunting." The film does not so much "return" to an origin as it celebrates a refrain. The pattern of oscillating *between* opposites has been hinted at in the beginning of the film. A grand sunrise at Ibo Landing opens the story, along with Nana Peazant's voice-over: "I am the first and the last. I am the whore and the holy one. I am the wife and the virgin. I am the barren one and many are my daughters. I am the silence that you cannot understand. I am the utterance of my name."[27] The lines of verse come from "Thunder: Perfect Mind," Nag Hammadi Gnostic gospels.[28] In them, "the first" and "the last," "the whore and the holy one," and so on, according to scholars, suggest that the divine should be understood as a dynamic, harmonious relation of opposites. Here, the peculiar sense of merging binaries speaks to the criteria of the philosophy promoted in the film. The film then unfolds its multilayered narration, braiding the evocative vision of the opposites: "I am the first and the last," "the last of the old and the first of the new," and so forth. African diasporic experience is then woven into a dynamic whole exuberant with rich cultural significance to inform the dislocated Africans with cultural identity.

The film is a story about African Americans whose ancestors were slaves, but its title is based on a meaningful passage from the Bible, with "sons" having been changed to "daughters": "'Upon your knees, sons of the dust!'

And the Lord said unto Abram, 'get thee out of thy country, out of thy birthplace, and from thy father's house, unto the land that I will show thee.' So Abram departed as the Lord had spoken to him."[29] In the Bible, God wants Abram to leave his father's house and to move to the place that will be his. Under a title alluding to the biblical story of Abram, the film seems to carry an allusive urge for the Gullah people, especially the women, to set out to claim their cultural territory.

Accordingly, *Daughters of the Dust* not only depicts the marginalization experienced by African Americans and the ensuing pursuit of cultural identity but also launches an active intervention in mainstream culture in the hope of creating a more nuanced articulation of ethnicity. The film's deliberate elaboration of the sense of "temporality" and its legitimization of the culture of the African diaspora actually resort to a process more complicated than a simple binary opposition or cultural hybridity. The film complicates the dialogics of "sameness" and "difference," "fixed" and "permeable" borders, "here" and "there," "the past" and "the future," "roots" and "routes" with a gesture of cultural resistance. While the very vocabulary of representational resistance often adopts some types of filmic conventions and images, *Daughters of the Dust* presents rural Gullah community, using the characters not as traditional victims in African American movies but as black people reclaiming their cultural richness.

AESTHETICS OF HAUNTING

Daughters of the Dust, exquisitely photographed by Arthur Jafa, is narrativized and focalized from a circumspectly aesthetic concern. The landscape consists of splendid scenery with the richest of colors—the light blue sky, the pure white beach, the azure ocean, along with the soft sounds of water. With its intense attention to the picturesque view that the small island has to offer, *Daughters of the Dust* presents a poetic series of pastoral images, rituals, music, and voice. The scene of family celebration, the bountiful feast, the wonderful patterns of the women's hair, the rich quilts, the lovely "bottle trees," and even the graves covered with the possessions of the deceased are an indispensable part of the whole grand picture. Significantly, the film uses many aesthetic visual elements to help build up its space and convey Dash's critical concept of diasporic art. With this film, Dash offers her distinct and unconventional visions and narrative techniques to the cinematic world.

She uses color, for example, in the film to signal the nuance of the diaspora culture. The film's use of indigo blue, both in miserable and memorable memories, is striking. Indigo appears to be one of the "scars" of slavery, as the West Africans were brought to the New World partly because they knew how to work indigo. The close-ups show that Gullah women's hands are still stained with the blue of indigo.[30] Indigo becomes the color of sorrow; yet, it also represents something to be embraced. Indigo, or royal navy, is the color of their legacy. It symbolizes the continuity of the West African culture in America. Throughout the film, Nana, the grandmother, wears a long dress in bleached indigo; Unborn Child, the great-granddaughter, who wears mainly white, has an "indigo-colored bow"[31] in her hair. The color is so visible in the film that it illustrates Dash's diasporic art and also begins to "haunt" viewers. The film thereby promotes the aesthetics of haunting as a mode of cultural remembering, as historical reinscription, and as a particularized diasporic art. *Daughters of the Dust* explores how the aesthetics of haunting relates to memory and ethnicity through an investigation of the retold stories of Ibo Landing, the recurrent images of the floating African warrior, and the color indigo. The film, which engages with the spectral aura that haunts, eventually calls to American mainstream culture to appreciate the diasporic art of displaced African American culture.

Regarding this diasporic art, bell hooks insightfully uses "mythopoetic" aesthetic to refer to *Daughters of the Dust*. According to hooks, this aesthetic means "bring[ing] certain factual information into a kind of mythopoetic context."[32] She continues, "It's interesting that whenever an artist takes a kind of mythic universe and infuses it with aspects of everyday reality, like the images of women cooking, often the cinema audience in this society just isn't prepared."[33] As bell hooks asserts, the location of a black feminist take is always "a radical standpoint, perspective position. The politics of location necessarily calls those of us who would participate in the formation of counter-hegemonic practice to identify the spaces where we begin the process of revision."[34] In the recovery of her people's past, Dash draws on an ingenious "politics of location" that enables her to restore and recover what cannot be retrieved through written archives. Drawing on Robert Farris Thompson's studies on African and Afro-American art, the film utilizes a traditional African American aesthetic that "decorates the decorations." "Decorates the decorations," a phrase paraphrased from Zora Neale Hurston, denotes the way that the film adds "layer upon intricate layer of meaning and beauty to objects of nature and artifacts of everyday use."[35] Thompson's focus on the artifacts of everyday use seems to correspond to hooks's point in evaluating the film by mythologizing the everyday reality of black culture. To evaluate the film's centering on the sense of "beauty," Jacquie Jones states:

> Finally, on the screen, African American life is freed from the urban, from the cotton picking, from the tragic integrationist ladder-climbing. Here, in the unlikely arena of American film, the complexity and shaded histories of Black women's lives take center stage. . . . *Daughters of the Dust* offers a historical moment in African American culture, plain and imperfect, blended with such subtle charm, such careful technique that the presentation of food and a stroll

along the beach become overwhelming in their beauty. And Dash has conceded that the film does have a certain preoccupation with beauty.[36]

The film dexterously cultivates varied visual elements as a means to achieve a sense of beauty. These illustrations of diasporic art embody the film's central motif and message: the inscription of the ethnic past with a critical aesthetic sensibility. The island's "Edenic" space is textured into a multiplicity of visual narratives, intertwining the mythic aura and imagery with the very fabric of daily existence. Yet, Dash's diasporic art is not easily intelligible to the audience. Therefore, as Nana explains the meanings of the "bottle tree," she is also explaining to the audience the way to view their culture in the right perspective: "You're a natural fool, Haagar Peazant. Nobody ever said that the old souls were living inside those glass jars. The bottle tree reminds us of who was here and who's gone on. You study on the colors and shapes. You appreciate the bottle tree each day, as you appreciate your loved ones."[37] With those delicate details, the film's endeavor to offer aesthetically complex and compelling images of African Americans is remarkable. The African diasporic cultural specificities and aesthetic sensitivities that create the film's unique cinematic style owe much of their power to the diasporic art that Dash makes so much effort to demonstrate.

In this film, Dash seeks to eschew traditional narrative in favor of a poetic and multilayered presentation, which gives rise to a film that cultivates female genealogy, conveys a particular sense of temporality, and finally elaborates a unique aesthetics of haunting. Dash engages in revisiting her people's histories to recover the old lives, to honor the cultures, to connect the past to the present, and to highlight the people who crossed the waters and thrived on the island, and thereafter on the American mainland.

In her review of the film, Anna Everett asserts, "It has often been stated that history is less concerned with an accurate accounting of the past events than it is with providing a framework from which to apprehend the future."[38] In *Daughters of the Dust*, we see how Dash adds a spectral figure to enrich the film, which not only negotiates cultural memories but also envisions the future, a changing world, for the continuity of cultural histories. As Jeffrey Andrew Weinstock suggests, in literary works, the ghost often comes back to shed light on the layers of hidden histories:

> The ghost is that which interrupts the presentness of the present, and its haunting indicates that, beneath the surface of received history, there lurks another narrative, an untold story that calls into question the veracity of the authorized version of events. As such, the contemporary fascination with ghosts is reflective of an awareness of the narrativity of history.[39]

While in Gothic fiction the dead return either to tell stories or to block the progress of narration, in Dash's film the Unborn Child returns to the past to mobilize the narrative. The spirit girl in the film opens up other possibilities for scrutiny across time and space. Indeed, this film provides a good index for a more inclusive, culturally diverse, and in-depth point of view of the cultures of the African diaspora, while offering us a more complex version of the spectral figure.

NOTES

1. *Daughters of the Dust*, directed by Julie Dash (1991; New York: Kino on Video, 2000, DVD). Dash says of the islands, "The Sea Islands represents Ellis Island for us; that is where the slave ships came in. That is our Ellis Island. It is sacred ground for us." In reality, geographically, Ellis Island, located at the mouth of the Hudson River in New York Harbor, was the main entry facility for immigrants entering the United States from January 1, 1892, until November 12, 1954. Today, over 100 million Americans can trace their ancestry to the immigrants who first arrived in America through the island before dispersing to other destinations all over the country.

2. Ibo is the name of a tribe in Nigeria. The legend spread widely in African American lore.

3. The African slaves who were shipped to the United States during the eighteenth and nineteenth centuries brought with them their language, culture, and traditions. Collectively, these traditions and languages have merged into one form—Gullah. The word "Gullah" itself in some books is thought to be a derivative of Angola and the Gola tribe. Today, Gullah represents a unique branch of black history. Because they have preserved so much of their African cultural history, arguably, the Gullah is thought to be the most authentic African American community in the United States. See Marquetta Goodwine's *The Legacy of Ibo Landing, Gullah Roots of African American Culture* (Atlanta, GA: Clarity Press, 1998) and Morris Jenkins's "Gullah Island Dispute Resolution: An Example of Afrocentric Restorative Justice," *Journal of Black Studies* 37, no. 2 (2006): 299–319.

4. *Daughters of the Dust* is the first full-length feature by an African American writer/ director. Before making the film, Dash had already established herself as a filmmaker of considerable note with shorts such as *Illusions*, about a black woman who passes for white in Hollywood during the 1940s. *Daughters of the Dust* fulfills Dash's project to construct a history of the African American experience. In this film, Dash honors the black family with the beauty and grace that has been obscured by a colonial past.

5. Julie Dash, Daughters of the Dust: *The Making of an African American Woman's Film* (New York: New Press, 1992), 5. The phrase comes from Shakespeare's *Tempest*, act II, scene i, lines 257–58. The quotation comes from Julie Dash's "Screenplay" in her 1992 book. "The Script: *Daughters of the Dust*" ("Screenplay" [73–164] is a typewritten "screenplay" with Dash's handwritten notes in the margins, like an "authentic" archive). Because the characters in the film mostly speak the "Gullah" language, which can be ambiguous even to native speakers, the "Screenplay" becomes very useful in helping viewers interpret the film.

6. Generally, "Geechee" is also referred to as "Gullah" in some parts of the U.S. South. Anthropologists, however, tend to classify those people living on the South Carolina coast as "Gullah" and those living on the Georgia islands and their mainland relatives as "Geechee."

7. Manthia Diawara, ed., *Black American Cinema* (New York: Routledge, 1993), 417.

8. Dash, *The Making of an African American Woman's Film*, 55.

9. Ibid., 83.

10. Ibid., 48.

11. Ibid., 69.

12. Ibid., 52. Indeed, in Yellow Mary, the intertextual echoes are rich. The first anecdote seems to allude to sorrow-song and blues tradition, which Alice Walker also utilizes in her black woman singer, Shug Avery, in *The Color Purple*. There is an allusion to Toni Morrison's *Beloved* in Yellow Mary's second anecdote.

13. Ibid., 77.

14. Ibid., 6.

15. Jacqueline N. Stewart, "Negroes Laughing at Themselves? Black Spectatorship and the Performance of Urban Modernity," *Critical Inquiry* 29 (2003): 650.

16. As discussed in the beginning of this chapter, the spirit girl strongly resonates intertextually with Toni Morrison; see Morrison, *Beloved* (New York: Knopf, 1987). In addition, intertextual allusions to other African American writers' works are abundant in the film, which, though not the main concern of this chapter, suggest the strong bond between writing and black womanhood.

17. Dash, *The Making of an African American Woman's Film*, 67.

18. Ibid., 65.

19. According to Dash, the elaboration of the Ibo Landing scene is based on historical records from logs of slave ships (Dash, 1995 DVD interview) and from black oral history. Yet, she chooses to enrich it with symbolic significance. In her film, Dash uses the image of a carved wooden African warrior floating in the river off the Ibo Landing inlet to symbolize the fact that Africans revolted against slavery by suicidal drownings.

20. Dash, *The Making of an African American Woman's Film*, 59.

21. Ibid., 32.

22. Toni Cade Bambara, "Reading the Signs, Empowering the Eye: *Daughters of the Dust* and the Black Independent Cinema Movement," in *Black American Cinema*, ed. Manthia Diawara (New York: Routledge, 1993), 124.

23. Dash, *The Making of an African American Woman's Film*, xiii.

24. Quoted in Joel R. Brouwer, "Repositioning: Center and Margin in Julie Dash's *Daughters of the Dust*," *African American Review* 29, no. 1 (1995).

25. Bambara, "Reading the Signs," 123.

26. Caroline Brown, "The Representation of the Indigenous Other in *Daughters of the Dust* and *The Piano*," *NWSA Journal* 15, no. 1 (2003): 2. In the opinion of Brown, *Daughters of the Dust* contains at its core "the complementary tension of nostalgia and radical transformation." Here, I use only part of her statement, "a return to the past," for I do not think that the film aims at nostalgia and radical transformation of that past. Rather, I think that the film seeks to retrieve the past in a symbolic and creative way. Dash's attempt is by no means nostalgic, because "the past" is still within "the present."

27. Dash, *The Making of an African American Woman's Film*, 2.

28. Dash jots down "Thunder: Perfect Mind," from the Nag Hammadi Gnostic gospels in the margin of *The Making of an African American Woman's Film*, 2. The Gnostic gospels were dug out from Nag Hammadi, Egypt, in 1945. In the 1960s, scholars began to get access to the precious archives in the United States and sought to interpret them. Various research results can be found on websites as well as in books, journals, and monographs.

29. Gen. 12:1.

30. In "Dialogue between bell hooks and Julie Dash" (in Dash's Daughters of the Dust: *The Making of an African American Woman's Film*), Dash explains that she uses indigo as "a symbol of slavery" to replace "the traditional showing of the whip marks or the chains. Because we've seen all those things before. . . . I wanted to show [slavery] in a different way." Actually, indigo "would not have remained on the hands of the old folks who had worked the indigo processing plant" (Dash, *The Making of an African American Woman's Film*, 31).

31. Dash, *The Making of an African American Woman's Film*, 25.

32. Dash, "Dialogue," 29.

33. Dash, *The Making of an African American Woman's Film*, 30. This point refers to "oppositional gaze," a term hooks uses to describe the way African American women engage cinematic images critically. In this sense, *Daughters of the Dust* indeed presents alternating viewpoints, which *both* celebrate a stance of "resistant spectator" (i.e., the act to negate the representational politics of individual film texts) *and* embrace black spectatorship by featuring a tale steeped in mysticism and ethnic history, creating a shift between "vulnerable" and "aggressive" spectatorship positions.

34. Quoted in Carole Boyce Davies, *Black Women, Writing and Identity: Migrations of the Subject* (New York: Routledge, 1994), 154–55. Dash accepts this rubric because it accommodates her film's speculative fiction or "what if" scenario, as she calls it. Dash reminds hooks

that "myth, of course, plays a very important part in all our lives, in everyone's culture. Without myth and tradition," she asks, "what is there?" (Dash, *The Making of an African American Woman's Film*, 29).

35. Quoted in Robert Farris Thompson, *Flash of the Spirit: African and Afro-American Art and Philosophy* (New York: Random House, 1983), 132.

36. Jacquie Jones, "The Black South in Contemporary Film," *African American Review* 27, no. 1 (1993): 19.

37. Dash, *The Making of an African American Woman's Film*, 74.

38. Anna Everett, "Toward a Womanist/Diasporic Film Aesthetic," in *Film Analysis: A Norton Reader*, ed. Jeffrey Geiger (New York: Norton, 2005), 865.

39. Jeffrey Andrew Weinstock, "Introduction: The Spectral Turn," in *Spectral America: Phantoms and the National Imagination*, ed. Jeffrey Andrew Weinstock (Madison: University of Wisconsin Press, 2006), 5.

Chapter Nine

Women as Cultural Wound

Korean Horror Cinema and the Imperative of Han

Andrew Hock Soon Ng

In Korean philosophy, the term *han* (or *haan*) alludes to the symbiotic relationship between the individual and the nation, "the logic of emotions" and "the logic of the dominant social order."[1] A concept that eludes translation, *han* came to the forefront of Korean ideology during the 1960s when the *Minjoong* ("people" or "mass") movement to reclaim "Koreanness" from centuries of dissipation by its various colonizers was at its height, although its rootedness within the Korean thought-system reaches further back in history. *Han,* on the one hand, distinguishes the prolonged suffering of a people who have been repeatedly colonized, which has led to socioeconomic and educational deprivation and backwardness when compared to Korea's neighboring countries. On the other hand, *han* can also be used to characterize interpersonal relationship and the dynamics of power and feelings, usually negative, embedded in it. *Han* often carries connotations of regret, anger, and "resentment of injustice related to social contradictions,"[2] which can manifest itself in paradoxical ways: The bitterness engendered by such a resentment can be expressed in "indifference, subservience, humor, or even love"[3] and "can be directed, either constructively or destructively, to others or oneself. In other words, *han* is both emotion and energy, which can result in favorable or unfavorable consequences."[4]

But one aspect of *han* that must be stressed is that it is ultimately irresolvable. The "consequences" achieved by the release of *han*'s energy may temporarily alleviate it, but this does not suggest its dissolution. One undertheorized but interesting development of this concept is that although *han* infiltrates the fabric of Korean society without discriminating by gender or class, women seem to somehow have a unique relation to *han*. As Young-Hee Lee argues, for example, appreciating Korean women's literature would require an understanding of the way *han* operates in their work. Recurrent themes such as the domination of men over women, the prohibition against remarriage, the strict Confucian injunction to uphold virtue (especially chastity), and concubinage are fundamental traces of *han* in women's writings.[5] This is possibly because under the Confucian dictates that regulate the Korean social order, the oppressions and disadvantages experienced by Korean women far exceed those experienced by men, and as such, they epitomize the *han* in their very subjectivity. Korean women, in this sense, not only suffer *han*, but their very "existence [is] *han* itself."[6]

This association between Korean women and *han* provides an important and useful starting point for meditation on the predominance of female specters in Korean horror cinema, which is the focus of this chapter. If women carry a great deal of *han* within them and thus provoke "much unhappiness among the living,"[7] how much more augmented would this circumstance be if a woman were to die horrifically and turn into a malevolent spirit seeking revenge? The situation is particularly acute if she is an unmarried woman, because there will be no one to worship her as an ancestor, thus leaving her spirit dissatisfied.[8] Within the strict gender coding prescribed by Confucianism, a woman gains status as an "ancestor" only if she engenders sons; hence, to die unmarried and childless is to die with deep regret and resentment toward the living, especially those who have directly perpetrated her death. Such intense emotions carry into the afterlife, accumulating over time even as the yearning to release them (*hanpuli,* or releasing *han*) takes on harmful dimensions.[9] Her return embodies negative emotions insinuated by *han*, which will manifest as destructive energies. Read within this framework, the nonclosure of some Korean horror films such as *Cello*,[10] in which the perpetuity of the haunting is suggested, seems to further substantiate *han*'s irresolvability.

But *han* has another side to it, one that is often elided by critical exegesis. In a keynote speech on Korean literature at a colloquium held at the University of Paris in 1994, one of Korea's most distinguished writers, Kyong-Ni Park, argued that *han* "is an expression of complex feeling which embraces both sadness and hope."[11] Her elaboration suggests that while existence acknowledges the death and decay of all that lives, there is the hope that beyond death is another universe that parallels, rather than opposes, this one. As such, *han* is a paradoxical concept that plots sadness and hope, death and life—not within a binary structure but as existential modes complementing and relying on each other. In view of this, I argue that the haunting portrayed by some Korean horror films does not necessarily insinuate the pursuit of redress by the dead, although narratives about ghosts seeking revenge are often read in this perspective, but an invitation to enter into a higher form of existence, one where the bitterness and regret of *han* give way to selflessness and reparation.

To illustrate this contradictory nature of *han,* two Korean horror films, *Cello* and *Wishing Stairs*,[12] will be discussed. Although Korean horror films tend to follow a rather strict formula (the ghost and victim are almost always female; the story tends to implicate the modern woman; there is always a fantastic possibility to the text—i.e., the haunting may ultimately be the woman's hysterical delusion after all), my choice of these two films is largely guided by similar subtexts that are significant for my analysis. First, both stories revolve around a female friendship that turns sour because of an education system that pits students against each other. The enmity gradually escalates into a fatal consequence, after which the one who dies returns to haunt her rival. Without commenting on the facticity of a Korean education system that promotes such extreme competition among students, the subtext of the "school" in both films nevertheless allows for an investigation of its potential metaphor as a Confucian system that simultaneously encourages academic excellence and punishes women for being modern and independent (because this, allegedly, violates the dictates of Confucian codes). Arguably, in both films, the "killer"/perpetrator and the "killed"/ghost are victims of a larger enemy against which there is no victory. Second (and related to the first), the manner in which friendship is represented in both films also requires careful deliberation. In *Wishing Stairs*, the strong friendship carries a powerful subtext of homoeroticism, which offers paradoxical readings (this feature is less obvious in *Cello*). On the one hand, this friendship borders on forbidden sexuality and must be overcome; the rivalry and eventual death of one girl can be interpreted as a narrative strategy to suppress this aberration. Furthermore, the homoerotic subtext is necessitated by the narrative in order to remove the threat of the modern, sexually polymorphous (that is, independent) woman and to reestablish the (heterosexual) Symbolic (Confucian) order. On the other hand, the dead girl's return to haunt her rival could imply not so much a desire for revenge, but rather for a restoration of what the Confucian order has disrupted; haunting her rival to death is not, in this sense, an act of destruction but of restitution: to restore a (homoerotic) friendship that henceforth can only be possible outside the existing order. The fact that the perpetrator is often deeply guilt-ridden and wishes to reverse her actions so as to have her friend back demonstrates a reciprocal desire on her part. Both girls thus harbor the sadness of *han,* whose hope for redress can only occur in the afterlife, where the self-as-constructed by the Symbolic order is dissolved, but leaving the desire unaffected. This subtext is notably missing in *Cello*, but the narrative's heterosexual premise that becomes exposed to a feminine attack may point to a criticism of a system that denies close friendship between women in order to ensure their conformity to Confucian paradigms.

CELLO

After recovering from a horrific car accident, Mi Ju, a professor at a music school, tries to reestablish some kind of normalcy in her professional and family life. A surprise birthday gathering organized by her family seems to suggest that all is gradually becoming well, but soon tragedy strikes. The family dog dies under mysterious circumstances and Mi Ju's sister-in-law apparently commits suicide because of a failed love affair (the viewer knows, however, that it is a ghost who kills her). One after another, Mi Ju's family members perish horrifically—her two daughters and her husband—and all of these deaths are somehow connected to a cassette tape containing a single cello track that she finds in her locker. After the death of her younger daughter, the narrative begins to revisit the memory of a past misdeed that Mi Ju has long repressed. Apparently, the cello piece was a favorite of Mi Ju's close friend, Tae Yon Kim, back when they were at music school. But, as Mi Ju tells her husband, despite their closeness, Yon Kim had always been jealous because Mi Ju was the better student. Mi Ju also believes that although there was bitterness in her friend's heart, Yon Kim never meant her any harm. One day, while driving home together, a heated quarrel between them led to a car accident, and Yon Kim was killed. Since then, Mi Ju has given up her dream of becoming a concert cellist, focusing her attention instead on teaching the instrument.

This confession sets Yon Kim's ghost as a vengeful spirit whose jealousy lingers beyond death. Sympathy is therefore channeled toward Mi Ju and her family who are victimized, but the narrative curiously never portrays the malevolent spirit's direct responsibility for the deaths of Mi Ju's family members. Mi Ju's younger daughter falls to her death because her deaf and dumb older sister misunderstands her plight to be a game, with a fatal result. How she ends up hanging by the edge of the roof is supposedly the spirit's conduct, but this is ambiguous as well. A heated quarrel ensues between Mi Ju and her husband after the latter discovers his daughter's demise. Already distraught, she suddenly "sees" her husband as Yon Kim, and in a moment of fright, pushes him against a wall, where he is pierced to death by a protruding nail. Mi Ju then proceeds to "murder" her maid (whom she again "sees" as Yon Kim), and she brutally murders her older daughter because the spirit tricks her into believing that the daughter is really the accursed cello, which Mi Ju violently bashes up.

Between these acts of graphic brutality, the "true" story of the original rivalry unfolds as a telling juxtaposition. It was Mi Ju who was jealous and resentful of Yon Kim. Yon Kim, by contrast, sincerely desired Mi Ju's support and friendship. A scene just before the accident shows the two women engaged in a moment of intimacy, but Mi Ju is clearly upset and caustically dismisses Yon Kim's pledge of friendship forever. A cut transports the two women to the scene of their fateful quarrel and the subsequent accident that leads to the damaged car hanging precariously on the edge of a cliff, with Yon Kim jettisoned and hanging desperately between Mi Ju and a certain plunge to death. Mi Ju reaches out to save her, but unhappy thoughts immediately assail her, and Mi Ju lets go of Yon Kim's hand—an eerie precursor to the way in which Mi Ju's older daughter will later cause her sister's death.

The revelation of Mi Ju's crimes toward the end of the film is shocking precisely because it disrupts our point of identification. In other words, the film's false suturing has managed to hold us to its deception, compelling us in the process to identify with a morally reprehensible individual. When the truth is revealed, and with all the other characters eliminated, the point of identification can no longer be displaced onto another character. As Mi Ju, no longer in control of herself, picks up a broken piece of glass to thrust into her own throat, the frame is constructed in reverse shots that simultaneously place us as observer and point of identification, thus reinforcing our witness to, and collusion with, Mi Ju's crimes by compelling us also to bear the narrative punishment. But as the glass is raised and lowered for the kill, a quick cut transfers Mi Ju back to the hospital, waking from a coma after her motor accident. Mi Ju is relieved to see her family and realizes that her "experiences" were nothing more than a prolonged nightmare. In the following scene, a fully recovered Mi Ju leaves work for home and arrives to find a surprise birthday gathering organized by her family. Before long, however, a horrible awareness dawns on Mi Ju that she is about to relive her nightmare all over again, and the film breaks off here.

As a spirit seeking revenge, the ghost in *Cello* embodies much destructive *han* energy precisely because she is an unmarried woman whose life has been stolen and "replaced" by her rival. The unspoken and secret injustice she suffers compounds the harnessing of *han*, and the *hanpuli* that follows will inevitably be terrible. The fact that the narrative remains inconclusive, however, suggests that the profundity of Mi Ju's crime will endlessly perpetuate the force of *han* in the lives (and afterlife) of all who are directly involved with her. For Mi Ju, there will be no end, and therefore no awakening, from the nightmare of her own engendering. The endless loop within which she is trapped compels her to revisit not only her crime but the subsequent murder of her family by her own hands. In this sense, as much as the specter of Yon Kim harbors the terrible energies of *han*, so does Mi Ju, whose resentment and anger were what initially motivated the series of violent events. If, in the end, Mi Ju's horrifying experience is nothing more than a perpetually repeating nightmare, the fact that the narrative is structured around this loop asserts the traumatic memory Mi Ju has suppressed, which is subsequently triggered by a car accident. The fact that she will awaken again and again to this nightmare corresponds to van der Kolk and van der Hart's observation that "traumatic memory is inflexible and invariable."[13]

In this sense then, it is not so much a vengeful ghost that haunts Mi Ju, but the resurfacing of a traumatic past that is suffused with resentment, fear, and guilt. If *Cello* is a trauma narrative, as I am suggesting, then Mi Ju's transfiguration of her trauma into a ghost is appropriate: both refuse symbolism because they remain outside the "rational" signifying order. The fact that only *she is aware of and can see* this "ghost" further reinforces the view that such a traumatic memory "has no social component; it is not addressed to anybody, the patient does not respond to anybody; it is a solitary activity."[14] In the guise of a ghost bent on doing her harm, Mi Ju's trauma takes on an entity-less configuration against which her struggle is futile, for how can she—the embodiment of her own guilt and terror—defeat herself? The possibility that it is not the return of a spirit after all, but trauma translated into haunting, profoundly deepens the narrative horror: The fear that structures Mi Ju's nightmare is, at the end of the day, fundamentally an *absence*—the most "effective element of . . . horror."[15] For trauma is that empty space, the "nothing," which the subject (patient) can never fill because it is unsymbolizable, and thus signals the subject's loss of itself.[16] Subjectivity here is replaced by its own void, or impossibility, which in turn refracts its own abjection. In other words, the self becomes a monster unto itself.

The nonclosure that suggests an interminable loop is, moreover, the narrative's denial of death to Mi Ju. Such is the terrible punishment that she must henceforth bear: to never find respite in obliteration. This is perhaps the film's most augmented moment of horror: Mi Ju's realization that her nightmare will never end. As Susan Stewart argues, "The horror story presents a repetition that is cumulative. Rather than canceling the significance of the original event by displacing it, the horror story increases that event's significance, multiplying its effect with each repetition. . . . [In] the horror story [death] may threaten an infinity of reversibility; it becomes the finale which is not final, whose limits are determined by its narrative possibilities."[17] Indeed, Stewart's point aptly describes *Cello*'s "paradox of reversibility and irreversibility."[18] In the scene that is to break the traumatic (anti)climax before the loop begins again, Mi Ju's death is revealed to be simultaneously certain and yet impossible. Her "death" does not displace the preceding episodes of horror but makes them more insistent. The fact that Mi Ju can never escape the narrative's "infinity of reversibility" is what also delivers— paradoxically—the final shock to the viewers. Unlike the standard denouement of many (Western) horror films, where the defeated monster/ghost makes a final, if subtle, reappearance to signal a potential sequel (the *Nightmare on Elm Street* series is exemplary of this tendency), in *Cello*, the horror's refusal to end is not insinuating a sequel because its continuous recurrence is already a "finale" that is definite. Its irreversibility is contained within the perpetual looping in this single narrative that cannot spill into a sequel because there is no possibility of continuity for Mi Ju. But even more frightening is that *there is no possibility of an end for her, either.*

As noted, the narrative strategically refuses to portray Yon Kim's ghost as the agent of the destruction of Mi Ju's family, but places Mi Ju instead at the center of this atrocity. In wanting to symbolize Yon Kim as evil and the source of her woe, Mi Ju instead faces the impossibility of her own desire, which becomes manifest as acts of murder. To put it differently, it is the inability, or refusal, to acknowledge the "nothing" that centers her trauma, which then compels her to project onto "reality" a ghost who would bear the burden of her trauma. The paradox is significant: Mi Ju, in translating trauma into a ghost, is simultaneously denying and acknowledging her own impossibility. Therefore, although she believes that it is Yon Kim who is harming her family, what we see is Mi Ju violently eliminating her husband and children. Such a paradox is not unfamiliar in trauma. As Dori Laub has observed, trauma is a dialectical relationship between "the imperative to tell and the impossibility of telling."[19] Through the ghost of Yon Kim, Mi Ju is articulating in extremis her trauma, even as she (unconsciously) is shielding herself from confronting the trauma itself. Within such a framework, it is not surprising that it is Mi Ju, not Yon Kim, who is the monstrous feminine.

The destructive energy of the two women generates an unrelenting cycle of *han*, but the predominance of *han* in their lives is ultimately related to the social structure they inhabit. The music school the two women attend serves as a Confucian microcosm, where correct order is carefully maintained and prescribed. Here, teachers and music directors are largely male, and the students primarily female. Academic excellence that will elevate only the best student to social privileges is to be pursued above all else, including friendship. It is unsurprising that it is Mi Ju who succeeds, because she practices calculated ruthlessness. Becoming a professor at a music school later in life demonstrates her identification with the Confucian regulation, for which she is not only granted a status usually accorded to men, but rewarded with a family. Yon Kim, rather, is disqualified although she is the better student, because she prizes friendship over academic endeavors. Her death, unmourned and forgotten, attests to her punishment by the Confucian order for "wasting" her abilities over matters of the heart.

But within the strict Confucian system that structures Korean gender ideology, the fact that Mi Ju exemplifies the modern woman runs counter to what Confucianism dictates for women: In the capacity of a successful music professor, she violates the stereotypical social categories prescribed for Korean women (such as filial daughter, dedicated mother, and dutiful wife), for which the narrative reveals her "lack" in initially subtle but later more blatant ways. The fact that she has no sons already points to her "lack" as a wife, whose duty, according to Confucianism, is to bear a male offspring to continue her husband's lineage. The fact that she is the mother of a handicapped child further compromises this duty and attenuates her lack; later, when she directly causes the deaths of her family (even if she has been "compelled" to do so by a ghost), the glaring reality of her inadequacy as a Confucian woman takes on monstrous proportions. Telling, for example, is her attendance at a concert while her younger daughter perishes. The narrative seems to be asking: What is she doing at a concert when she is supposed to be at home caring for her children? In his assessment of contemporary Korean horror cinema, Chris Berry argues, "Although women are represented as monstrous, it seems they are monstrous because modernity offers them a certain leverage and opportunity."[20] It is, however, unclear from his comments whether he views modernity as empowering or reductive. In allowing women certain "leverage and opportunity," which in turn transform them into monsters, does modernity enable women to circumvent their limitations, or does it further implicate them in their lack? In *Cello*, the latter certainly seems more evident. Here, more than the string of atrocities committed by a desperate Mi Ju and the terrifying vengeance meted out by the malevolent Yon Kim, is the reality that there is no escape for a Korean woman from Confucian strictures. She must either conform to the gender codes prescribed for her or embrace monstrosity. Yet both are, in the final analysis, transposable roles because they prescribe the woman as Other. She can only ever be either a Confucian woman or a threat, but never her-Self.

The seamless continuum between the Confucian woman and the monstrous alternative that *Cello* demonstrates can be further examined via the notion of doubling, a familiar motif in Gothic narratives. Indeed, the facts that Mi Ju reverses the story of rivalry to cast herself as victim and that she could so effortless assume Yon Kim's place on the stage of academic excellence (and later social recognition) suggest that the two women are each other's double. Interestingly, Andrew J. Webber, in his study of the motif in nineteenth-century German literature, asserts that whenever female doubling is present, "it would have little to do with altered or divided states of female subjectivity. Instead, female Doppelgängers are typically in the service of male fantasies of the other, corresponding to the time-honored polarization of Madonna and whore, the sexless and the oversexed."[21] Such an observation is equally useful in the context of *Cello*, although the cultural premises are different. Mi Ju's transformation from a successful modern woman to a murderer who destroys her own family conforms to Confucian (male) fantasies of the Other, whether polarized as the Confucian-coded woman or her malevolent antithesis. In a sociocultural system that supports and continuously reinforces the primacy of maleness and masculinity, the signifier "woman" must constantly be installed as lack. In this sense, it makes no difference whether the woman is the Confucian ideal or its contrast. Even when alive, her being coded as "lack" already implies a metaphorical death, a disturbing conundrum that *Cello* forcefully demonstrates. Notably then, it is Mi Ju, not her rival, who is her own ghost (trauma).

Standard theorizing of the double tends to relegate it as the self's alter ego externalized, whose inevitable and eventual dissolution would also mean the destruction of the self. In the case of *Cello*, it is arguable to a point that the act of murdering Yon Kim is also Mi Ju's self-destruction; but following what I have discussed thus far, if Yon Kim is nothing more than Mi Ju's trauma projected, then the destructive desire is not in the end located in an alter ego, "but within the very ego itself, which now functions as both the locus of desire and satisfaction, of presence and nonpresence."[22] Elsewhere, appropriating Derrida's concept of the hymen, I proffered an alternative model to theorize the literary double:

> Derrida's "hymen" therefore, signals the double on both rhetorical and themat-
> ic levels. In the case of the literary double, its presence at once suggests a
> rupture, or split, in the self, as well as points to, when considered alongside the
> self, a fusion, or consummation with the self. Or, to state it in a different way:
> the double, because it announces the incompleteness of the self, is therefore
> ultimately not the "other" of the self . . . but is integral to self—"no longer
> difference but identity.". . . As such, whether the double is personified by a
> character in a narrative or whether it is the hymen operating rhetorically, its
> essential characteristic is "inscribed at the very tip of . . . indecision."[23]

This reading of the double, in my opinion, is useful in describing the protago-nist's situation in *Cello*. Mi Ju's traumatic guilt creates a rupture within herself, which she has successfully repressed until another accident rehabili-tates it. The unconscious then attempts to counter this by projecting onto Mi Ju's reality the ghost of her past rival, but this ghost, as emphasized, is really Mi Ju's self refusing her a sense of completeness. Yon Kim then, is Mi Ju's "incompleteness of the self," not an Other but "integral to self." In the final analysis, the text remains ambiguous as to whether Yon Kim's presence signifies a haunting or the resurgence of trauma (either way, however, it is the return of the repressed); yet this imprecision is what characterizes the double in its most interesting and effective deployment.

WISHING STAIRS

Wishing Stairs is the third of a tetralogy of horror films that centers on schools for girls.[24] The principal difference in this installment from the other three is the dimension of folk superstition involved. It is a belief in this superstition that precipitates the haunting. According to a legend, if a magi-cal twenty-ninth step appears while a person climbs the concrete stairs that lead up to the school, she will be granted a wish by the fox spirit. In an elite art school rife with bitter rivalry, harmful wishes are bound to be made. Jin Sung, jealous of So Hee's superior talent as a ballet dancer, makes a wish to the fox spirit of the wishing stairs to gain entry to an international ballet competition. She gets her wish, but at the expense of So Hee, who incurs an injury and eventually commits suicide out of sadness and frustration. Though they were once close friends, the intense competition between students encouraged by the school system and the overt favoritism on the part of the dance teacher toward So Hee succeed in tearing apart the friendship. It is also evident that So Hee's love for Jin Sung carries strong homoerotic overtones. She often declares that all she needs is her friend, and she even suggests to Jin Sung that when they turn twenty, they should live together. But the intensity of So Hee's desire remains unreciprocated. Just as Jin Sung's "success" is the result of a wish, So Hee's return is a wish granted to Hae Ju, a school misfit who deeply admires So Hee. So Hee's angry spirit then possesses Hae Ju in order to get close to Jin Sung. Hae Ju eventually kills herself out of fear, confusion, and guilt when another student who often victimizes her is found murdered. Hae Ju realizes that So Hee is growing malevolent and that she is no longer able to contain her. In a final confrontation between So Hee and Jin Sung on the steps of the wishing stairs, Jin Sung tells her friend that she had never hated her but had only wanted to "win, just once." So Hee reaffirms her love for Jin Sung and proceeds to "embrace" the latter to death.

In *Wishing Stairs*, the metaphor of the school as a system that breeds competitiveness, jealousy, and rivalry is undeniable. Social acceptance is based on popularity and ability, and the more popular and able a student is the more accepted she becomes. Inevitably, the most outstanding student would find it difficult to have friends, as her "sublimated" status would make others feel inferior. Although So Hee clearly loves her friend above the praises of her teachers, popularity, and talent, Jin Sung's damaged self-esteem breeds bitterness and causes her to increasingly distance herself from So Hee. But unlike *Cello*, which seems to reiterate Confucianism's repressive stance toward women and its repudiation of homoerotic bonding, *Wishing Stairs* is more directly critical of such an ideology and potentially reinvests the women with power. Importantly, this power is arguably drawn from a belief system that precedes Confucianism in Korea and is believed to be more prejudiced toward the feminine (if not to women per se): shamanism. Within the competitive environment of the school, Jin Sung can finally "succeed" because she relies on the magic of the fox spirit. Later, it is Hae Ju's passionate wish that brings So Hee back from the dead. In the end, Jin Sung's desperate plea to the spirit for everything "to go back to the way it was before" brings about her final confrontation with So Hee and a resolution. In death, the two friends will be reunited once again, and the terror that shadows the school will end. As Chongho Kim observes, despite the mistreatment of shamanism by Confucianism (and later by Christianity and the Japanese Occupation), it continues to occupy a vital place in contemporary Korean society (especially among women) because it has long been "a cultural domain of misfortune in Korea" that helps people deal with "the dark side of . . . life."[25] Evidently then, for Korean women who bear a profound repository of *han*, shamanism is a countersite for personal empowerment to deal with the daily repression they face as women.

The conflict between Confucianism and shamanism is already evident in the first of the school horror series. In *Whispering Corridors*, the victimized student who will eventually die and return as a vengeful ghost is the daughter of a shaman, and the girl drawn to her has shamanistic proclivities because of her ability to contact spirits. It is apparent that the helplessness of the women in this film and *Wishing Stairs* compels their invocation of shamanism to reverse their disenfranchised status, and despite tragic consequences, it, at the very least, provides them with a modicum of influence and agency. In *Whispering Corridors,* for example, it is finally the student with mediumistic powers who can appease the vengeful spirit and restore order. In *Wishing Stairs,* it is not the fox spirit that harms the students; it merely grants them their wishes. It is ultimately the Confucian system (represented by the school) that encourages the competition and interpersonal contempt that motivates the discouraged and marginalized students to seek alternative modes of self-actualization or fulfillment.

Like *Cello*, the strong friendship bordering on homoeroticism between the two principal characters in *Wishing Stairs* is denied by a competitive system whose underlying objective is not only to isolate the academically superior student from "contamination" by her weaker friends, but to stamp out any aberrant relationship that subverts the Confucian heterosexual imperative. Tellingly, it is always the "superior" student who expresses overt homoeroticism, which then precipitates her doom. This is ironic but perhaps not unexpected. The superior student's homoerotic propensity is, as the films imply, a *signifier* of her modernist potential, and both mark her out as defiant against the established gendered and sexual codes of Confucianism. As such, she must be punished, but her punisher is also the one who would eventually occupy the "privileged" space that the former has vacated, thus becoming, in turn, a threat. In the end, as in *Cello*, both women in *Wishing Stairs* are each other's double, and the destruction of one inevitably spells the negation of the other. Alternatively, the fact that So Hee privileges friendship above her academic and professional calling labels her as aberrant because this also violates the Confucian imperative to excel. From a psychoanalytical viewpoint, such desire identifies her as a potential infraction, or "a *future* wound that will destroy" the Confucian regulation.[26] In directly plotting herself as a "lack" so as to retain her affinity with Jin Sung (even to the point of knowingly wearing a pair of ballet shoes that Jin Sung has secretly embedded with shards of broken glass in order to ruin her audition), So Hee reveals that her desire is not identified with the school's (her "self" as ultimately an extension of her school's desire), but with that of "the Other" (Jin Sung). Rather than conforming to the Symbolic order, which constructs her subjectivity, she chooses instead to enable "the Other's enjoyment." This directly marks her own loss—"the death of the self to oneself"[27] —which also implies repudiation, and therefore, a wounding of the regulating system itself. So Hee's punishment is therefore swift and ironic. The Other for whom she sacrifices much will become the very agent that the system mobilizes to destroy her.

There is, however, another way of appreciating the motif of haunting in the film, one that complements the paradoxical nature of *han* as described by Kyong-Ni Park earlier in this chapter. Significantly, Park's interpretation of *han* is guided by her support for and appreciation of Korean shamanism. As she asserts:

> We cannot however completely deliver ourselves from *Han* in this world because *Han* is also a hope for the future. This is how *Han* becomes more profound and touches upon shamanism. Shamanism is based on life and extends to the infinite universe. We Koreans believe that the dead have only left this world, that they are not completely dead and that they are still living somewhere in this universe. That is why we say, when someone dies, that he has left this world or that he has returned. . . . Our ancestors did not consider death as the end. . . . Moreover, we long ardently to communicate with the souls of the dead. It is our will to overcome the contradictions of life. We do not wish to destroy the laws of the universe, but to arrive at a place where there are no longer any contradictions.[28]

As such, Park does not consider *han* as only insinuating profound sadness and resentment; in her redefinition, which is inflected with a shamanist worldview, *han* embeds within it a hope for a future when contradictions (life/death; love/hate) are resolved. Reading *Wishing Stairs* from this perspective, So Hee's return is not motivated by revenge but by reconciliation. The impossibility of the two women's homoerotic desires, the drive toward excellence, and the subsequent rivalry that have brought profound misery to their lives can, through death, be overcome so that So Hee never has to be, in her words, "kept waiting" for Jin Sung's love and friendship anymore. In death, the girls have "arrive[d] at a place where there are no longer any contradictions," and where they can, as Jin Sung wishes, go back to the way things were. It seems from the film, however, that it is not only the living that "ardently [longs] to communicate with the souls of the dead" but vice versa as well. The strength of the two girls' intimacy compels a "returned" So Hee to seek out Jin Sung and reunite.[29]

In horror films, the body is often designated the site of transformations that explode the self's sense of unity. Whether it is the body morphing into an unspeakable creature, or the body haunted, or the body brutalized into dismembered parts, horror alters the qualities of coherence and stability that the body supposedly represents and turns the human into an object. Korean horror films, in persistently reducing women's bodies to mutilated, bloodied materiality, reveal through such exaggerations women's profound constriction by the status quo. The fact that these bodies, allegedly toughened by competition, can be ultimately fragile and so easily broken attests to the horror of a sociocultural system that marks them with self-hatred and the terror of failure, which in turn invite sadomasochistic performances upon the self and others. It is interesting, therefore, that the final shots in *Cello* and *Wishing Stairs* are the protagonists' countenances. In the former, Mi Ju's increasing terror is registered in a close-up face shot as a withered hand slowly embraces her from behind. In the latter, a new student, given the room Jin Sung once occupied, finds a photo portrait of the two girls as the camera slowly zooms into their faces.

To appreciate the significance of the close-up face shot in these two films, I turn to Gilles Deleuze's insightful reading of this camera technique. In *Cinema 1*, speaking of the face in a close-up shot, Deleuze postulates:

> When part of the body has had to sacrifice most of its motoricity in order to become the support for organs of reception, the principal feature of these will now only be tendencies to movement or micro-movements which are capable of entering into intensive series, for a single organ or from one organ to the other. The moving body has lost its movement of extension, and movement has become movement of expression. It is this combination of reflecting, immobile unity and of intensive expressive movements which constitutes the affect.[30]

The reduction of the totality of the body to a single "organ of reception" is most successfully rendered through the close-up shot of the face. The rest of the body, now eclipsed (because it is outside the frame), must depend on the face to convey its circumstances. This is possibly what Deleuze means by the "tendencies to movement or micro-movement," in which the "moving body" is no longer capable of "movement of extension," only "movement of expression." The face must, in this sense, register all the modalities the body is undergoing. This directly contributes to the facial close-up's "reflecting, immobile unity" and its "intensive expressive movements which constitutes the affect": the face reflects the overall, "unified" experience of the body, which is now denied presence and visibility, and from this, affects the way in which the viewer would interpret the shot. Appropriating Deleuze's meditation to my discussion of the two films, I want to suggest that the close-up shots that conclude both films reflect the terrifying immobility that women face in

Korean culture. The rigid codes that Confucianism enforces leave very little room for self-maneuvering, and as a result, crystallize women in their stereo-typical categories. Whether as ideal Confucian women or monsters, women are, metaphorically, nothing more than set pieces designed to satisfy the male gaze and imperative.

In *Cello*, Mi Ju's mounting terror is not just the dawning realization of an endless nightmare; when read against a larger cultural context, it signifies her entrapment in a social system that denies her identity and individuality. In the case of *Wishing Stairs*, the fact that the narrative takes place within a school—a microcosm of the Confucian order—makes the doubled framing of the two girls in the last shot (the photograph and the camera frame) all the more urgent. Although the girls are now beyond the pale of the regulating system, it is at such tremendous cost, and there will be more girls who will continue to bear the burden of such a system.

Diane Hoffman's thesis that contemporary Korean culture tends to oper-ate on the blurring of genders seems untenable in light of what Korean horror films persistently insinuate. If, as Sheila Miyogi Jager observes, Korean nar-ratives continue to "shape Koreans' thinking about the history of collective suffering . . . in terms that are strikingly gendered,"[31] Korean horror films certainly conform to this trend with unwavering consistency. As noted earli-er, although *han* is collectively experienced by all Koreans, it is the women who have a stronger affinity with it. As I have attempted to demonstrate in my reading of two Korean horror films, the various forms that the female embodiment of *han* can take should not be regarded only for their destructive propensities, but for their hopeful ones as well. Likewise, the focus on pri-marily women in Korean horror should not be perceived as a generic reduc-tion of women to hysterical, monstrous beings whose only salvation lies in their rehabilitation and return to the Confucian status quo. These films, for all of their objectification and abject-ifying of women, are actually profoundly feminist in their concerns as they highlight the powerful circumscriptions that Korean women endure in a society that denies them a sense of indepen-dent selfhood. Sara Maitland once said that Victorian women share an affin-ity with ghosts because they both belong to a "tradition in the shadow,"[32] which is why the ghost story genre is especially favored by women writers. With some modification, the same could be said of Korean women and ghosts. The fact that Korean horror cinema simultaneously portrays women as ghost and victim reveals, in the end, that all three (women, ghosts, vic-tims) share a similar tradition of prejudice, oppression, and silence. Rendered invisible, the only way they can assert a presence, and hence a history, is by marking themselves as bloodied—a wound—to rupture the fantasy of their culture's male-inflected ideology.

It is noteworthy that *Wishing Stairs* has a more redemptive dimension to it (at least in my reading) than *Cello*, whose implication of persistent torment suggests that the protagonist will loop endlessly in a nightmare from which she will never wake. While I am not in favor of reading a fictive text based on its author's gender because this is reductive, in the case of these two Korean horror films under discussion, however, there may actually be worth in deploying such an interpretative approach (but without stretching the point too far). Both films, I maintain, are profoundly feminist in that they highlight the ideological straitjackets women experience within a highly Confucian and patriarchal society, but *Cello*, whose director is a man, is decidedly limited in its inability to envision emancipation for women; in this text, *han* bears only a single quality, and whoever embodies it will be channeled toward devastation. As a result, ties like friendship and family become impossible in life, and in death, these relationships turn into knots that bind the victim to perpetual grief. Mi Ju is possibly cursed to relive her trauma indefinitely; neither she nor the viewer is sure if she is alive, trapped in between worlds, or is already dead and must henceforth endure eternal punishment. On the other hand, *Wishing Stairs*, which is directed by a woman, adopts what I argue to be a more conciliatory tenor. It is possible that like the author Kyong-Ni Park, Jae-Yeon Yun also rejects the male-defined, limited significations of *han*, but appreciates its potential for reparative capacities while acknowledging its destructive nature. In her film, Yun demonstrates that *han* can sometimes be evoked at another stage in our existence to undo the damage caused by an earlier stage: A friendship ravaged by rivalry in life finds restoration in the afterlife. This suggests that *han* accommodates oppositional qualities and does not only signify profound wretchedness (as *Cello* seems to intimate); there are facets to it that can be harnessed for self-expansion and healing. *Han* may be the cause of suffering, but it can also be affected to bring suffering to an end and, consequently, to help the victim find liberation.

NOTES

1. Eungjun Min, Jinsook Joo, and Han Ju Kwak, *Korean Film: History, Resistance, and Democratic Imagination* (Westport, CT: Praeger, 2003), 8.

2. Kilsŏng Ch'oe, "Male and Female in Korean Folk Belief," *Asian Folklore Studies* 43, no. 2 (1984): 231.

3. Min, Joo, and Kwak, *Korean Film*, 9.

4. Ibid., 8.

5. Young-Hee Lee, "Women's Literature in the Chosŏn Period: *Han* and the Songs of Women," in *Korean Studies: New Pacific Currents*, ed. Dae-Suk Soh (Honolulu: Hawaii University Press, 1994): 101–2.

6. Nam-Dong Suh, "Towards a Theology of *Han*," in *Minjung Theology: People as Subjects of History*, ed. The Commission on Theological Concerns of the Christian Conference of Asia (Singapore: Christian Conference of Asia, 1981), 58. As scholars have consistently noted, "Confucianism has a stronger hold in Korea than in any other nation in the world." Joyce Gelb and Marian Lief Palley, *Women of Japan and Korea: Continuity and Change* (Philadelphia: Temple University Press, 1994), 3. This sometimes requires women to play conflicting roles:

On the one hand, they are to remain sexually active for and attractive to their husbands, while on the other, they must uphold the Confucian virtues of self-effacement, demureness, and passivity. See Young-hee Shim, "Feminism and the Discourse of Sexuality in Korea: Continuities and Changes," *Human Studies* 24 (2001): 141. Despite recurrent and vital feminist movements to educate and improve the status of Korean women, Confucianism's entrenched presence in the Korean society remains difficult to counter.

7. Ch'oe, "Male and Female," 231.

8. Ibid.

9. Hagen Koo, *Korean Workers: The Culture and Politics of Class Formation* (Ithaca, NY: Cornell University Press, 2001), 136.

10. *Cello*, directed by Woo-cheol Lee (2005; New York: Tartan Asia Extreme, 2006), DVD.

11. Kyong-Ni Park, "The Feelings and Thoughts of the Korean People in Literature" at http://web.archive.org/web/20021126053722/http://www.keganpaul.com/articles_main.php?url=main_file.php/articls/30/ (accessed September 22, 2008).

12. *Wishing Stairs*, directed by Jae-yeon Yun (2003; New York: Tartan Video, 2005), DVD.

13. Bassel A. van der Kolk and Onno van der Hart, "The Intrusive Past: The Flexibility of Memory and the Engraving of Trauma," in *Trauma: Explorations in Memory*, ed. Cathy Caruth (Baltimore: Johns Hopkins University Press, 1995), 163.

14. Ibid.

15. Linda Williams, "When the Woman Looks," in *Horror: The Film Reader*, ed. Mark Janovich (London: Routledge, 2002), 61.

16. Slavoj Žižek, *The Sublime Object of Ideology* (London: Verso, 1989), 196.

17. Susan Stewart, "The Epistemology of the Horror Story," *Journal of American Folklore* 95, no. 375 (1982): 36.

18. Ibid.

19. Dori Laub, "Truth and Testimony: The Process and the Struggle," in *Trauma: Explorations in Memory*, ed. Cathy Caruth (Baltimore: Johns Hopkins University Press, 1995), 64.

20. Chris Berry and Kim So-Young, "'Suri Suri Masuri': The Magic of the Korean Horror Film: A Conversation," *Postcolonial Studies* 3, no. 1 (2000): 55.

21. Andrew J. Webber, *The Doppelgänger: Double Vision in German Literature* (Oxford: Clarendon Press, 1996), 20.

22. Andrew Hock Soon Ng, "Introduction: Reading the Double," in *The Poetics of Shadows: The Double in Literature and Philosophy* (Stuttgart: Ibidem-Verlag, 2008), 7.

23. Ibid., 6–7. Inset quotation from Jacques Derrida, *Dissemination*, trans. Barbara Johnson (London: Continuum, 2004), 220.

24. The first two are *Whispering Corridors*, directed by Park Ki-Hyung (1998; London: Tartan, 2005), DVD, and *Memento Mori*, directed by Kim Tae Yeon, Kim Tae-Yong, and Min Kyu-Dong (1999; London: Tartan, 2005), DVD, while the fourth is *Voice*, directed by Equan Choi (2005; Seoul: CJ Entertainment, 2008), DVD. In all three films, the themes of academic rivalry, bitter friendship, and of course, haunting, are paramount. Homoeroticism is also a subtext threaded through them.

25. Chongho Kim, *Korean Shamanism: A Cultural Paradox* (Aldershot, UK: Ashgate, 2003), 63.

26. Elizabeth Cowie, "The Lived Nightmare: Trauma, Anxiety, and the Ethical Aesthetics of Horror," in *Dark Thoughts: Philosophical Reflections on Cinematic Horror*, ed. Steven J. Schneider and Daniel Shaw (Lanham, MD: Scarecrow Press, 2003), 33.

27. Ibid.

28. Kyong-Ni Park, "The Feelings and Thoughts of the Korean People in Literature," at http://web.archive.org/web/20021126053722/http://www.keganpaul.com/articles_main.php?url=main_file.php/articles/30/ (accessed September 22, 2008).

29. According to Diane Hoffman, intimacy in Korea "involves a fundamental shift in the way the self is constituted that is variously experienced as a loss of self, a merging of self with that of the other, or an all-enveloping acceptance of the other as part of the self. In this process of identification the very boundaries of self, including sex and gender, become blurred, subsumed in a union that represents the end point of the continuum of 'social relatedness' or state of embeddedness that characterizes self's relations with others." Diane M. Hoffman, "Blurred

Genders: The Cultural Construction of Male and Female in South Korea," *Korean Studies* 19 (1995): 128. This seems to contradict contemporary Korean sociocultural reality: Confucianism demands a hierarchical social structure so that one's self-worth is locatable and obvious. Hoffman, on the other hand, insists that Korean intimacy instigates a "blurring" of self from other; the self incorporates the other so as to mark a loss in oneself. But from what many Korean horror films have demonstrated, it is difficult to see how Hoffman's view can be plausible. Her observation, I would argue, suggests a more shamanistic dynamic of self/other interrelatedness that is clearly at odds with the existing "'social relatedness' or state of embeddedness" in Korean culture. Of course, it is possible that an excellent student can still maintain close friendships, but the school system in the Korean horror films blatantly discourages this. In the end, for intimacy to be at all possible, the self and the other must be released from their entrapment within the existing regulating system. *Wishing Stairs* achieves this with the afterlife reunion of the two protagonists. In the fourth high-school horror installment, *Voice*, the dead girl attains this through possessing the body of her best friend.

30. Gilles Deleuze, *Cinema 1: The Movement Image*, trans. Hugh Tomlinson and Barbara Habberjam (London: Athlone Press, 1986), 87.

31. Sheila Miyoshi Jager, "Woman and the Promise of Modernity: Signs of Love for the Nation in Korea," *New Literary History* 29, no. 1 (1998): 126.

32. Sara Maitland, "Introduction," in *The Virago Book of Ghost Stories*, vol. 2, ed. Richard Dalb (London: Virago, 1991), xiii.

Chapter Ten

"Help Me"

Interrogating Capitalism, the Specter of Hiroshima, and the Architectural Uncanny in Kiyoshi Kurosawa's Pulse

Paul Petrovic

Kiyoshi Kurosawa's film *Pulse*[1] (originally released as *Kairo*) exists as perhaps the apotheosis of the recent Japanese horror craze. The film frames the uncanny effects of late capitalist alienation and social estrangement in Japan today, themes that Kurosawa likewise explores in his films *Cure* (1997) and *Bright Future* (2003), among others; yet in *Pulse* these effects are mediated through a spectral haunting that exists as a symbolic critique. Utilizing the generic framework of specters that first haunt Tokyo through modern technology, Kurosawa soon expands on this thematic coverage, exploring space and representation to suggest, however liminally, an interrogation of the cultural memory of Hiroshima. *Pulse* initially appears as little more than another in a long tradition of J-horror films, but its subtextual engagement allows for a matrix of historical, psychological, and sociocultural concerns to come to the foreground. These issues of visibility and witnessing disrupt the generic conventions that ground *Pulse* and privilege instead the allegorical nature inherent to Kiyoshi Kurosawa's filmmaking.

Consideration of the cultural memory of Hiroshima, and similarly, Nagasaki, is important since so little of Japan's popular film history considers it in any explicit manner, perhaps precisely because it remains such a potent signifier. Indeed, the cultural memory of Hiroshima signifies no less than the Japanese people's survival of the nuclear apocalypse. Expanding that idea out more broadly, Joshua La Bare asserts that "in its capacity to survive apocalypses, Japan marks our futuristic *imaginaire*."[2] However, La Bare concerns himself with images of Japan as seen from American cyberpunk authors Neal Stephenson and William Gibson, and consideration of the apoc-alyptic, especially in genre cinema, has received little sustained attention from critics of Japanese film. For example, Hayao Miyazaki's anime, espe-cially *Nausicaä of the Valley of the Wind* (1984) and *Spirited Away* (2001), often dwell on images of desolate and postindustrial wastelands, but these films ultimately critique humanity's unwillingness to care for its environ-ment rather than bearing witness to Hiroshima's cultural memory. Even Shinya Tsukamoto's classic cyberpunk film *Tetsuo: The Iron Man* (1989) is more interested in documenting how man destroys nature and neglects any outward gesture toward Hiroshima. More direct coverage of Japan's cultural memory can be found in Mori Masaki's *Barefoot Gen* (1983), which adapts Keiji Nakazawa's manga narrative of the same name, an anime that is based loosely on Nakazawa's own experiences with Hiroshima's atomic destruc-tion. Some of Japan's early 1980s anime aesthetic hinders *Barefoot Gen*, but the film does reach for flourishes of expressionism, especially when the film begins depicting images of the destruction wrought by the atomic blast in Hiroshima. Those scenes, with flesh curdling and eyeballs distending from the skeletal remains, achieve a haunting, stark grace. Similarly, the way it covers abandoning family to survive in the aftermath of radiation, pika don, and collapsed architecture is convincing, especially when framed against the autobiographical coverage of the tale. Yet against those weighted moments, the film's rudimentary animation and coming-of-age narrative cannot capture the full weight of historical emotions. Shōhei Imamura gives perhaps the strongest direct memorial to Hiroshima in *Black Rain* (1989), documenting both the immediate destruction of the bomb and the lingering after-effects that continue to ravish Hiroshima's citizens years after the dropping. Imamu-ra shows flesh hanging loose from bones, bodies turning to hard shells of ash, dust clouds covering the ruins of the cityscape, and the lasting psychological trauma that the bomb comes to inflict.

Despite these more direct approaches that Masaki and Imamura present, Kiyoshi Kurosawa's cinema becomes one of the veiled arenas in which con-sideration of Hiroshima's cultural memory is most actively played out, even if it is frequently hidden because of his films' ostensible genre limitations. Though *Pulse* bears the mark of a conventional horror film, this same frame-work allows it the leeway to contextualize modern anxieties about the condi-tion of Japanese life after the Hiroshima attacks. Using an allegory of translu-cent specters that plague Tokyo, and by extension all of Japan, Kurosawa assesses the ways in which existential surrender gives way to smudges of body and ash, subtextually memorializing the dead of Hiroshima's and Naga-saki's atomic attacks.

Kurosawa suggests a permanence about the specters' haunting within *Pulse*, situating their surveillance of Japanese society vis-à-vis their trans-gressive infringement upon the anxieties of contemporary life. For example,

Pulse documents a technology-dependent society that is unable to handle the phantasmatic breach of the specters, as characters commit suicide to avoid further confrontation with these hauntings; likewise, the film documents a preternatural disconnect between familial generations, wherein parents are "irrelevant," if noted at all; and it documents *hikikomori,* an extreme form of social withdrawal exhibited by Japanese adolescents, where characters resort to a psychological abandonment of others and thereby remain physically and emotionally rootless. Consequently, Kurosawa chronicles a social milieu in which isolation forms the dominant mode of thought.

This same isolation only eases the characters' surrender to death, for they possess little in the way of optimism or a positive belief system to combat the existential dread that the specters emit. Instead, *Pulse*'s characters simultaneously embrace and fear these encounters, dissolving into, as Jeremiah Kipp contends, "Hiroshima smudges of black on the wall" once they are too weak to counter the specters. [3] Such scenes carry with them an obviously subtextual weight, for these scenes are, to use Kathleen Brogan's words, full of "cultural transmission." [4] That is, these scenes bear witness to the "cultural haunting" in their exploration "of a people's historical consciousness." [5] Kurosawa problematizes the cultural memory of Hiroshima. The film is textually amnesic, refusing to directly negotiate or otherwise engage the atomic bombings on Japan; in its subtextual engagement with images of psychical and bodily disintegration, however, *Pulse* disentangles notions of cultural amnesia and exists as an unambiguous referent to Hiroshima. Even though Kipp notes the historical resonance of the ultimate self-erasure into "smudges of black," neither he nor other critics study this aspect of the film in any sustained analysis. In response to this lack of analysis, this chapter first traces the production and systemization of capitalism's alienating effects. Second, and most vitally, this chapter traces how Kurosawa interrogates the cultural memory of Hiroshima, analyzing how the invisible mnemonic site in *Pulse* is rendered visible through liminal representations. Finally, this chapter traces Kurosawa's dependence on architecture and representational space to transmit his social and epistemic ideas of how physical, though not emotional, rootlessness aids survival.

First, it is necessary to frame the complexities that await any storyteller who wishes to draw upon the liminal cultural memory of Hiroshima rather than the direct historical memory of Hiroshima. In her study *Hiroshima Traces: Time, Space, and the Dialectics of Memory,* Lisa Yoneyama notes that when the storyteller produces a testimony of Hiroshima that is apart from the event's mimetic representation, it is rendered as an "alternate trajector[y]." [6] She continues, "The moment the storyteller desires his or her [Hiroshima] testimony to be heard as a prophecy, or as a possible future event, the past event is relentlessly made allegorical," until it is "transfigured into a future happening in a fictive timespace." [7] Kurosawa fashions *Pulse* as a transfigured metaphor, for the film is relentlessly allegorical, complicating conventional approaches to the atomic destruction in Hiroshima and thereby extending its symbolism to an apocalyptic timespace, one where the disintegrated bodies of the dead become ontologized as mnemonic sites of Hiroshima. As such, while the interrogation of late capitalist society should not be neglected in studies of *Pulse*, neither should readings of Hiroshima's uncanny textual (in)visibility within the work, for this hermeneutic reveals a strain of cultural commentary that is initially invisible.

Pulse opens and closes on a lone ship surrounded by the ocean. As Jerry White notes, the ship is "a paragon of isolation."[8] While this isolation creates discomfort, White identifies the principal quality for Kurosawa's auteurist intentions. White's linguistic choice of the ship as "paragon" highlights the positive status that lies within the nonanchored vessel. Whereas the rest of the film posits the alienating effect that burdens so much of Tokyo's postindustrial, late capitalist relations, this moment exists in direct opposition to it, suggesting a potential freedom that is demarcated visually through its spatial separation from conflicts on land. In that sense, landed properties become the first ghost to appear through their very invisibility. So even though this opening bears the weight of a dystopic timespace, it also harbors traces of a transcendent timespace. Kurosawa first establishes the film's consideration of being rootless here, though this chapter will discuss that theme in greater detail later.

To begin, though, the ship captain (Kôji Yakusho) governs a small crew and steps out on the ship's deck for "navigational information."[9] The sense of implied dislocation offers a preliminary understanding that some catastrophic event has estranged them from land. While roaming the ship, the ship captain comes upon Michi Kudo (Kumiko Aso), one of the film's two leads. She appears lost in thought, and she soon alerts the spectator to the framework of bookends by situating the events through voice-over: "It all began one day, without warning, like this."[10] Within such an opening, Michi references the sense of an everyday normalcy beneath the eruption of this cultural haunting. That is to say, *Pulse* directly references the familiar, but the film is just as emphatic about referencing the unfamiliar. In this sense, the unfamiliar encompasses the specters, but the unfamiliar is also the specters' allegorical (in)visibility when seen through the lens of Hiroshima. As such, the uncanny effect of the specters is doubled: first they are an infringement upon the homely, and second they are an infringement upon a society that outwardly neglects any cultural marker of Hiroshima.

Pulse, then, powerfully evokes the uncanny. As a literary term, the uncanny reaches all the way back to Sigmund Freud's unsuccessful attempts to articulate precisely what is uncanny about the uncanny, a concept that itself seems ineffable, and more contemporary theorists have problematized and noted the slippage inherent to seemingly disparate notions of the homely and unhomely. For the sake of brevity, this chapter will rely on the archetypal uncanny, or, to use art historian Anthony Vidler's definition, "the contrast between a secure and homely interior and the fearful invasion of an alien presence."[11] Yet Kurosawa immediately denaturalizes this central dichotomy of the homely and unhomely, generating much of the film's tension and unease precisely through the collapse of such binaries. Prior to any introduction of the specters, homely spaces in *Pulse* are already defamiliarized and contaminated with disquietude, and this spatial uncanny "no longer serves to center, to fix, or to stabilize."[12] Kurosawa presents space in *Pulse* as an agent that partitions and denies closeness, as in the many shots of workplaces that always privilege spatial avoidance over intimacy. Instead, the space further represents the horrific, estranging spatial divide between individuals and their once stable home, and only Michi and Kawashima, a character introduced later in the film's narrative, are able to circumvent that destabilizing sense.

After the voice-over opening, *Pulse* cuts to the immediate past, where Michi works in a rooftop nursery, Sunny Plant Sales, with her friends. Yet Kurosawa reveals the estrangement and *hikikomori* that his characters exhibit vis-à-vis their approximation of space. Michi's workplace is not docile but rather alienating, with its high-rise building existing as an architectural metonym of spatial separation. The nursery produces a sense of the uncanny that is marked by its stark contrast between placid ordinariness and its distance from the humanity below them. Indeed, this sense of spatial dislocation is doubled by the workers' own disconnection, which is itself symptomatic of capitalism, where the primary affect is one of labor and, as Marx notes, "active alienation, the alienation of activity, the activity of alienation."[13] For example, Michi does not voice any concern over coworker Taguchi's disappearance until "it's been a week."[14] Furthermore, Michi and Junco, a coworker, seldom appear close to one another in the cinematic space, instead favoring distance and separation. Kurosawa accentuates this aspect by using little in the way of close-ups during scenes on the rooftop; the camera is largely positioned in medium- and long-shot to further the dehumanization process.

Michi is eventually unsettled by Taguchi's absence and goes to visit him in his apartment, though Kurosawa notes that the visit is primarily to retrieve from him a computer disc for work, reinforcing the depersonalization of capitalism. When Michi leaves work to visit Taguchi, she goes by bus. Here, Kurosawa frames Michi in terms of her physical isolation from society; she exists on the bus, which is, naturally enough, driven by a phantom driver, as a solitary figure. There are no signs of life beyond her presence, and Michi herself appears almost ghostly despite her corporeality, as she is devoid of any facial expression. This sense of the phantasmatic is doubled by the film's refusal to orient the spectator to known space, which is evident when Kurosawa situates the shot of Michi on the bus against an indistinguishable back-projection of cityspace. Because of this denial of spatial representation, Kurosawa arranges these shots as a crossing of liminal thresholds, so that the bus is a transport that denies any approximation of spatial memory. As such, the film's mise-en-scène orchestrates the selfsame alienation, becoming a facsimile of the fractured, disembodied cityspace.

Michi enters Taguchi's apartment and its sprawl of technology welcomes her, even though the dark space enshrouding the room is disorienting. Evoking the film's nearly constant sense of alienation, she concerns herself first with locating the computer disc and demonstrates little concern for his physical safety, fumbling at his worktable prior to ever searching the home for him. In the space behind Michi, a body rises from behind a plastic film curtain, which is the first real cinematic, and genre-specific, horror, as it seems disembodied from behind the plastic. She starts; she soon realizes, however, that it is merely Taguchi, and again feels as though she resides in a homely space. For his part, Taguchi seems distant, detached from her concerns, as he has already been victimized by the specters. He lacks any real characterization, instead offering only monosyllabic answers when Michi finally voices concerns over his health. Yet her tacit acceptance of these conditions further identifies the alienation produced by capitalism. Kurosawa gestures toward Michi's obliviousness at this early stage by showing Taguchi wander off, secure some rope, and return to his quarters without receiving any inquiry from her. When Michi investigates, she discovers his body hanging from a noose, and such a visceral image highlights the film's social critique between the delay of Michi ever expressing concern and Taguchi's surrender to hopelessness. The unhomely, then, has penetrated and contaminated the homely.

Remarkably, Yabe, a coworker, realizes that Taguchi, though dead, still exists in the representational space on the disc that Michi retrieved, and it is here that the film's cultural haunting truly begins. Yabe calls Michi and Junco into the nursery office and they study the image. When he magnifies the resolution, Taguchi appears, desolate but discernibly there. Again the uncanny intrudes upon the seemingly docile workspace. Moreover, shortly thereafter, Yabe is alone and he receives a call from Taguchi's phone. It is, apparently, Taguchi, who whispers, "Help me," a mantra that assumes import both through its unchanging repetition and through its linguistic traces back to Hiroshima. Though the words have a primacy that will always be invoked in emergencies, this phrase specifically haunts the cultural memory of Hiroshima. Later, even though they lack any corporeal form, the smudges of ash themselves whisper this repetitive plea, and in this way the mantra lifts up from *Pulse*'s subtext and skirts the film's surface.

For example, in *City of Silence: Listening to Hiroshima*, Rachelle Linner shares the story of Sadako Ueno, a *hibakusha*, or a survivor of the atomic bomb. In her own words, Sadako narrates how she fled the screams and debris that immediately followed the explosion, noting how she repeatedly heard, "Help me, help me."[15] This is but one example of many *hibakusha* testimonies where survivors heard their countrymen and women crying out for help, and the urgency of these words bespeak the hidden horrors that Hiroshima survivors witnessed. Likewise, Imamura's *Black Rain* also legitimizes the testimony by applying the stark difficulty of the plea directly to the aftermath of Hiroshima. When Imamura's protagonist and Hiroshima survivor, Shigematsu Shizuma (Kazuo Kitamura), meets an old neighbor, they converse about the destruction that they witnessed firsthand. The neighbor tells how his son had been caught in the wreckage wrought by the bomb and screamed "Help me" to his father, who could only watch as the fires swept through the wreckage and consumed his son. This linguistic parallel affirms the symbolic need to reconcile oneself against the plea and the inability to save those intoning it. Much like *Black Rain*'s direct approach to Hiroshima, *Pulse* insinuates the phantom text of Hiroshima, and Kurosawa himself has acknowledged his propensity to craft apocalyptic scenes, where "'you see cities destroyed, and perhaps even hints that the end of civilization is near.'"[16] Considering this trend of thematic coverage, it does not seem improbable to suggest that, at least on an allegorical level, the repetition of the words "Help me" bear a linguistic trace to Hiroshima. This is, however, likely the most explicit audible marker of Kurosawa's reference to the cultural memory of Hiroshima.

Indeed, the words, with their encoded infraction of the dead terrorizing the living by pleading for help, deeply disturb Yabe. He goes to Taguchi's apartment to investigate this corporeal impossibility, and again Kurosawa references the crossing of liminal space vis-à-vis the bus. Upon his arrival at the apartment, Yabe's dread is at a higher peak simply because everything is so mundane, and Taguchi is nowhere to be seen. When Yabe turns on the light and checks the spot where Taguchi hanged himself, though, he comes across the smudge. The smudge maps the liminal space of death's existential horror, authored through Taguchi's surrender; it is the visual representation through which Kurosawa references the charred corpses of Hiroshima, their bodies reduced to ash and dust. After gazing at it, Taguchi turns off the light and leaves the room momentarily. When he returns, the smudge assumes the corporeal body of Taguchi, though only fleetingly. While the representation of Taguchi vanishes, its traces linger within the liminal space of the smudge, and it is these traces that provide much of *Pulse*'s allegorical impact. As Avery F. Gordon argues, "The ghost is not simply a dead or a missing person, but a social figure, and investigating it can lead to that dense site where history and subjectivity make social life."[17] With respect to *Pulse*, the ghostly specters approximate a return to the cultural memories of Hiroshima—as if such memories ever truly left Japanese culture—and by probing the depths of the allegory that Kurosawa placed in the film's cinematic elements, the historical weight of *Pulse*'s visual and auditory designs is revealed. Whether tracing the ashes of the dead or ontologizing the Hiroshima smudges themselves with an utterance of the film's unchanging plea, Kurosawa is endlessly fascinated by tracing the density of his film's ideas.

As such, the density of the cultural memory of Hiroshima in *Pulse* is the essential entryway into reading the film. In fact, the half-buried mnemonic sites of Hiroshima bear much of the film's visceral power. Though *Pulse* is densely allegorical, themes of visibility and invisibility have long been studied. For instance, Laura Kipnis argues, "Visibility is a complex system of permission and prohibition, of presence and absence, punctuated alternately by apparitions and hysterical blindness."[18] If the specters are hypervisible, as they indeed are after Taguchi visits the apartment, then what systems of representation remain blind, closed off, or underrepresented but the subtextual—that is to say, the liminal? As such, Kurosawa's production of Hiroshima is seen through this spectacle of horror, its terrors operating as allegory, as fictional testimony.

Yabe, too, is soon infected by the specters, and Kurosawa finally lets the spectator see the enemy. In this instance, the specter is personified as an indistinct woman who steps out of the shadows, her menace offset only by her slow, dance-like walk. Though the specter lacks speed, the terror she exudes smothers any chance of escape. As Jerry White explains, "The woman in the black dress is horrifying because she's not clearly defined, falls beyond such comforting labels as ghost or vampire or demon. She is beyond our realm of understanding."[19] Though Kurosawa lets the climax of the encounter occur off-screen, Yabe's absence from work the next day telegraphs his contamination. When Michi decides to visit him and see what is wrong, Junco recoils. Her demeanor, physical and psychological, suggests instead a suppression of reality, and she contends that "nothing strange has happened yet" and that they should "just act normal."[20] Her willingness to abandon others for her own material self-interest is clear. Much like Taguchi before him, when Yabe returns to work he is perceptibly alien. He is even more preternaturally estranged from his coworkers, shutting them all out by closing the nursery office door, and he remains aloof until he surrenders to the effects of the haunting despair, becoming merely a smudge on the office walls.

As the film continues, Michi watches the infected build in number. Still, she realizes that the specters can be contained in rooms with red tape, a color that seemingly bears no direct signification. When she is leaving work, for example, she witnesses a woman barricade a house in this manner. Despite testimony from a secondary character Yoshizaki, who states otherwise (as this chapter discusses later), such attempts at containment are merely temporary because that same woman is soon seen jumping to her death from the top of a water tower. In a film with many outwardly nihilistic moments, this scene is perhaps the worst, for it fully communicates the horror and inevitability of the despair that they all come to feel. The visualization of the devastation that consumes these characters, in fact, far outweighs any generic horror spectacle, for the film exhibits a panorama of emotional defeat and growing architectural ruin that transcends the film's ostensible origins as a "ghost story."

Eventually, Junco enters a room covered in red tape, a telltale sign that specters reside inside, and she is infected. Though Michi pulls her out of the room, Junco devolves quickly into a cowering ball in the middle of Michi's apartment. Much like those before her, Junco is reduced to a cold, cringing mass of flesh that adopts that monosyllabic plea that signifies her imminent death: "Help me."[21] All of Junco's ontological memory, or identity, evaporates, and her stand against oblivion is reduced to the whimpering plea that occurs after she is enveloped by the specter's despair. As Lisa Yoneyama notes concerning the Hiroshima survivor, "When claims about the incommunicability of the experience shift from the individual level of coping with remembering and forgetting to universal generalizations regarding the authenticity of memory and the essential meaning of survival, they begin to repress and control heterogeneous voices and contestatory forms of memory."[22] That is to say with regard to *Pulse*, that the subjectivity of the individual disintegrates and shifts instead to governed and preconditioned uniformity: "Help me." There is nothing to ward off the isolation. Once the cultural haunting penetrates the victims through their exposure to the specters and that sense of overwhelming estrangement takes its hold, the plea for help is codified into a single monologism. In this way, the specters control the material production of the survivor until the transmitted despair conquers them, at which point they hang themselves, jump to their deaths, or simply become smudges on the wall.

Moreover, the specters deny any rigid categorization. Though they are, as Kurosawa conceives them, the uncanny embodiment of all of capitalism's excess and estranging materialism, their objective is never fully clear with regard to the existential despair that they produce in society. Do they merely wish to procure another timespace because the afterlife is full? Though a graduate student in the film, Yoshizaki, notes that the "souls have no choice but to ooze into our world,"[23] Kurosawa biographer Jerry White rightly asserts that this rationalization is strained precisely because the "fact that an impossibly knowledgeable scientist conveniently appears in order to explain the mysterious events . . . smacks of fifties sci-fi movies."[24] White thereby suggests that the specters be conceived apart from any narratological explanation. At their core, the specters are ontologically allegorical and must be seen as such. Psychologically, then, the specter is that which, to use Jacques Lacan's terminology, "resists symbolization completely."[25]

The specters' haunting of the ubiquitous technology available in Tokyo allows them a direct panoptic lens with which they can haunt and survey the estranged society at will. The specters are thus conveyors of meaning, yet their reach is not abbreviated merely by a resistance to technology. To believe that survival from *Pulse*'s specters merely means that one maintain an independence from mediums of modern technology, as some critics of Kurosawa's film derisively contend, is to miss the larger commentary. The specters exist in any unhomely space, which inherently suggests any space of late capitalism. They exist in any place where characters see "space as threat, as harbinger of the unseen, [which] operates as medical and psychical metaphor for all the possible erosions of bourgeois bodily and social well being."[26] Though the specters do not materially kill the victim, they authorize the conditions for the victim's remaining life. Metaphorically, they are an uncanny by-product of capitalism, dispensing their despairing ideology into the bodies they have victimized. As Michel Foucault writes of the subject and his power, "To govern, in this sense, is to structure the possible field of action of other people."[27] The victims abandon all agency and potential, wallowing instead in the despair produced by the ghosts. Not only do the specters produce a constant surveillance and a sense of hopelessness, but they also systematize their ideology so that all the victims are coerced into willful suicide.

Kurosawa foregrounds these issues by doubling up the film's oppressive imagery. First, Kurosawa's camera settles again on the water tower, that oppressive symbol of inevitability, even though the architectural landscape is barren. A woman's scream is heard suddenly in the nondiegetic space, and the camera pans down to the ground below, coming to rest on the smudge that represents metaphorically all of the suicide jumper's corporeality. Kurosawa manipulates temporal logic subversively by ontologizing the smudge; the camera is still statically trained on the smudge when it whispers the film's haunting refrain, "Help me."[28] The (in)visibility of this mnemonic site of Hiroshima parallels with the immediate cut to Junco, who is gazing inconsolably out of an open window in Michi's apartment. While Michi cleans the apartment, Junco turns and blankly asks, "Am I going to die, just like this?" Junco's social withdrawal, her *hikikomori*, is impenetrable. When Michi asserts that Junco will survive, Junco counters that initial layer of optimism by noting the inherent estrangement that will exist, "I'll keep on living, all alone."[29] She has no other possible course of action, as her responses are fielded and systematically produced by the specters, and she too surrenders, evaporating into the now prototypical smudge on the wall. Kurosawa amplifies this sense of despair when a gust of wind blows in through the window and scatters the smudge, so that Junco's corporeal remains become all but ash. The uncanny cultural memories this evokes of Hiroshima, where the dead collapsed into bone and ash, are obvious as Michi tries futilely to snatch the ashes from the air. Such an injunction speaks of the need to remember Hiroshima and to hold onto those memories, however fleeting and ephemeral one's body might become. By sustaining the memory of the dead, Michi can bear witness to their legacy. As such, whereas Michi was formerly bound by the ontology of capitalist alienation, her encounters with the specters, seen through her struggles to care for and nurture Junco, now lead her to a more humanized and, by proxy, humanistic mentality.

In a parallel narrative, though one largely devoid of any traces of Hiroshima, Kurosawa reveals the way out of such desolation: direct human contact and human need. The estrangement of late capitalism and the apocalyptic oppression of the specters must be battled with emotional rather than physical willpower. As Joshua La Bare notes, "Ever since Hiroshima and Nagasaki the bomb is the symbol of the apocalypse, and through it the Japanese themselves have come to be imagined as an apocalyptic people," yet such representation yields its opposite in that "the Japanese represent not only the apocalypse, but the fact of its transcendence: the finite and, through it, the infinite."[30] As such, Kurosawa fashions a narratological path where college student Ryosuke Kawashima (Haruhiko Kato) appears lost as he links his computer to the Internet and is immediately, albeit ominously, greeted with contact from the specters, who ask via the computer, "Would you like to meet a ghost?"[31] Kawashima recoils and shuts down the connection at once. Later, they contact him again and show live images of the victims, all of whom are overwhelmed with despair and unease. Their demonstration of power is meant to certify to Kawashima their pervasive impact on Japan's population by testifying to the impossibility of finding a location safe from their influence. This demonstration also positions the idea of the ghosts as ubiquitous and overwhelming, and thus forces Kawashima to surrender to the inevitability of his death. When an attraction develops between Kawashima and computer lab manager Harue (Koyuki), however, she helps him combat the specters' continuing advances. During a scene in her apartment, she even gathers surveillance on the infected, as live feeds of their estranged and systematized activities are all broadcast onto her multiple computers.

Despite Harue's own misgivings about the sociocultural landscape of Tokyo and Japan at large, she seems amenable to Kawashima's advances. That said, their personalities are diametrically opposed. Whereas Kawashima is generally sociable, Harue's ethos is summed up in her statement, "We all live totally separately." She has internalized the estrangement that is contained in capitalism; Kawashima has not. Their relationship is thereby fraught with the slow splintering of different epistemic realities. Still, when the Japanese population edges toward obsolescence, the two flee together, seeking haven on a train where they are, in a parallel to the instances with Michi and Yabe on the bus, the only passengers moving through the liminal space of the cityscape. This revelation is simultaneously comic and dramatic, as the two crane their heads and realize that their society may be all but gone. Such a realization is both liberating and profoundly alienating. In one of the most affecting shots, Kurosawa orchestrates both reactions simultaneously and repudiates any claim that he is anything but a humanist. Harue places her head on Kawashima's shoulder wordlessly. He soon returns the gesture, and the chasms and emotional estrangements that have engulfed the entirety of the film thus far evaporate. Kawashima epitomizes this sentiment, stating, "I'm here beside you. Even if there's no one else, it doesn't matter. We're both definitely here."[32]

Yet this moment is transient, which suggests that the production of alienation inherent to capitalism cannot be easily transcended. When the train stutters to a stop, Harue flees and draws upon the literal as well as the metaphorical when she says, "This is the end of the line."[33] She feels adrift and abandoned, and even the possibility of a relationship with Kawashima cannot counter her epistemic mentality. She escapes back to her apartment, where she turns on her multiple computers and their surveillance of the infected; however, they all show only empty space. The conduit of surveillance is subverted when the screen cuts to an image of Harue herself watching the computer monitor framed through her bedroom, which at once reifies the notion that the specters govern and structure the field of possible actions. This uncanny doubling of voyeurism, where the invisible ghosts watch Harue while she watches herself being watched, is an epiphany for Harue, and she heads into her bedroom, her face growing more ebullient with each step. In a shot framed through the specter's subjective experience, Harue comes to the entity and embraces it, whispering, "I'm . . . not alone."[34] She can simply no longer reconcile her pessimistic ideology with any counterideology. Though Harue does not die immediately, her subjectivity is absorbed just like that of the others, and the potential for any transcendence is seemingly abolished. The specters offer her a community, but it is one that is self-denying and fatalistic, and Harue's trust in their offering is foolhardy precisely because any community is predicated on self-surrender. Consequently, Harue becomes like all of the other victims who have yielded to the specters, an empty vessel that the specters can use to force Kawashima and Michi to dwell on the stark prospects that await them in Tokyo.

For his part, Kawashima has also alighted on an epiphany. He arrives outside Harue's apartment door and shouts, albeit too late, his suggestion that "the two of us live together. That way, we can always be together. If we keep living alone, we'll get worse and worse because we're weak. We'll balance each other out."[35] This epistemic principle is the central idea behind *Pulse*—society must struggle on and not surrender to the apocalypse, even if all seems lost. In this manner, Kurosawa's humanism interrogates responses to this imagined memory of the apocalypse and elides all responses save for a tempered sanguinity. These ideas likewise exist as Kurosawa's treatise on ways to view the cultural memory of Hiroshima. Human connection, or at least the potential for such connection, is a necessity to survive amid the emotional and psychical despair that afflicts survivors. This is not to say, however, that one can exhibit a blithe refusal to accept pessimism; moderation is the key.

Eventually, Kawashima breaks through Harue's door, and when he finds neither Harue's physical body nor any representational smudge in her apartment, he takes to the streets in absentminded wandering. In another ode to nuclear disaster, the television now broadcasts and memorializes the missing, and these representational spaces certify that the specters have infiltrated all of Japanese society and not merely Tokyo. Kawashima walks down an abandoned street, and at last the two parallel narratives connect as he comes upon Michi asleep in her broken-down car. The two work on repairing her car, and this labor exists as a metaphor to mend their own damaged psyches. Their meeting exists as confirmation that there are people who are still alive and unaffected by the specters, though Michi confirms that she is otherwise alone when Kawashima asks whether her mom or dad made it through. Regardless, their meeting reconfigures the potential for transcendence of this liminal space once more.

First, though, Michi suggests they make one last effort to save Harue, even though Kawashima believes that Harue is already lost to the specters. This attempt at recovering the lost affirms Michi's central humanity and her refusal to submit to the alienated mindset of society, and she becomes the exemplar of faith that Kawashima tries to emulate. When they arrive at a factory where they think she might be, however, Kawashima notes, "This is the last stop. After that we go as far as we can."[36] This pronouncement asserts the need that they not just abandon themselves to the specters' production of obsolescence, no matter if they are infected; and it exemplifies their need to situate themselves in relation to a destination, regardless of whether any such destination exists. As such, they are thinking beyond the countrywide apocalypse that surrounds them and projecting instead a liminal space of potential. In this sense, a borderless destination haunts the thinking of both of them.

Naturally, Michi and Kawashima encounter the systematized and governed body of Harue, and, despite their attempts to allay her fears, they are unable to prevent her suicide when she fires a pistol into her temple. Harue, the embodiment of pessimism, merely fashions her own pessimistic demise. Before Michi and Kawashima can begin their attempt at finding some liminal space of safety, they need to retrieve more gas for Michi's car. Here is where Kurosawa's epistemic ideas invariably become problematized, for Kawashima becomes weighted down in horror films' clichéd behavior and follows the machinations of horror tropes. He goes after the lid when it pops off of the gas can and rolls through a door that was formerly covered shut with red tape. Even these machinations can be explained away, for Kawashima has never been as strong at resisting the specters as Michi. The door slams shut, barricading Kawashima inside, and a specter manifests itself, producing the representative traces of alienation, with its assertion that "death was . . . eternal loneliness."[37] Though Kawashima counters, it is with an absurdity based on the experiences of the film thus far. He states, "I refuse to acknowledge death." Yet death and its various representational forms, whether through Hiroshima or through specters of horror, must be acknowledged and remembered. One must, like Michi, possess a healthy and moderate fear; a glib refusal of death is as damning as an epistemic pessimism.

Though Kawashima is infected, Michi is able to rescue him and help him back into the car. Michi breaks into tears immediately, but Kawashima again voices, albeit weakly, that they go "as far as they can."[38] So Michi starts the car and heads into the ruinous cityscape, and Kurosawa, at long last, gives the spectator an intimate architecture of the city. Yet this space has long since elided any notions of being a homely space and now exists as an apocalyptic space where, in Anthony Vidler's words on posturban architecture, as there is no

> systematic map that might be carried in the memory, we wander . . . surprised but not shocked by the continuous repetition of the same, the continuous movement across already vanished thresholds that leave only traces of their former status as places. Amidst the ruins of monuments no longer significant because deprived of their systematic status, and often of their corporeality, walking on the dust of inscriptions no longer decipherable because lacking in so many words, whether carved in stone or shaped in neon, we cross nothing to go nowhere.[39]

As Kurosawa frames his mise-en-scène, Tokyo's architecture itself is dismembered, barren, and devoid of stable comfort or safety. The spectral haunting has reformulated the city and produced a space of a postindustrial material wasteland. Explosions rock the cityscape repeatedly, and the city is eroded by dust, ash, and all the representational space of the (un)dead. Heightening this sensation is the apocalyptic vision that Kurosawa employs when Michi witnesses a plane plummet from the skies and explode into the center of the cityspace. In another (in)visible reference to the site of Hiroshima, Michi enters a room awash with the ashes of the dead in order to retrieve the keys to a small boat so that she and Kawashima can escape the haunted terrain of the land. Michi and Kawashima soon steer the boat into the waters, leaving behind the ghostly vestiges of the apocalyptic land.

At this point, Kurosawa returns the spectators to the bookends, where they are greeted with Michi's voice-over. She considers her decision to keep struggling, noting that "death comes to us all. If so, maybe we would have been happier if we had gone with the rest. But we chose to keep going . . .

into the future."[40] If one extrapolates from *Pulse*'s apocalyptic narrative, nothing but more water awaits Michi and the survivors on the boat. To dock at any harbor is to risk contamination. As the ship captain approaches her, Michi looks to him for confirmation and asks, "Have I done the right thing?" In a moment rife with metatextual references back to actor Kôji Yakusho's many roles in Kiyoshi Kurosawa's filmography, the ship captain looks at Michi and steadfastly offers her certain faith and assurance in this world, saying, "You're doing the right thing."[41]

Indeed, if the spectators consider the multitude of (in)visible referents to Hiroshima in Kurosawa's *Pulse*, then they must also consider the ultimate way to pay tribute to the legacy of the apocalyptic memory, regardless of whether it is generated by an atomic blast or by specters. As Lisa Yoneyama notes, those exposed to the bombs in Hiroshima and Nagasaki, and therefore, for this chapter's purposes, those exposed to the specters, must continue to survive and endure, "because telling *is* an act, 'relating' and 'witnessing' become nothing less than proof of existence after survival."[42] Michi must survive precisely because her testimony is necessary to historicizing the specters, which in turn prevents history from becoming liminal or otherwise lost. This refusal to submit to the will of the apocalypse is a resolutely humanistic choice, and it is one that Kurosawa fosters throughout in his filmography. As Kurosawa noted in an interview, "Many people construe those [apocalyptic] images and ideas as negative and despairing, but I actually see them as just the opposite—as the possibility of starting again with nothing; as the beginning of hope."[43]

Similarly, *Pulse* highlights precisely the value that Kurosawa places on physical rootlessness as a key to survival in this production of a late capitalist ideology, which recalls Martin Heidegger's maxim "Homelessness is coming to be the destiny of the world."[44] Though Heidegger invokes this condition as a negative, where society's world-historical Being is becoming uprooted by a materialistic existentialism, this phrase exists for Kurosawa as a positive, for it possesses a potential that is contrary to the estrangement and alienation produced by capitalism. Social critic Slavoj Žižek offers a contemporary view of Heidegger's maxim in the critical companion piece to Alfonso Cuarón's *Children of Men* (2006), *The Possibility of Hope* (2007). Cuarón's film bears remarkable similarities to *Pulse* in terms of its thematic coverage and its notions of the ideal representational space as one that is rootless, which makes Žižek's comment doubly fascinating: "The solution is the boat. It's rootless; it floats around. That's the solution. We must accept really how we are rootless."[45] Kurosawa seems to suggest that, lacking any anchor, the boat possesses limitless potential. Indubitably, the boat exists beyond any liminal sense of borders or bounded space, and it therefore exists as both a homely and unhomely home; it is this twinning that establishes its unique power for Kurosawa.

Therefore, Kiyoshi Kurosawa's *Pulse* epitomizes the horror film of ideas. As Harmony Wu theorizes, critics must track the liminal and subversive commentary that haunts deep within horror media, since this "remarkably protean substance of horror, seemingly endlessly adaptable to different contexts, offers a highly charged and usefully pliable framework for articulating diffuse, intangible and various anxieties."[46] In *Pulse*, then, Kurosawa uses the horror film's generic conventions as a way to question and interrogate the long-term consequences of an alienating and estranging capitalism, which is embodied through his framing of architectural high-rise buildings and physical separation. Secondly, Kurosawa imbues his film with (in)visible referents back to the cultural memory of Hiroshima, allowing the scattering smudges of these mnemonic sites and the linguistic markers to carry import through their psychical proximity to the legacy of the atomic blasts. Lastly, Kurosawa comments on the effects of the slow disintegration of the cityscape that implodes beneath the weight of ruinous monuments, becoming a ghost of its former capitalistic import. Instead, all of the value that was once privileged in the cityscape is now culturally transmitted into the rootless boat, which affirms that Japanese society, and if we extrapolate further, any society, must be willing to abandon the haunted landscapes of the past for the protean dwelling of the future. In other words, Kiyoshi Kurosawa's *Pulse* exists as an uncanny web of meaning that renders visible the ghostly anxieties that plague much of Japanese society.

NOTES

1. *Pulse*, directed by Kiyoshi Kurosawa (2001; New York: Magnolia Pictures, 2005), DVD.
2. Joshua La Bare, "The Future: 'Wrapped in That Mysterious Japanese Way,'" *Science Fiction Studies* 27, no. 1 (2000): 41. La Bare asserts an appreciation for the ambiguity of the French term *imaginaire* over a more conventional translation of the term to a more exact (for all its problematic rigidity) term like *imagination*. I am adopting his terminology for this chapter.
3. Jeremiah Kipp, "Movie Review: *Pulse*," *Slant Magazine*, June 20, 2005, http://www.slantmagazine.com/film/film_review.asp?ID=1661 (accessed March 13, 2008).
4. Kathleen Brogan, *Cultural Haunting: Ghosts and Ethnicity in Recent American Literature* (Charlottesville: University Press of Virginia, 1998), 6.
5. Ibid., 5.
6. Lisa Yoneyama, *Hiroshima Traces: Time, Space, and the Dialectics of Memory* (Berkeley: University of California Press, 1999), 212.
7. Ibid.
8. Jerry White, *The Films of Kiyoshi Kurosawa: Master of Fear* (Berkeley, CA: Stone Ridge Press, 2007), 163.
9. *Pulse*.
10. Ibid.
11. Anthony Vidler, *The Architectural Uncanny: Essays in the Modern Unhomely* (Cambridge, MA: MIT Press, 1994), 3.
12. Ibid., 70.
13. Karl Marx, *The Economic and Philosophic Manuscripts of 1844*, ed. Dirk J. Struik, trans. Martin Milligan (New York: International Publishers, 1964), 110.

14. *Pulse.*

15. Rachelle Linner, *City of Silence: Listening to Hiroshima* (Maryknoll, NY: Orbis, 1995), 40.

16. Chuck Stephens, "High and Low: Japanese Cinema Now; A User's Guide," *Film Comment* 38, no. 1 (2002): 36.

17. Avery F. Gordon, *Ghostly Matters: Haunting and the Sociological Imagination* (Minneapolis: University of Minnesota Press, 1997), 8.

18. Laura Kipnis, "Feminism: The Political Conscience of Postmodernism?" in *Universal Abandon? The Politics of Postmodernism*, ed. Andrew Ross (Minneapolis: University of Minnesota Press, 1988), 158.

19. White, *The Films of Kurosawa*, 167.

20. *Pulse.*

21. *Pulse.*

22. Yoneyama, *Hiroshima Traces*, 89.

23. *Pulse.*

24. White, *The Films of Kurosawa*, 168.

25. Jacques Lacan, *The Seminar of Jacques Lacan*, vol. 1, *Freud's Papers on Technique, 1953–1954*, ed. Jacques-Alain Miller, trans. John Forrester (New York: Norton, 1988), 167.

26. Vidler, *The Architectural Uncanny*, 167.

27. Michel Foucault, "The Subject and Power," in *Michel Foucault: Beyond Structuralism and Hermeneutics*, 2nd ed., ed. Hubert L. Dreyfus and Paul Rabinow (Chicago: University of Chicago Press, 1982), 221.

28. *Pulse.*

29. Ibid.

30. La Bare, "The Future," 38, 43.

31. *Pulse.*

32. Ibid.

33. Ibid.

34. Ibid.

35. Ibid.

36. Ibid.

37. Ibid.

38. Ibid.

39. Vidler, *The Architectural Uncanny*, 185.

40. *Pulse.*

41. Ibid.

42. Yoneyama, *Hiroshima Traces*, 103.

43. Stephens, "High and Low," 36.

44. Martin Heidegger, *Basic Writings: From* Being and Time *(1927) to* The Task of Thinking *(1964)*, ed. David Farrell Krell (New York: Harper and Row, 1977), 219.

45. Slavoj Žižek, *Possibility of Hope*, *Children of Men*, directed by Alfonso Caurón (2006; Universal City, CA: Universal Studios, 2007), DVD.

46. Harmony Wu, "Trafficking the Horrific," *Spectator* 22, no. 2 (2002): 3.

Bibliography

Anatol, Giselle. "Transforming the Skin-Shedding Soucouyant: Using Folklore to Reclaim Female Agency in Caribbean Literature." *Small Axe* 7 (2000): 44–59.

Anderson, Melanie R. "'What Would Be on the Other Side?': Spectrality and Spirit Work in Toni Morrison's *Paradise*." *African American Review* 42, no. 2 (2008): 307–21.

Ang, Ien. *On Not Speaking Chinese: Living between Asia and the West.* London: Routledge, 2001.

Anolik, Ruth Bienstock. "The Missing Mother: The Meanings of Maternal Absence in the Gothic Mode." *Modern Language Studies* 33, no. 1/2 (2003): 24–43.

Appiah, Kwame Anthony. "Cosmopolitan Patriots." In *Cosmopolitics: Thinking and Feeling beyond the Nation*, edited by Pheng Cheah and Bruce Robbins, 91–114. Minneapolis: University of Minnesota Press, 1998.

Austen, Jane. *Northanger Abbey, Lady Susan, The Watsons, and Sanditon.* Edited by John Davie. Oxford: Oxford University Press, 1998.

Bambara, Toni Cade. "Reading the Signs, Empowering the Eye: *Daughters of the Dust* and the Black Independent Cinema Movement." In *Black American Cinema*, edited by Manthia Diawara, 118–44. New York: Routledge, 1993.

Becker, Gay, Yewoubdar Beyene, and Pauline Ken. "Memory, Trauma, and Embodied Distress: The Management of Disruption in the Stories of Cambodians in Exile." *Ethos* 28, no. 3 (2000): 320–45.

Bennet, Andrew, and Nicholas Royle. *Elizabeth Bowen and the Dissolution of the Novel.* London: Macmillan, 1995.

Bennett, Gillian. *Alas, Poor Ghost! Traditions of Belief in Story and Discourse.* Logan: Utah State University Press, 1999.

Berry, Chris, and Kim So-Young. "'Suri Suri Masuri': The Magic of the Korean Horror Film: A Conversation." *Postcolonial Studies* 3, no. 1 (2000): 53–60.

Birch, Tony. "Returning to Country." In *A Museum for the People: A History of Museum Victoria and Its Predecessors 1854–2000*, edited by Carolyn Rasmaussen, 397–400. Melbourne: Scribe, 2001.

———. "Surveillance, Identity, and Historical Memory in Ivan Sen's *Beneath Clouds*." In *Empires, Ruins + Networks: The Transcultural Agenda in Art*, edited by Scott McQuire and Nikos Papastergiadis, 185–201. Melbourne: Melbourne University Press, 2005.

Blodget, Harriet. *Patterns of Reality: Elizabeth Bowen's Novels.* The Hague: Mouton, 1975.

Bohannan, Heather. "Quest-tioning Tradition: Spiritual Transformation Images in Women's Narratives and *Housekeeping*, by Marilynne Robinson." *Western Folklore* 51, no. 1 (1992): 65–79.

Bowen, Elizabeth. *Bowen's Court* (London: Longmans, Green & Co., 1942). In *Bowen's Court and Seven Winters* (London: Virago, 1984).

————. *The Collected Stories of Elizabeth Bowen*. London: Jonathan Cape, 1980. Reprint, London: Vintage, 1999.

————. *The Death of the Heart*. New York: Alfred Knopf, 1938.

————. *The Demon Lover and Other Stories*. London: Jonathan Cape, 1945.

————. *Encounters*. London: Sidgwick & Jackson, 1923.

————. *The Heat of the Day*. London: Jonathan Cape, 1949. Reprint, London: Vintage, 1998.

————. *The Mulberry Tree: Writings of Elizabeth Bowen*. Edited by Hermione Lee. London: Virago, 1986. Reprint, London: Vintage, 1999.

Boyce Davies, Carole. *Black Women, Writing, and Identity: Migrations of the Subject*. New York: Routledge, 1994.

Briggs, Julia. *Night Visitors: The Rise and Fall of the English Ghost Story*. London: Faber, 1977.

Brogan, Kathleen. *Cultural Haunting: Ghosts and Ethnicity in Recent American Literature*. Charlottesville: University Press of Virginia, 1998.

Broome, Richard. *Aboriginal Victorians: A History since 1800*. Crows Nest, NSW: Allen & Unwin, 2005.

Brouwer, Joel R. "Repositioning: Center and Margin in Julie Dash's *Daughters of the Dust*." *African American Review* 29, no. 1 (1995): 5–17.

Brown, Caroline. "The Representation of the Indigenous Other in *Daughters of the Dust* and *The Piano*." *NWSA Journal* 15, no. 1 (2003): 1–19.

Buse, Peter, and Andrew Stott, eds. *Ghosts: Deconstruction, Psychoanalysis, History*. New York: St. Martin's Press, 1999.

Calder, Robert L. "'A More Sinister Troth': Elizabeth Bowen's 'The Demon Lover' as Allegory." *Studies in Short Fiction* 31, no. 1 (1994): 91–98.

Carpenter, Lynette, and Wendy K. Kolmar, eds. *Haunting the House of Fiction: Feminist Perspectives on Ghost Stories by American Women*. Knoxville: University of Tennessee Press, 1991.

Castillo, Debra. *Talking Back: Toward a Latin American Feminist Literary Criticism*. Ithaca, NY: Cornell University Press, 1992.

Caver, Christine. "Nothing Left to Lose: *Housekeeping*'s Strange Freedoms." *American Literature* 68, no. 1 (1996): 111–38.

Cello. Directed by Woo-cheol Lee. 2005. New York: Tartan Asia Extreme, 2006. DVD.

Ch'oe, Kilsŏng. "Male and Female in Korean Folk Belief." *Asian Folklore Studies* 43, no. 2 (1984): 227–33.

Clemens, Valdine. *The Return of the Repressed: Gothic Horror from* The Castle of Otranto *to* Alien. Albany: State University of New York Press, 1999.

Colley, Linda. *Britons: Forging the Nation 1707–1837*. Rev. ed. New Haven, CT: Yale University Press, 2009.

Corcoran, Neil. *Elizabeth Bowen: The Enforced Return*. Oxford: Oxford University Press, 2004.

Cowie, Elizabeth. "The Lived Nightmare: Trauma, Anxiety, and the Ethical Aesthetics of Horror." In *Dark Thoughts: Philosophical Reflections on Cinematic Horror*, edited by Steven J. Schneider and Daniel Shaw, 25–46. Lanham, MD: Scarecrow Press, 2003.

Cruz, Angie. *Soledad*. New York: Scribner, 2001.

Dash, Julie. Daughters of the Dust: *The Making of an African American Woman's Film*. New York: New Press, 1992.

Daughters of the Dust. Directed by Julie Dash. 1991. New York: Kino on Video, 2000. DVD.

Davison, Carol Margaret. "Haunted House/Haunted Heroine: Female Gothic Closets in *The Yellow Wallpaper*." *Women's Studies* 33 (2004): 47–75.

Dawson, Ashley. *Mongrel Nation: Diasporic Culture and the Making of Postcolonial Britain*. Ann Arbor: University of Michigan Press, 2007.

Dayan, Joan. "'A Receptacle for That Race of Men': Blood, Boundaries, and Mutations of Theory." *American Literature* 67, no. 4 (1995): 801–13.

DeLamotte, Eugenia C. *Perils of the Night: A Feminist Study of Nineteenth-Century Gothic.* New York: Oxford University Press, 1990.

Deleuze, Gilles. *Cinema 1: The Movement Image.* Translated by Hugh Tomlinson and Barbara Habberjam. London: Athlone Press, 1986.

Derrida, Jacques. *Dissemination.* Translated by Barbara Johnson. London: Continuum, 2004.

———. *Specters of Marx: The State of the Debt, the Work of Mourning, and the New International.* Translated by Peggy Kamuf. New York: Routledge, 1994.

D'Hoker, Elke. "Confession and Atonement in Contemporary Fiction: J. M. Coetzee, John Banville, and Ian McEwan." *Critique: Studies in Contemporary Fiction* 48, no. 1 (2006): 31–43.

Diawara, Manthia, ed. *Black American Cinema.* New York: Routledge, 1993.

Edelman, Lee. *No Future: Queer Theory and the Death Drive.* Durham, NC: Duke University Press, 2004.

Ellmann, Maud. *Elizabeth Bowen: The Shadow across the Page.* Edinburgh: Edinburgh University Press, 2003.

———. "The Shadowy Fifth." In *The Fiction of the 1940s: Stories of Survival*, edited by Rod Mengham and N. H. Reeve, 1–25. New York: Palgrave, 2001.

Everett, Anna. "Toward a Womanist/Diasporic Film Aesthetic." In *Film Analysis: A Norton Reader*, edited by Jeffrey Geiger, 850–71. New York: Norton, 2005.

Faulkner, William. *Requiem for a Nun.* New York: Vintage, 1975.

Finney, Brian. "Briony's Stand against Oblivion: The Making of Fiction in Ian McEwan's *Atonement*." *Journal of Modern Literature* 27, no. 3 (2004): 68–82.

Fleenor, Juliann E. "Introduction: The Female Gothic." In *The Female Gothic,* edited by Juliann E. Fleenor, 3–28. Montreal: Eden Press, 1983.

Foucault, Michel. "The Subject and Power." In *Michel Foucault: Beyond Structuralism and Hermeneutics*, edited by Hubert L. Dreyfus and Paul Rabinow. 2nd ed. Chicago: University of Chicago Press, 1982.

Fraustino, Daniel V. "Elizabeth Bowen's 'The Demon Lover': Psychosis or Seduction?" *Studies in Short Fiction* 17, no. 4 (1980): 483–87.

Gelb, Joyce, and Marian Lief Palley. *Women of Japan and Korea: Continuity and Change.* Philadelphia: Temple University Press, 1994.

Gelder, Ken. *Reading the Vampire.* London: Routledge, 1994.

Gelder, Ken, and Jane Jacobs. *Uncanny Australia: Sacredness and Identity in a Postcolonial Nation.* Carlton: Melbourne University Press, 1998.

Geyh, Paula E. "Burning Down the House? Domestic Space and Feminine Subjectivity in Marilynne Robinson's *Housekeeping*." *Contemporary Literature* 34, no. 1 (1993): 103–22.

Gibson, Ross. *Seven Versions of an Australian Badland.* St Lucia: University of Queensland Press, 2002.

Gilman, Charlotte Perkins. *The Yellow Wallpaper: A Sourcebook and Critical Edition.* Edited by Catherine J. Golden. New York: Routledge, 2004.

Gilroy, Paul. *"There Ain't No Black in the Union Jack": The Cultural Politics of Race and Nation.* Chicago: University of Chicago Press, 1991.

Glendinning, Victoria. *Elizabeth Bowen: Portrait of a Writer.* New York: Avon, 1977.

Goodwine, Marquetta, ed. *The Legacy of Ibo Landing: Gullah Roots of African American Culture.* Atlanta, GA: Clarity Press, 1998.

Gordon, Avery F. *Ghostly Matters: Haunting and the Sociological Imagination.* Minneapolis: University of Minnesota Press, 1997.

Gunew, Sneja. *Haunted Nations: The Colonial Dimensions of Multiculturalism.* London: Routledge, 2004.

Hage, Ghassan. *Against Paranoid Nationalism: Searching for Hope in a Shrinking Society.* Annandale, NSW: Pluto Press, 2003.

———. "Polluting Memories: Migration and Colonial Responsibility in Australia." In *"Race" Panic and the Memory of Migration*, edited by Meaghan Morris and Brett de Bary, 333–62. Hong Kong: Hong Kong University Press, 2001.

———. *White Nation: Fantasies of White Supremacy in a Multicultural Society.* Sydney: Pluto Press, 1998.

Heath, William. *Elizabeth Bowen: An Introduction to Her Novels*. Madison: University of Wisconsin Press, 1961.

Heidegger, Martin. *Basic Writings: From* Being and Time *(1927) to* The Task of Thinking *(1964)*. Edited by David Farrell Krell. New York: Harper and Row, 1977.

Hildebilde, John. *Five Irish Writers: The Errand of Keeping Alive*. Cambridge, MA: Harvard University Press, 1989.

Hodge, Bob, and John O'Carroll. *Borderwork in Multicultural Australia*. Crows Nest, NSW: Allen & Unwin, 2006.

Hoeveler, Diane Long. *Gothic Feminism: The Professionalism of Gender from Charlotte Smith to the Brontës*. University Park: Pennsylvania State University Press, 1998.

Hoffman, Diane M. "Blurred Genders: The Cultural Construction of Male and Female in South Korea." *Korean Studies* 19 (1995): 112–38.

hooks, bell. "Eating the Other: Desire and Resistance." In *Media and Cultural Studies: Key-Works*, edited by Meenakshi Gigi Durham and Douglas M. Kellner, 424–38. Malden, MA: Blackwell, 2001.

Howard, John. Opening Address to the Australian Reconciliation Convention, Melbourne. May 26, 1997. http://www.austlii.edu.au/au/other/IndigLRes/car/1997/4/pmspoken html (accessed August 4, 2012).

Huggan, Graham. "Vampires, Again." *Southerly* 66, no. 3 (2006): 192–204.

Hughes, Douglas A. "Cracks in the Psyche: Elizabeth Bowen's 'The Demon Lover.'" *Studies in Short Fiction* 10, no. 4 (1973): 411–13.

Ippolito, Emilia. *Caribbean Women Writers: Identity and Gender*. Rochester, NY: Camden House, 2000.

Irwin, John T. *Doubling and Incest / Repetition and Revenge: A Speculative Reading of Faulkner*. Expanded ed. Baltimore: Johns Hopkins University Press, 1996.

Jager, Sheila Miyoshi. "Woman and the Promise of Modernity: Signs of Love for the Nation in Korea." *New Literary History* 29, no. 1 (1998): 121–34.

James, Henry. *The Turn of the Screw and Other Short Novels*. New York: Signet/Penguin, 1995.

Jays, David. "First Love, Last Rites." *Sight and Sound* 17, no. 10 (2007): 34–35.

Jenkins, Morris. "Gullah Island Dispute Resolution: An Example of Afrocentric Restorative Justice." *Journal of Black Studies* 37, no. 2 (2006): 299–319.

Johnson, Erica. "Giving Up the Ghost: National and Literary Haunting in *Orlando*." *Modern Fiction Studies* 50, no.1 (2004): 110–28.

Jones, Jacquie. "The Black South in Contemporary Film." *African American Review* 27, no. 1 (1993): 19–24.

Kahane, Claire. "The Gothic Mirror." In *The (M)other Tongue: Essays in Feminist Psychoanalytic Interpretation*, edited by Shirley Nelson Garner et al., 334–51. Ithaca, NY: Cornell University Press, 1985.

Kaivola, Karen. "The Pleasures and Perils of Merging: Female Subjectivity in Marilynne Robinson's *Housekeeping*." *Contemporary Literature* 34, no. 4 (1993): 670–90.

Kiberd, Declan. *Inventing Ireland: The Literature of the Modern Nation*. London: Jonathan Cape, 1995.

Kim, Chongho. *Korean Shamanism: A Cultural Paradox*. Aldershot, UK: Ashgate, 2003.

King, Richard H. *A Southern Renaissance: The Cultural Awakening of the American South, 1930–1955*. Oxford: Oxford University Press, 1980.

Kingston, Maxine Hong. *The Woman Warrior: Memoirs of a Girlhood among Ghosts*. New York: Random House, 1989.

Kipnis, Laura. "Feminism: The Political Conscience of Postmodernism?" In *Universal Abandon? The Politics of Postmodernism*, edited by Andrew Ross, 149–66. Minneapolis: University of Minnesota Press, 1988.

Kipp, Jeremiah. "Movie Review: *Pulse*." *Slant Magazine*, June 20, 2005. http://www.slantmagazine.com/film/film_review.asp?ID=1661 (accessed March 13, 2008).

Koo, Hagen. *Korean Workers: The Culture and Politics of Class Formation*. Ithaca, NY: Cornell University Press, 2001.

Kristeva, Julia. *Revolution in Poetic Language.* Translated by Margaret Waller. New York: Columbia University Press, 1984.

La Bare, Joshua. "The Future: 'Wrapped in That Mysterious Japanese Way.'" *Science Fiction Studies* 27, no. 1 (2000): 22–48.

Lacan, Jacques. *The Seminar of Jacques Lacan.* Vol. 1, *Freud's Papers on Technique, 1953–1954.* Edited by Jacques-Alain Miller. Translated by John Forrester. New York: Norton, 1988.

Lassner, Phyllis. *British Women Writers of World War II: Battleground of Their Own.* London: Macmillan, 1997.

———. *Elizabeth Bowen.* London: Macmillan, 1990.

———. *Elizabeth Bowen: A Study of the Short Fiction.* New York: Twayne, 1991.

Laub, Dobi. "Truth and Testimony: The Process and the Struggle." In *Trauma: Explorations in Memory,* edited by Cathy Caruth, 61–75. Baltimore: Johns Hopkins University Press, 1995.

Lee, Young-Hee. "Women's Literature in the Chosŏn Period: *Han* and the Songs of Women." In *Korean Studies: New Pacific Currents,* edited by Dae-Suk Soh, 101–12. Honolulu: Hawaii University Press, 1994.

Linner, Rachelle. *City of Silence: Listening to Hiroshima.* Maryknoll, NY: Orbis, 1995.

Lorde, Audre. *Sister Outsider.* Freedom, CA: Crossing Press, 1984.

MacCannell, Dean. *Empty Meeting Grounds: The Tourist Papers.* New York: Routledge, 1992.

Maitland, Sara. "Introduction," *The Virago Book of Ghost Stories,* vol. 2, edited by Richard Dalby. London: Virago, 1991.

Margaronis, Maria. "The Anxiety of Authenticity: Writing Historical Fiction at the End of the Twentieth Century." *History Workshop Journal* 65 (2008): 138–60.

Marx, Karl. *The Economic and Philosophic Manuscripts of 1844.* Edited by Dirk J. Struik. Translated by Martin Milligan. New York: International Publishers, 1964.

Masse, Michelle A. *In the Name of Love: Women, Masochism, and the Gothic.* Ithaca, NY: Cornell University Press, 1992.

McEwan, Ian. *Atonement.* New York: Anchor Books, 2001.

Meese, Elizabeth. *Crossing the Double-Cross: The Practice of Feminist Criticism.* Chapel Hill: University of North Carolina Press, 1986.

Memento Mori. Directed by Kim Tae Yeon, Kim Tae-Yong, and Min Kyu-Dong. 1999. London: Tartan, 2005. DVD.

Min, Eungjun, Jinsook Joo, and Han Ju Kwak. *Korean Film: History, Resistance, and Democratic Imagination.* Westport, CT: Praeger, 2003.

Moers, Ellen. *Literary Women.* Garden City, NY: Doubleday, 1976.

Mohanram, Radhika. *Imperial White: Race, Diaspora, and the British Empire.* Minneapolis: University of Minnesota Press, 2007.

Montag, Warren. "The Universalization of Whiteness." In *Whiteness: A Critical Reader,* edited by Mike Hill, 281–93. New York: New York University Press, 1997.

Mooney, Sinéad. "Unstable Compounds: Bowen's Beckettian Affinities." *Modern Fiction Studies* 53, no. 2 (2007): 238–55.

Morrison, Toni. *Beloved.* New York: Knopf, 1987.

Newman, Beth. "Getting Fixed: Feminine Identity and Scopic Crisis in *The Turn of the Screw.*" *Novel* 26, no. 1 (1992): 43–63.

Ng, Andrew Hock Soon. "Introduction: Reading the Double." In *The Poetics of Shadows: The Double in Literature and Philosophy.* Stuttgart: Ibidem-Verlag, 2008.

Ochoa Fernández, María Luisa. "Family as the Patriarchal Confinement of Women in Sandra Cisneros' *The House on Mango Street* and Loida M. Pérez's *Geographies of Home.*" In *Evolving Origins, Transplanting Cultures: Literary Legacies of the New Americans,* edited by Laura P. Alonso Gallo and Antonia Domínguez Miguela, 119–28. Huelva, Spain: Universidad de Huelva, 2002.

Owens, E. Suzanne. "The Ghostly Double behind the Wallpaper in Charlotte Perkins Gilman's *The Yellow Wallpaper.*" In *Haunting the House of Fiction: Feminist Perspectives on Ghost Stories by American Women,* edited by Lynette Carpenter and Wendy K. Kolmar, 64–79. Knoxville: University of Tennessee Press, 1991.

Oyeyemi, Helen. *White Is for Witching.* New York: Doubleday, 2009.

Park, Kyong-ni. "The Feelings and Thoughts of the Korean People in Literature," at http://web.archive.org/web/20021126053722/http://www keganpaul.com/articles_main.php?url=main_file.php/articles/30/ (accessed September 22, 2008).

Pearlman, Mickey. "Introduction." In *Mother Puzzles: Daughters and Mothers in Contemporary American Literature*, edited by Mickey Pearlman, 1–9. New York: Greenwood Press, 1989.

Pérez, Loida Maritza. *Geographies of Home*. New York: Penguin, 1999.

Pham, Hoa. *Vixen*. Sydney: Hodder Headline, 2000.

Plain, Gill. *Women's Fiction of the Second World War: Gender, Power, and Resistance*. Edinburgh: Edinburgh University Press, 1996.

Pulse. Directed by Kiyoshi Kurosawa. 2001. New York: Magnolia Pictures, 2005. DVD.

Radcliffe, Ann. *The Mysteries of Udolpho*. Edited by Bonamy Dobrée. Oxford: Oxford University Press, 1996.

Radcliffe, Mary-Anne. *Manfroné: Or, the One-Handed Monk*. New York: Arno, 1972.

Read, Peter. *Haunted Earth*. Sydney: UNSW Press, 2003.

Robinson, Marilynne. *Housekeeping*. New York: Farrar, 1980.

Roche, Regina Maria. *Clermont*. Edited by Natalie Schroeder. Chicago: Valancourt Books, 2006.

Romanow, Rebecca Fine. *The Postcolonial Body in Queer Space and Time*. Newcastle upon Tyne, UK: Cambridge Scholars Publishing, 2008.

Russ, Joanna. "Somebody's Trying to Kill Me and I Think It's My Husband: The Modern Gothic." In *The Female Gothic,* edited by Juliann E. Fleenor, 31–56. Montreal: Eden Press, 1983.

Schneider, Karen. *Loving Arms: British Women Writing the Second World War*. Lexington: University Press of Kentucky, 1997.

Schroeder, Natalie. "Introduction." In *Clermont*, by Regina Maria Roche. Chicago: Valancourt Books, 2006.

———. "*The Mysteries of Udolpho* and *Clermont*: The Radcliffean Encroachment on the Art of Regina Maria Roche." *Studies in the Novel* 12, no. 2 (1980): 131–43.

Sheller, Mimi. *Consuming the Caribbean: From Arawaks to Zombies*. New York: Routledge, 2003.

Shim, Young-hee. "Feminism and the Discourse of Sexuality in Korea: Continuities and Changes." *Human Studies* 24 (2001): 133–48.

Singh, Amritjit, Joseph T. Skerrett Jr., and Robert E. Hogan, eds. "Introduction." In *Memory, Narrative, and Identity: New Essays in Ethnic American Literatures* . Boston: Northeastern University Press, 1994.

Solomon, Deborah. "A Sinner's Tale." *New York Times*, December 2, 2007. http://www nytimes.com/2007/12/02/magazine/02wwln-Q4-t.html?_r=1 (accessed August 4, 2012).

Stein, Karen F. "Monsters and Madwomen: Changing Female Gothic." In *The Female Gothic*, edited by Juliann E. Fleenor, 123–37. Montreal: Eden Press, 1983.

Stella, Maria. "Territorio di guerra." In Elizabeth Bowen, *È morta Mabelle*, edited by Benedetta Bini and Maria Stella, 105–15. Verona: Essedue Edizioni, 1986.

Stephens, Chuck. "High and Low: Japanese Cinema Now; A User's Guide." *Film Comment* 38, no. 1 (2002): 35–36.

Stephenson, Peta. "New Cultural Scripts: Exploring Dialogue between Indigenous and 'Asian' Australians." *Journal of Australian Studies* 77 (2003): 57–68, 189–91.

Stevenson, John Allen. "A Vampire in the Mirror: The Sexuality of *Dracula*." *PMLA* 103, no. 2 (1988): 139–49.

Stewart, Jacqueline N. "Negroes Laughing at Themselves? Black Spectatorship and the Performance of Urban Modernity." *Critical Inquiry* 29 (2003): 650–77.

Stewart, Susan. "The Epistemology of the Horror Story." *Journal of American Folklore* 95, no. 375 (1982): 33–50.

Stone, Elena. *Rising from Deep Places: Women's Lives and the Ecology of Voice and Silence*, vol. 2 of *Feminism and the Social Sciences*. New York: Peter Lang, 2000.

Suh, Nam-Dong. "Towards a Theology of *Han.*" In *Minjung Theology: People as Subjects of History.* Edited by The Commission on Theological Concerns of the Christian Conference of Asia, 57–69. Singapore: Christian Conference of Asia, 1981.

Taylor, Gary. *Buying Whiteness: Race, Culture, and Identity from Columbus to Hip Hop.* New York: Palgrave Macmillan, 2005.

Teo, Hsu-Ming. "Future Fusions and a Taste for the Past: Literature, History, and the Imagination of Australianness." *Australian Historical Studies* 33, no. 118 (2002): 127–39.

Thompson, Robert Farris. *Flash of the Spirit: African and Afro-American Art and Philosophy.* New York: Random House, 1983.

Todorov, Tzvetan. *The Fantastic: A Structural Approach to a Literary Genre.* Translated by Richard Howard. Ithaca, NY: Cornell University Press, 1975.

Tumarkin, Maria. *Traumascapes: The Power and Fate of Places Transformed by Tragedy.* Carlton: Melbourne University Publishing, 2005.

Turcotte, Gerry. "Vampiric Decolonization: Fanon, 'Terrorism,' and Mudrooroo's Vampire Trilogy." In *Postcolonial Whiteness: A Critical Reader on Race and Empire,* edited by Alfred J. López, 103–18. Albany: State University of New York Press, 2005.

van der Kolk, Bassel A., and Onno van der Hart. "The Intrusive Past: The Flexibility of Memory and the Engraving of Trauma." In *Trauma: Explorations in Memory,* edited by Cathy Caruth, 158–82. Baltimore: Johns Hopkins University Press, 1995.

Vidler, Anthony. *The Architectural Uncanny: Essays in the Modern Unhomely.* Cambridge, MA: MIT Press, 1994.

Voice. Directed by Equan Choi. 2005. Seoul: CJ Entertainment, 2008. DVD.

Walton, Priscilla. "'What Then on Earth Was I?': Feminine Subjectivity and *The Turn of the Screw.*" In *The Turn of the Screw,* edited by Peter Beidler, 253–67. Boston: Bedford-St. Martin's, 1995.

Ward Smith, Jeannette. "Being Incommensurable/Incommensurable Beings: Ghosts in Elizabeth Bowen's Short Stories." MA thesis, Georgia State University, 2006. http://etd.gsu.edu/theses/available/etd-04282006-181909/unrestricted/ward_jeannette   _w_200605_ma.pdf (accessed October 6, 2008).

Webber, Andrew J. *The Doppelgänger: Double Vision in German Literature.* Oxford: Clarendon Press, 1996.

Weinstock, Jeffrey Andrew, ed. "Introduction: The Spectral Turn." In *Spectral America: Phantoms and the National Imagination.* Madison: University of Wisconsin Press, 2006.

Werbner, Pnina. "Vernacular Cosmopolitanism." *Theory, Culture, and Society* 23, nos. 2–3 (March–May 2006): 496–99.

Werner, E. T. C. *Myths and Legends of China.* Singapore: Graham Brash, 1991.

Whispering Corridors. Directed by Park Ki-Hyung. 1998. London: Tartan, 2005. DVD.

White, Jerry. *The Films of Kiyoshi Kurosawa: Master of Fear.* Berkeley, CA: Stone Ridge Press, 2007.

Williams, Linda. "When the Woman Looks." In *Horror: The Film Reader,* edited by Mark Janovich, 61–66. London: Routledge, 2002.

Wishing Stairs. Directed by Jae-yeon Yun. 2003. New York: Tartan Video, 2005. DVD.

Woolf, Virginia, "A Haunted House." In *Monday or Tuesday.* London: Hogarth Press; New York: Harcourt, Brace, 1921. Reprint *A Haunted House: The Complete Shorter Fiction,* edited by Susan Dick, 116–17. London: Vintage, 2003.

Wu, Harmony. "Trafficking the Horrific." *Spectator* 22, no. 2 (2002): 1–11.

Yoneyama, Lisa. *Hiroshima Traces: Time, Space, and the Dialectics of Memory.* Berkeley: University of California Press, 1999.

Žižek, Slavoj. *Possibility of Hope. Children of Men.* Directed by Alfonso Caurón. 2006. Universal City, CA: Universal Studios, 2007. DVD.

———. *The Sublime Object of Ideology.* London: Verso, 1989.

Index

Aboriginal, 75, 84–86. *See also* Indigenous
    Australians
abuse, 92–94, 98
The Amityville Horror, x
the "Angel in the House," 31, 61–62
anime, 137
Asia, 79, 81–82
Atonement (novel and film), xiii, 47–57,
    57n3; and Elizabeth Bowen, 57n2
Austen, Jane, 3, 9; *Northanger Abbey*, 3–5,
    9–10
Australia, xiii, 75–78, 80–87

Bambara, Toni Cade, 111–112
Beloved, ix; and *Atonement*, 49; and
    Daughters of the Dust, 106, 116n12
Bennett, Gillian, ix
Bible, 109, 112
Bohannan, Heather, 39–40
Bowen, Elizabeth, xiii, 15–24; connection
    to *Atonement*, 47, 57, 57n2
Briggs, Julia, ix–x
Brogan, Kathleen, xi–xii, 49, 77, 79, 81,
    92–93, 96, 139

Carpenter, Lynnette and Wendy K.
    Kolmar, x, xii
Caver, Christine, 36–37
Cello, 120–132
China, 75, 82, 84

class-consciousness (and classism), 47–57,
    94
Colley, Linda, 60
colonization, 76, 78, 83–87
communism, 76
complex personhood, 55–56
Confucianism, 120, 125, 128–129, 132,
    133n6, 135n29
Corcoran, Neil, 16
Cruz, Angie, xiv, 91–94, 99–100; *Soledad*,
    xiii, 91–99, 101n44
Cuarón, Alfonso, 151; *Children of Men*,
    151; *The Possibility of Hope*, 151
cultural haunting, x–xiv; in *Atonement*,
    49–53, 57; in *Daughters of the Dust*,
    112, 114; in *Pulse*, 139–140, 142, 145
cyberpunk, 137

Dacre, Charlotte, 4
Dash, Julie, xiv, 105–106, 109–115,
    116n1, 116n4, 117n19, 117n28,
    117n33–117n34; *Daughters of the
    Dust*, xiv, 105–115, 116n1, 116n4
Dawson, Ashley, 60–61, 63
The Death of the Heart, 47, 49, 53–54, 57.
    See also Elizabeth Bowen
decolonization, 76
DeLamotte, Eugenia, 34–35
Deleuze, Gilles, 131
The Demon Lover and Other Stories,
    15–16, 21–22. *See also* Elizabeth

Bowen
Derrida, Jacques, x, xii, 16, 19–20, 26n36, 127
diaspora, 80, 101n44, 105–106, 108–110, 113, 115
dispossession, 75, 84–85
Dominican Republic, 93, 96
dreams, 18, 38, 95–96

Edelman, Lee, 66
Ellmann, Maud, 19
England, 4, 61. *See also* Great Britain
exorcism, 91, 96

Faulkner, William, x, 64
Fleenor, Juliann, 30
fox fairy, 75–82, 84–87
France, 78–79

Geechee, 107, 116n6. *See also* Gullah
Geyh, Paula, 40
ghost, ix–xiv, xvn12, xvin14, 4–5, 7–12, 15–24, 25n10, 26n54, 29–34, 35–41, 47–49, 50–52, 54–56, 59, 77–79, 82, 84–87, 91–93, 95–96, 106, 115, 120–127, 129, 132, 140–141, 143–144, 146–148, 150, 152. *See also* specters
ghosting, xii, xiii–xiv, 9–12, 52
ghost-related semantics, 15, 18
Gilman, Charlotte Perkins, xiii, 29, 33–36, 40–41; *The Yellow Wallpaper*, 29–30, 33–36, 40
Gilroy, Paul, 60–61
Gordon, Avery F., x, xi–xii, 4, 10, 55–56, 91–92, 96–97, 100, 143
Gothic, xiii, xiv, 3–12, 30–31, 115, 126; in Elizabeth Bowen's writing, 15–16; Female Gothic, 3–6, 12, 13n18, 30; in *White Is for Witching*, 59, 65; in *The Yellow Wallpaper*, 33–35
Great Britain, 59–60
Gullah, 105, 107, 111–113, 116n3, 116n5–116n6

Haiti, 62
han, xiv, 119–121, 123, 125, 128, 130, 132
The Heat of the Day, 17, 20, 24, 25n15. *See also* Elizabeth Bowen
Heidegger, Martin, 151

hikikomori, 138, 141, 146
Hildebilde, John, 21
Hiroshima, xiv, 137–140, 142–152
historical fiction, 49, 76
Hoeveler, Diane Long, 3–4
hooks, bell, 69, 114, 117n30, 117n33, 117n34
Howard, John (Australian prime minister, 1996–2007), 86
Hurston, Zora Neale, 114

Imamura, Shōhei, 137–138, 142; *Black Rain*, 137, 142
immigration, 75, 81, 83, 87–88
incest, 60, 64–65, 71
Indigenous Australians, 75, 85–86
Irwin, John T., 64

James, Henry, xiii, 29, 33, 35; *The Turn of the Screw*, 29–34, 35, 37, 40
Jays, David, 56–57

Kahane, Claire, 34, 37
Kaivola, Karen, 39–40, 42n40
King, Richard H., 64–65
Korea, 119–121, 125, 128, 130–132, 133n6, 134n28
Kristeva, Julia, 98
Kurosawa, Kiyoshi, xiv, 137–152; *Bright Future*, 137; *Cure*, 137; *Pulse*, xiv, 137–152

Lacan, Jacques, 145
Lorde, Audre, 94

MacCannell, Dean, 70
McEwan, Ian, xiii, 47–50, 52–53, 57n3. *See also Atonement*
Moers, Ellen, 13n18, 30
Mohanram, Radhika, 61–62
Montag, Warren, 60
Morrison, Toni, ix, xvin14, 49, 98, 106, 111, 116n12, 117n16. *See also Beloved*
multicultural(ism), 60, 76–77, 80, 82–84, 86–88, 89n30

Nagasaki, 137–138, 147, 151
Nag Hammadi Gnostic gospels, 112, 117n28

New York City, 109
ningaui, 75–78, 82, 84–87

the Other, 32, 35, 38, 62, 69, 126, 129–130
Ottley, C. R., 67
Oyeyemi, Helen, xiii, 59–62, 65; *White Is for Witching*, xiii, 59–71

Park, Kyong-Ni, 120, 130, 132
patriarchy, 4, 31, 37, 40, 94, 98–99
Pérez, Loida Maritza, xiv, 91–93, 99, 101n50; *Geographies of Home*, xiv, 91–92, 97–99, 101n44, 101n50
Pet Sematary, x
Pham, Hoa, xiv, 75–78, 80, 82, 84, 87, 88n7; *Vixen*, xiii, 75–87
pica, xiii, 59–61, 63, 66, 71
postcolonialism, 75, 82–83, 86–87

racism, 60–61, 70, 81, 94
Radcliffe, Ann, 3–4, 8, 10, 12, 13n18, 13n26; *The Mysteries of Udolpho*, 3–6, 8, 10, 12
Radcliffe, Mary-Anne, 4, 10, 12, 13n26; *Manfroné; Or, the One-Handed Monk*, 10–12
rebirth, 38, 96
repression, xiii, 40, 94, 128
revenant, 19, 20–21, 26n36
Robinson, Marilynne, 29, 36, 40–41; *Housekeeping*, 29–30, 36, 40–41
Roche, Regina Maria, 3–10, 12; *Clermont*, 3, 5–10
Romanow, Rebecca Fine, 66
Rudd, Kevin (Australian Prime Minister, 2007–2010), 87

Seventh-Day Adventist, 92, 97
sexism, 94
shamanism, 128–130
Sheller, Mimi, 62, 69
silence, xii, xvn12, 34, 91–99, 112, 132
slavery, 49, 60, 67–68, 105, 110, 113, 117n19, 117n30; postslavery migration,

110
social death, 30, 40
social ghost, xii, xiv, xvin14, 4, 10, 32
soucouyant myths, 67–68, 69–70
specters, ix–xiv, 4, 5, 10, 12, 19–20, 26n36, 29, 40, 59, 93, 99, 120, 123, 137–151
spectrality, x, xii, xiv–xv, xvin14, 11, 97, 99–100
Stein, Karen, 32–33
Stevenson, John Allen, 69–70
Stolen Generations, 87

Taylor, Gary, 60
telepathy, 91, 99
Todorov, Tzvetan, 21
Tokyo, 137–138, 140, 146–150
trauma, ix, xiii–xiv, 15, 18–19, 36, 47–48, 84, 93–94, 108, 123–127, 132, 137
Tsukamoto, Shinya, 137; *Tetsuo: The Iron Man*, 137
Turcotte, Gerry, 70
twin, 63–64, 68, 76, 151

vampire, xiv, 59, 63, 66, 68–70, 76, 78–79, 144
Victorian, 30–34, 61–62, 69, 106, 132
Vietnam, 75–82, 84–87; Vietnam War, 81
voodoo, 91, 93, 99

Walker, Alice, 116n12
Walton, Priscilla, 31
Weinstock, Jeffery Andrew, 115
Wharton, Edith, xiv
White Australia policy, 81, 83
Wishing Stairs, 121, 127–132, 134n28
women's supernatural fiction, x–xi
World War I, 20
World War II, xiv, 15, 20–21, 24, 48, 60, 71

Žižek, Slavoj, 151

About the Editors and Contributors

Karley K. Adney received her PhD from Northern Illinois University in sixteenth- and seventeenth-century British literature. Her research interests include adaptations of Shakespearean plays for children, literature and film, and women in literature. She currently serves as the senior department chair for ITT Technical Institute, Online.

Melanie R. Anderson is an instructional assistant professor of American literature for the University of Mississippi. Her research interests include spectrality, gender, and trauma in twentieth-century American writing. She has published work on Toni Morrison and Louise Erdrich, among other writers.

Jessica Carniel holds a doctorate in Australian Studies from the University of Melbourne, where she has taught on issues of migration and identity for several years. Her research interests include cultural diversity and identity, place, multiculturalism and cosmopolitanism, and cultural texts, such as film and literature. She is currently developing research focusing on soccer as a particular site at which Australian multicultural belonging can be examined and understood.

Amy K. King is a doctoral student at the University of Mississippi, where she is focusing her studies on circum-Atlantic anglophone literature and film. Her dissertation project examines relationships of violence between women in novels and films of the American South and Caribbean.

Lisa Kröger is a freelance writer, who also teaches academic writing to graduate students at Mississippi State University. Her research interests include everything from Anne Radcliffe to Shirley Jackson. She has worked with Udolpho Press, annotating a new edition of Mary Charlton's *Phedora; or, The Forest of Minksi*. She has also published on the Gothic novel and horror fiction, most recently in *The Encyclopedia of the Vampire*.

Yu-yen Liu, assistant professor at Huafan University, Taiwan ROC, specializes in contemporary fiction. She was a visiting scholar at the University of California, Berkeley (2006–2007). Recently, she has centered her research on issues such as the geopolitics of memory, affect, and transnational studies, as shown in her publications.

Andrew Hock Soon Ng is senior lecturer in literary studies at Monash Malaysia. His publications include *Dimensions of Monstrosity in Contemporary Narratives* (2004), *Interrogating In terstices* (2007), and *Intimating the Sacred* (2011), and his articles have appeared in journals such as *Symploke*, *Journal of the Fantastic in the Arts*, and *Pedagogy*.

Paul Petrovic recently defended his dissertation at Northern Illinois University, which considers the intersections between nationalism and national trauma in American and Japanese media about 9/11 and Hiroshima. He has articles published in the journals *Asian Cinema*, *Studies in American Naturalism*, *Journal of Graphic Novels and Comics*, and *ImageTexT: Interdisciplinary Comics Studies*, and in the book collection *Sexual Ideology in the Works of Alan Moore: Critical Essays on the Graphic Novels*.

Stefania Porcelli is an adjunct professor at Sapienza University of Rome, where she teaches courses in English language. Her research focuses on wartime fiction by female writers, the representation of trauma in literature, and the rewriting of ancient myth. She has published articles on Elizabeth Bowen, Christa Wolf, and Hannah Arendt, and she is currently writing a book on the relationship between propaganda and literature in the Second World War.

Betsy A. Sandlin is an associate professor of Spanish at Sewanee: The University of the South (Sewanee, Tennessee). Her research interests include gender and sexuality in contemporary U.S. Latino/a and Hispanic Caribbean literature. She received her PhD from the University of North Carolina at Chapel Hill.

Jana M. Tigchelaar is a doctoral candidate in English at the University of Kansas, where she teaches classes in American literature and culture. Her article "Empathy or Expectation of Return: Relationships, Gifts, and Economy in Edith Wharton's *Summer*" can be found in *The Edith Wharton Review*.